MW01026708

The Passions of Peter Sellars

# The Passions of Peter Sellars
## Staging the Music

Susan McClary

**University of Michigan Press • Ann Arbor**

Published in the United States of America by the
University of Michigan Press
Manufactured in the United States of America
Printed on acid-free paper
First published January 2019

A CIP catalog record for this book is available from the British Library.

Library of Congress Cataloging-in-Publication Data

Names: McClary, Susan, author.
Title: The passions of Peter Sellars : staging the music / Susan McClary.
Description: Ann Arbor : University of Michigan Press, 2019. | Includes bibliographical references and index. |
Identifiers: LCCN 2018027556 (print) | LCCN 2018028800 (ebook) | ISBN 9780472124794 (E-book) | ISBN 9780472131228 (hardcover : alk. paper)
Subjects: LCSH: Sellars, Peter—Criticism and interpretation. | Opera—Production and direction—History—20th century.
Classification: LCC ML429.S415 (ebook) | LCC ML429.S415 M33 2019 (print) | DDC 792.502/33092—dc23
LC record available at https://lccn.loc.gov/2018027556

The University of Michigan Press gratefully acknowledges the Case Western Reserve University Department of Music's generous support of this publication.

Cover photograph of Peter Sellars, © Ruth Waltz.

# Acknowledgments

I never imagined myself writing such a book. Indeed, I thought I had finished with the ordeal of writing books of any kind. But this one was thrust upon me, and I should identify some of the culprits.

My colleagues at the University of Toronto—Sherry Lee, Linda Hutcheon, Caryl Clark—invited me repeatedly to speak before productions of the Canadian Opera Company, beginning with a production in 2012 of Kaija Saariaho's *L'amour de loin*. When I happened to be in town in 2013 for a doctoral oral, they happily included me in the entourage trucking off to see *The Tristan Project* by Sellars and Bill Viola. Whether or not they intended to serve as matchmakers, my Toronto friends pushed me into Sellars's proximity enough times that the contagion took.

At a party hosted by Linda and Michael Hutcheon following the *Tristan* performance, I engaged in a long boozy conversation with Vicki Cooper, then acquisitions editor at Cambridge University Press. When I wondered out loud to her why no one had written a book on Sellars, she suggested that I take on the task. I toyed with the idea for a while, but the project did not yet catch fire. That occurred only after I participated in a day-long session with Sellars in Toronto in conjunction with his 2014 production of Handel's *Hercules*. Over the course of that day we became fast friends, so much so that I seem to have known him forever, and the writing of this book became a necessity.

I have been aided by my many students at Case Western Reserve University who have taken my "Opera after *Einstein*" seminar. Together we have explored a wide range of new music theater works, including those by John Adams and Kaija Saariaho in which Sellars served as collaborator, and we have worked to develop a vocabulary for analyzing relationships between sound and motion, opera and ideology. Conversations with Nicholas Stevens, Sophie Benn, Kate Doyle, Alex Lawler, Dan Batchelder, Maria Parrini, April Sun, Brian Stuligross, and Taylor McClaskie have proved especially stimulating. I went into musicology because I love to teach, and all my ideas come from interactions in the classroom. More so than any of my other publications, this one represents a group effort.

At Case Western Reserve University I have not only spectacular students but also the most supportive colleagues one could ever hope to have. Particularly precious to me is the group of women—Georgia Cowart, Francesca Brittan, Kate Doyle, Kathleen Horvath, Julie Andrijeski, Debra Nagy, Judy Bundra—with whom I can share both the tribulations and joys of teaching and academic life. Magnificent scholars and musicians, as well as resourceful cooks, they have rallied around me in times of need. I also count among my departmental angels my chair, David Rothenberg, who manages to maintain a level of morale exceedingly rare among music programs.

I am grateful to my long-time editor, Mary Francis, who gave invaluable feedback as I wrote. I followed Mary from University of California Press to her new post at University of Michigan Press because I have such faith in her judgments. I must also thank Dr. Nathan Mesko and Dr. Jacob Scott who saved my life when I was in the final throes of producing this book.

My husband, Robert Walser, has helped in countless ways as I pursued this and all my other projects; the range of my intellectual pursuits owes everything to him and his encouragement. Over the course of our more than thirty years together, we have visited and established connections on every continent save Antarctica, which has not yet caught on to New Musicology. I drafted much of this book in Sitges, Catalunya: our chosen paradise.

Most of all, however, I am indebted to Peter himself: for his fascinating work, for his endless generosity, for his extraordinary humaneness. It is hard to know Peter and not adore him. I can dedicate this book to no one other than its subject, the inimitable Peter Sellars.

# Contents

Digital materials related to this title can be found on
the Fulcrum platform via the following citable URL:
https://doi.org/10.3998/mpub.10023187

# Introduction

## Who Is Peter Sellars?

In 1988, Peter Sellars stunned the opera world when he staged Mozart's *Le nozze di Figaro* in the Trump Tower, with the philandering Count Almaviva implicitly as Donald himself. Many critics saw this affront as just one more example of Sellars's penchant for playing classic works for laughs: the topicality of Donald Trump in this production seemed to operate as a piece with other contemporary references, such as the branded cleaning products lined up in the room of Almaviva's servants, Susanna and Figaro.

The 2016 presidential election, however, incited a plethora of opera stagings that alluded to Trump, suggesting that we revisit Sellars's prescient production of 1988.[1] As Sellars explained tirelessly at the time, his decision to set Mozart's masterwork in present-day Manhattan emerged from his unswerving commitment to translating the volatile class and gender tensions of Beaumarchais's revolutionary (and censored) play into a North American context. In breaking *Figaro* out of the quaint, comfortable, white-wigged past, he intended to alert us to present dangers already lying right on our doorstep thirty years ago.

But a great many viewers saw Sellars's Trump as a joke—an insider joke at best, for few outside New York City at the time knew about Trump's business machinations, his documented brutality toward women, his loudly trumpeted ambition to become president. Indeed, when I first started drafting this book in 2015, I considered it necessary to explain who Trump was; I revised that section a bit in mid-2016 when he became the unlikely Republican nominee for president, still little more than fodder for punch lines on late night talk shows. I could never have imagined that events would eventually push this discussion to my opening paragraphs. As it turns out, the joke was on us. We can't say we weren't warned.

Peter Sellars has been directing operas professionally for nearly forty years, since 1979, when he was a mere twenty-two years old. Over the course of his career, he has offered productions of plays and operas ranging from the Greek tragedies and Mozart to works in which he served as collaborator or even principal author. Whatever the source material, however, all of his productions manifest his determination to make staged works relevant to contemporary ethical problems, including capital punishment, human trafficking, income inequality, immigration, traumatized veterans, and domestic violence.

Yet Sellars invariably balances his political critiques with a deep investment in spirituality—an investment that saves these critiques from sliding over into cynicism. An idiosyncratic blend of Christian, Buddhist, Hindu, African American, and Native American elements, Sellars's nonsectarian faith in the possibility of redemption in a secular world underscores all his work. Themes such as Divine Union, penitence, and the mysterious liminal state between life and death appear with increasing regularity in his productions. Despite my recovering-evangelical allergy to all things religious, I find this aspect of Sellars's agenda deeply compelling.

I first heard of Sellars when I was completing my dissertation at Harvard in the 1970s. Ever the enfant terrible, he had burst on the scene with a production of Shakespeare's *Antony and Cleopatra* staged in the Adams House swimming pool. He already sported his now-familiar sartorial eccentricities: then kimono jackets, now loud Hawaiian shirts and strands of beads, and always the inimitable shock of hair, carefully groomed to stand straight up like a child's representation of a sudden brainstorm. Everyone was scandalized, everyone was titillated. His name quickly circulated far beyond the parochial confines of Cambridge.

Just prior to his senior year at Harvard, he served as artistic director for the 1979 Loeb Summer Season. Never one to shy away from challenges, he staged *Much Ado About Nothing*, Wedekind's *Lulu*, Mayakovsky's *The Bedbug*, and a version of Wagner's *Ring Cycle*; the following year saw productions of *Don Giovanni* at the Monadnock Music Festival and *Santur Opera* by Ivan Tcherepnin at the Festival d'Automne in Paris, among other works. Upon graduation, he visited China, where he first encountered Chinese theatrical practices, and he worked with the National Theatre of the Deaf to produce *Kabuki Western* in 1981. Sellars became the artistic director of the Boston Shakespeare Company in 1983 at the age of twenty-six, and the following year he assumed leadership of the American National Theater, where his antiwar production of Sophocles's *Ajax*—starring Howie Seago, a signing deaf actor in the title role—roiled the cultural community of Washington, DC.[2] Testifying to his prodigious rise, the John D. and Catherine T. MacArthur Foundation named him a Fellow in 1983, only the third year such "genius grants" had been awarded. The *Los Angeles Times* reported in 1985 that some critics were calling him "the brightest young man to come along in the theater since Orson Welles."[3]

Sellars continues to direct plays, of course, and to receive accolades in legitimate theater. Moreover, many of the trademark strategies I discuss in these chapters also appear in Sellars's interpretations of Euripides and Shakespeare. But I have to leave the examination of his nonmusical work to those who specialize in that area. As a musicologist, I focus in this book exclusively on his productions of operas and oratorios: the pieces that display his remarkable talent for bringing together elements for staging plays—acting, blocking, set design, lighting—with the particular demands of genres involving singing, dancing, and instrument music.

•     Although we had many colleagues in common, Sellars and I did not meet when we were both in Cambridge. I first had that pleasure in 1984 when Sellars produced his Brechtian mash-up of Maxim Gorky's play *Summerfolk* with Gershwin songs at the Guthrie Theater in Minneapolis. Then on the faculty at the University of Minnesota, I frequently gave talks before or after events at the Guthrie and the Walker Arts Center, and I was invited to speak to audiences who attended Sellars's *Hang On to Me*.

It should have come as no surprise that those who had come to wallow in Russian gloom found the interpolated show tunes offensive, while Gershwin fans found themselves bemused by the dour plot into which their favorite songs had been inserted. Even though the play finished much later than the time announced for the final curtain, many outraged individuals stayed on to express their indignation to me, their only available target. I fielded questions and complaints as best I could in Sellars's stead; it appears I have continued to do so for the last thirty years.

Those thirty years have seen the rise to dominance of *Regietheater*, a practice whereby stage directors claim license to do whatever they please with classic operas and plays. We have become accustomed to Valkyries on gigantic seesaws, Rigolettos tending bar for the Rat Pack in Las Vegas, characters from Ligeti's *Le Grand Macabre* entering and exiting through the orifices of a gigantic naked woman.[4] Such stunts often dwarf and sometimes even injure singers; the music may get lost in the shuffle, overwhelmed by the clanking of machinery and visual tomfoolery. But hey: it's all just postmodern—our arch way of relating to our shared cultural legacy, reveling in the guilty pleasures of favorite arias while maintaining ironic distance.

Some of the responsibility for this iconoclastic movement no doubt falls to Sellars, whose 1980s Mozart Trilogy updated *Le nozze di Figaro, Don Giovanni,* and *Così fan tutte* to present-day North American settings.[5] Yet if Sellars's work influenced some proponents of *Regietheater,* his work stands apart from that of most of his postmodernist colleagues in crucial respects. As a musicologist, I have little interest in writing about Robert Lepage or Michael Mayer or Barcelona's La Fura dels Baus. But Sellars's work continues to intrigue and move me.

Every year at the end of my undergraduate survey of music we arrive at the last two excerpts included in the *Norton Anthology of Western Music:* scenes from John Adams's *Doctor Atomic* and Kaija Saariaho's *L'amour de loin,* both of them Sellars collaborations. And each time we reach those two operas, I ask myself why I have not yet engaged in depth with Sellars's work, which demands most urgently to be taken seriously. Four events compelled me finally to begin this book. First, my viewing in Toronto in 2013 of the spectacular *Tristan Project* Sellars designed together with video artist Bill Viola;[6] second, a symposium on the occasion of his production in 2014 in Toronto of Handel's *Hercules;* third, the release on DVD of his Bach passions; fourth, his residency in June 2016 as director of the Ojai Festival, at which I had the honor of serving as co-interlocutor on daily panel discussions.

As even his detractors now have to agree, Sellars counts among the most significant artists working today. Most obviously, he has staged dozens of operas and plays in nearly all the world's most prestigious houses, influencing stage directors everywhere. But, even more important, he has acted as a kind of Johnny Appleseed, persuading composers who had never shown any interest in opera—foremost among them, John Adams and Kaija Saariaho—to collaborate with him, thereby creating many of the acknowledged masterpieces of our time;[7] the photograph by Ruth Walz on the cover captures something like that invitation to follow his lead.

Adams has written eloquently about Sellars's "peculiar gift for relating musical ideas to vivid corporeal images" and his extraordinary sensibility:

> Over time, one of life's great pleasures would be finding myself on the receiving end of one of Peter's monumental verbal riffs, usually a nonstop, wall-to-wall summation of a piece that he'd just heard, or a work of choreography or theater he'd witnessed. His quick, intensely reactive mind and endlessly resourceful gift for verbalization would illuminate the music of Mozart, Shostakovich, Bach, Stravinsky, Debussy, or Handel; the choreography of George Balanchine, William Forsythe, or Mark Morris; or the architecture of Philip Johnson or Frank Gehry. You would be left wondering, "How did I miss all that?"[8]

In fact, anyone caught up in the whirlwind of a Sellars disquisition will marvel not only at his wealth of knowledge (he appears to have read and listened to everything) but also at his ability to cite a staggering number of repertories and world cultures, to refer in detail to political crises all over the planet, and to make unexpected connections and syntheses. YouTube offers a seemingly endless array of Sellars interviews. In addition to all his other talents, he probably qualifies as the most effective public intellectual addressing music since Leonard Bernstein.

I hope in these pages to explore several of Sellars's artistic priorities: his engagement with present-day social tensions, his concern with spirituality in human life and the arts, his foregrounding of the body in dance and in his idiosyncratic gestural vocabulary, his empathetic commitment to women's experiences and modes of expression. But I intend to examine most particularly his deep responses to the music itself, which have characterized his work throughout his career. More than any other stage director I know, he concerns himself with the subtleties of musical scores and allows these to shape his decisions. As he says in the documentary concerning his production of Olivier Messiaen's *Saint François d'Assise*:

> Most people are busy staging the plot synopsis and not the opera. And so they don't really look at the score and see what the composer has already written in. . . . Anything that really matters doesn't appear in a plot synopsis. And so this history of staging the plot synopsis is what has made opera intellectually inert and expressively limited. Opera becomes incredibly expressive as soon as you forget about the story and try and stage the music.[9]

"Try and stage the music." This is why my attention continually returns to Sellars's performances, and it also explains why some of the most discerning of actor-singers—among them James Maddalena, Sanford Sylvan, Dawn Upshaw, Gerald Finley, Willard White, Eric Owens, Julia Bullock, the late Lorraine Hunt Lieberson, Mark Padmore, Magdalena Kožená, Christian Gehaher—have lined up to work in his rehearsal-heavy productions. Sellars cares if you listen, cares that you leave the theater powerfully affected by the ways he has brought together sonic nuance, visual imagery, and trenchant social criticism.

Sellars works with opera scores from multiple time periods, each of which brings with it a particular set of dramatic and syntactical conventions for shaping expression. Few other directors choose to engage with so broad a range, from the sixteenth century (Orlando di Lasso's penitential madrigals in *Lag-*

*rime di San Pietro*), to the seventeenth (Purcell), to the eighteenth (Bach, Handel, Mozart), to the nineteenth (Tchaikovsky), to the twentieth (Debussy, Stravinsky, Weill), to the twenty-first (Adams, Golijov, Saariaho). Although certain signature traits of Sellars show up all across this spectrum, he always designs his decisions in ways that respond to the details of the particular score. For him, meanings do not reside solely or even primarily in the words, but rather in the ways the composer has choreographed those words. He has even waded through modal theory for pertinent insights into Lasso, and he negotiates with expertise the thorny modernist scores of Messiaen and Ligeti.

Most opera directors find themselves having to construe their stagings in ways that accommodate principals who show up only at the last minute for blocking. Moreover, many of those principals acquire their roles primarily on the basis of vocal prowess, and all too often they hover anxiously over the prompter box or stand rigid as sticks as they sing; a stage director simply has to work within those conditions. By contrast, Sellars's productions depend on long, intensive rehearsal periods. Much as Philip Glass, Steve Reich, and Meredith Monk found it necessary to form their own ensembles to execute their work adequately, Sellars works very closely with a handful of carefully trained performers, sculpting along with them their every bodily, facial, and musical nuance. If he draws in rehearsals on the creative input of the troupe, he consolidates his interpretations by the time the run begins. It is for this reason that his performances invite and reward deep analysis.[10]

In addition to the cadre of singers in his cohort, Sellars also has partnered with a number of celebrated designers. James F. Ingalls, for instance, has collaborated from the outset to produce the lighting effects so crucial to Sellars's productions, and he attends even the earliest rehearsals of each new project. For stage sets Sellars has relied repeatedly on Adrianne Lobel and George Tsypin. Craig Smith conducted his early performances, with Esa-Pekka Salonen, William Christie, John Adams, Kent Nagano, Simon Rattle, Susanna Mälkki, Joana Carneiro, and Teodor Currentzis serving as music directors for later productions; Mark Morris and Lucinda Childs have provided choreographies. But all of these artists necessarily respond to Sellars's concepts when they work with him. His vision shapes the decisions made in every other area, including musical timing and nuance.

In this book, I will deal primarily with the productions available on commercial DVD or on YouTube, thereby allowing readers to consult the sequences I discuss. Doing so requires another layer of discussion: the process of rendering stage works in video format. Over the years Sellars has exerted increasing control over the filming of his stagings, and much of his oeuvre—even major productions such as Adams's *The Death of Klinghoffer* and Saariaho's *Adriana Mater*—remains tantalizingly out of reach because he was never sufficiently satisfied with the ways the various elements came together to release DVDs. Fortunately, however, we have easy access to filmed productions reaching back as far as 1988 (*Nixon in China*) and 1990 (the Mozart Trilogy and Handel's *Giulio Cesare*).

This span of thirty years allows me to trace the development of Sellars's craft: to deal with his interpretations of standard works, with the operas he himself instigated, with those for which he actually composed the libretti, with those for which he assembled both the texts and the music. Although his strategies have evolved considerably over the course of three decades, I hope to demonstrate that many of the elements now appreciated in his recent stagings of the Bach passions with the Berlin Philharmonic may be detected in retrospect even in his earliest productions—the very ones for which he used to be castigated. Sellars claims that the most important musical experience of his undergraduate years involved his singing Bach at Emmanuel Church in Boston, and the dramaturgical influences that finally became explicit in his stagings of the passions in Berlin show up already in the Mozart Trilogy. In this sense, all his entire career may be understood not only as the result of his various *passions*—music, theater, the body, social intervention, gender, spirituality, violence—but also as a series of tributes to those passions by J. S. Bach that so deeply influenced his aesthetic formation.

I have three principal purposes in writing this book. The first, as is already evident, is to examine in some detail the work of one of North America's foremost creative minds—one who has had an extraordinary international impact on music and theater. Although he will continue to develop and bring ever more surprising effects to the stage, Sellars has already accomplished much more than most artists do in a lifetime. A critical account of his work is long overdue.

The second involves a broader project. Many viewers ignore the apparatus, whether staging or cinematic decisions, that brings an opera to life for them. To be sure, they may notice if something goes contrary to their expectations: for instance, those moments of twentieth-century cultural vulgarity that popped up in adored pieces by Mozart or Handel. But a director's concept should penetrate far more deeply into what we see than the mere presentation of eye-catching props or unexpected settings. In the readings offered here I hope to make visible the kinds of choices Sellars makes in the process of enactment, in the moves from score and source materials to the stage and screen.

Finally, I want to explore the ways in which Sellars works through opera to encourage social reflection on ethical issues. A recent article in the *New York Times* asked if opera can become an agent of change.[11] For Sellars, performance never aims simply at aesthetic goals, no matter how beautiful his results. A practitioner of Vsevolod Meyerhold's and Berthold Brecht's alienation effects, he invariably seeks to dislodge viewers from their complacency to focus intently on their relationships to other individuals, their responsibilities for the advancement of greater global harmony. Many of the composers whose dramas he stages have shared this vision of deploying art for moral awareness, and his interpretations shatter the glass jars within which canonization has often confined them. I will examine the strategies by means of which Sellars connects these objects of adoration to the gritty conflicts of today's political contexts.

I will not, however, present a biography of Sellars, nor will I attempt to psychoanalyze him through his productions. Those looking for insider knowledge concerning his personal life—including an explanation of his hairstyle—should look elsewhere. Although I know Sellars and communicate with him with on a regular basis, I have conducted no formal interviews with him or his colleagues for this book. I did once ask his mother, the remarkable Patricia Sellars, how she managed to spawn such a creature, and I got nothing back but the exceedingly helpful comment, "He had a good education." For this project, I focus exclusively on his artistry as manifested in publicly available formats.

Chapter 1 deals with Sellars's Mozart Trilogy, the pieces that first attracted the attention of an extended audience. I introduce here several of his trademark strategies, including his insistence on updating of eighteenth-century classics to the context of contemporary North America; his critical emphasis on issues such as power, gender, and violence; and, above all, his deep engagement with and commitment to the music.

The second chapter moves to productions that foreground a kind of dramaturgy associated with ritual, focusing particularly on Olivier Messiaen's *Saint François d'Assise* and Handel's oratorio *Theodora*. In these works, the stylized use of gesture that marks much of Sellars's subsequent stagecraft starts to emerge, and the concerns with spirituality that later permeate his own libretti become prominent.

The pieces considered in these first two chapters existed before Sellars came to them; his task was to find ways of interpreting these works that would communicate with present-day audiences. But inspired by the model of Lorenzo da Ponte, whose alliance with Mozart yielded the most effective instances of opera buffa of the eighteenth century, Sellars began in the 1980s to seek out composers for potential partnerships. Although many composers were writing operas at that time, he set his sights on musicians whom he had to convince, artists who had affected him strongly through their instrumental music. John Adams and, later, Kaija Saariaho (both of whom had regarded opera as a hopelessly stale and outmoded medium) recall their resistance to Sellars's vade mecum. That he persevered in his quest—suggesting themes for potential pieces and putting together creative teams to serve as librettists, set designers, and singers—has resulted a series of works already acknowledged as classics. His efforts have helped to make opera viable once again for the twenty-first century.

Chapter 3 examines Sellars's collaborations with Adams and Alice Goodman. If at first he handed off the writing of the texts to Goodman (*Nixon in China*, *The Death of Klinghoffer*), Sellars later took on that role himself in what he has called "getting the car keys." Chapter 4 turns to the collaborations with Adams—*El Niño*, *Doctor Atomic*, *The Gospel According to the Other Mary*—for which he and the composer assembled their own libretti from sources ranging from scriptures (Christian, Hindu, Buddhist) to classified documents from Los Alamos and poetry by women in both English and Spanish. Qualities that might have passed unnoticed in the earlier work with Mozart and Handel suddenly become unmistakable when he produces his own scenarios and sense of pacing.

The strong feminist dimension of his work becomes ever clearer in his collaborations with Kaija Saariaho, with libretti by Amin Maalouf. It was Sellars's productions of *Don Giovanni* and Messiaen's *Saint François* that persuaded Saariaho to consider stage works, and Sellars has worked with her and Maalouf since *L'amour de loin*. Although Saariaho had long expressed reluctance to writing from a woman's point of view, her decision to write operas led her to develop musical simulations of childbirth, motherhood, and what I will call spectral sensualities. Chapter 5 turns to this extraordinary moment in music history with discussions of *L'amour de loin* and *La passion de Simone* and concludes with *Only the Sound Remains*, a collaboration between Saariaho and Sellars based on Ezra Pound's translations of two Noh plays.

In chapter 6, I focus on Sellars's 2015 production of Henry Purcell's *The Indian Queen*: a recent work for which he assembled not only the libretto but also the music. Purcell wrote only incidental music for the 1664 play by John Dryden and Sir Robert Howard, and the original play scarcely offers an appealing entertainment for today's audiences. For his production, Sellars created an entirely new plot drawn from a novel by Nicaraguan writer Rosario Aguilar and culled music from all of Purcell's oeuvre. His montage of found materials—Aguilar's words, Purcell's music—for *The Indian Queen* reveals a great deal about the aesthetic priorities that have driven his entire career. Indeed, this production resembles that of his 1984 pastiche, *Hang On to Me*, in that Sellars controls both the music and the libretto. If writing his own libretti counted as getting the car keys, he now takes over the car itself.

My final chapter returns to the source, the Bach passions that helped seed Sellars's entire oeuvre. Only after his journey through opera, oratorio, and his own dramatic collaborations did he take on the monumental task of staging these works, and these surely count among the crowning moments in his exceptional career. But in a sense, Sellars had been preparing for these productions for his whole life. It was from the dramaturgical impulses of the passions that he learned how to plumb the emotional depths of his conflicted operatic characters and to structure trajectories that effectively weave together communal and individual utterances. For even as he engages with Bach's texts, we might catch glimmers of Sellars's abandoned Donna Elvira, his conscience-stricken Guglielmo, his martyred Theodora, his poignant Pat Nixon, his tormented Jaufré, his community bearing witness to the testing of the first atomic bomb.

Although they never met, Sellars's priorities have much in common with those of the late Christopher Small. Small has transformed much of musicology, ethnomusicology, and music education by insisting that we should concentrate not on scores and composers but rather on the fundamental human act he termed "musicking."[12] In a piece discovered among Small's papers after his death in 2011, he wrote:

> Concepts of beauty are most fruitfully approached by thinking about our concepts of relationships, especially those relationships we believe we ought to have, with the creatures and objects with which we share our world. Concepts of beauty, in other words, follow from, rather than govern, our concepts of how we ought to relate. . . . Artistic creation is concerned not with the creation of beauty or of beautiful objects . . . but with the articulation of ideal, or perhaps desired, relationships. The sensation of beauty arises from the appreciation of those relationships.[13]

Sellars labels his equivalent practice "ritualizing": making use of sound, lights, motion, and bodies to encourage us to think more productively about our responsibilities to one another. He has labored throughout his career to call our attention to human frailty and to our infinite capacity for forgiveness. And he chose opera as the medium best suited to conveying his passions—musical, aesthetic, political, spiritual, human.

# 1 • American Mozart

## Le nozze di Figaro

Rush hour in Christmas-season Manhattan: shoppers, attaché-toting lawyers, ice-skaters, Santas. A low-aiming camera tracks busy legs as they bustle across intersections, dodging traffic and hurrying on to their next gig. Landmarks of New York architecture flash up, punctuating the flow of pedestrians with moments of still monumentality. The camera zooms in on a Macy's bag, then on one from Tiffany's. Beneath this footage and the running credits we hear the overture to Mozart's *Le nozze di Figaro* (*The Marriage of Figaro*).[1]

Or perhaps we do *not* hear the overture, distracted as we are by the jokey imagery. It is precisely this foregrounding of branded products—Coke cans, McDonald's hamburgers, bottles of lite beer—that has caused some viewers to write Sellars off as a bad boy, as he gleefully besmirches classic master-works with determined vulgarity.[2] Critic Karrie Jacobs offers a terrific parody of such responses:

> What has he done now? The enfant terrible, the precocious one, the spiky-haired iconoclast: What has he done? Most articles about the director Peter Sellars begin this way. Perhaps those aren't the exact words, but the question is always implied: What has this brat pack of one done? Which of Western civilizations most sacred cultural monuments has he desecrated this time?[3]

So why does he do this, knowing full well that he will offend and even alienate many opera fans when he does so?

Fundamental to his long-term project is a commitment to making works—whether old or new—relevant to contemporary audiences. As a professor in the Department of World Arts and Cultures at UCLA, Sellars offers a seminar titled Art as Social Action, in which he guides students from many different programs as they reconceive their work in ways that address cultural tensions. The lucky participants who manage to get into his seminar invariably claim that it changes not only their careers but also their lives.

In his documentary *Destination Mozart: A Night at the Opera with Peter Sellars*, Sellars states:

> When you do opera in America, you have to do it for Americans with Americans by Americans. So you have to do it such a way that people feel it is part of their own vocabulary. And you have to do this in such a way that Americans feel they own this and that the American public feels invited.[4]

The technique of hailing viewers through the very detritus of American pop culture allows him to make a quick connection from which he can develop the more urgent social critiques that drive his choice of pieces, themes, and particular directorial decisions.

Sellars frequently introduces these plebian elements with a kind of affection, recalling perhaps Monty Python's "wink wink, nudge nudge." But then he inevitably moves on to show us aspects of our lives we might rather not acknowledge. In doing this he may actually recall the music-appreciation scene in *Don Giovanni*, when Leporello and his master comment on a stream of current hits, thereby winking at their own audiences, just before the Stone Guest comes to claim this all-too-contemporary antihero—a hipster who knows how to sing along with the most recent pop tunes. In other words, Mozart and Da Ponte brought their own cultural detritus onto the stage for this sequence. No distanced mythological character, Giovanni is one with the original audience members as he gets dragged down into hell right after singing along to their own hit parade.

In the case of Sellars's mise-en-scène of the *Figaro* overture, the variety of shopping bags, as well as the stark contrast between ordinary pedestrians and luxury automobiles, gestures toward the class divisions and sexual abuses addressed so explosively in Beaumarchais's play of 1784 that the French authorities banned it. Mozart and Da Ponte sought to exploit the scandalous reputation of this exceedingly topical play when they chose to adapt it only two years later. This was not an opera in which quaint characters went traipsing around in long-forgotten fashions; this was how the collaborators themselves and all their acquaintances dressed. They *were* Figaro, Susanna, Almaviva, and Cherubino, and so were those who attended the first performances.[5]

Earlier I suggested that this barrage of images might prevent the viewer from actually attending to Mozart's music. To be sure, many moviegoers imagine themselves oblivious to the soundtracks that accompany the pictures they watch. But Hollywood producers would scarcely pay the likes of John Williams or the late James Horner if no one noticed.[6] Whether we pay explicit attention or not, the music of film—and of opera—predisposes us affectively, encouraging us to identify emotionally with the characters and stirring up sufficient excitement to make us invest in successive turns in the plot. Most people can discern within about five seconds of music whether a film is a chick flick, a thriller, or a horror movie, and they weep or whoop on cue, depending on what the music demands.

Sellars excels in his ability to deploy these habits, using the details of the music itself to further his agendas. He serves in his stage direction as a model listener, emphasizing particular features of scores for dramatic purposes. In his Bach passions, he goes so far as to have instrumental soloists interact on stage with those singing the arias, so that we cannot fail to observe Bach's intricate connections between voice and obbligato player (see chapter 7). As we shall see, that kind of commitment to the intricacies of the music runs all the way through Sellars's career.

In the overture to *Figaro*, Mozart signals to his own audiences the world of opera buffa: a genre that featured ordinary people, as opposed to the monarchs and deities who populated opera seria. The opening material scurries and even simulates sniggering with that exemplar of orchestral chortling, the bassoon (not surprisingly, the bassoon will often attend Figaro, thus underscoring the lower-body associations of both character and instrument). The very rhythms—whether on the surface with the wiggly figure of the opening or on the level of phrasing—contribute to the humorous effect. The late Wendy Allanbrook has argued persuasively that the entire classical style depends upon the gestural vocabulary of comic theater, and the *Figaro* overture exemplifies this link.[7]

When Sellars pairs those harried Manhattanites with Mozart's opening figures, he takes his cue from the quality of motion suggested in the score itself. The clothing we see may be updated, but that mode of locomotion may be as ageless as humanity itself. Still, it is partly the music's eighteenth-century idiom that makes this twentieth-century street scene so hilarious.

If the initial bars of the overture suggest the scene's bustling, its phrase structure informs its dramatic shape. A sequential buildup in the winds suddenly explodes with the entry of trumpets and timpani. Mozart's musical lexicon identified those instruments, and their key of D major, with royalty, and when they erupt the camera pauses on a close-up of a street sign for W. 58th Street. When they show up next, the camera stops to focus on the hood of a Rolls Royce, then on other fancy cars and hotels; Sellars pairs their appearances in the middle of the overture with the gilded storefronts of Fendi, Buccellini, and Gucci. Saving the best for last, he accompanies the overture's triumphant conclusion with the camera slowly panning the name of the Trump Tower. And since Mozart repeats his cadential arrival three times over for good measure, the camera too gets to keep flashing back on that gaudy sign.

In other words, Sellars choreographs the visual imagery of his opening in such a way as to highlight the overture's musical rhetoric (those sudden blasts from trumpets and drums, the redundant closing strategy) but also Mozart's own political dichotomy: the contrast between the bustling, everyday strings and a privileged nobility that does no work but simply intrudes with imperious demands. We are accustomed to hearing Mozart's instrumental music as perfect order, untainted by worldly issues—which means that we very often miss his musical and ideological points.[8] But Sellars teaches us how to hear both the hilarity and the social tensions so carefully articulated by Mozart in this opening sequence. Listen to it again after you have watched Sellars's presentation, and you'll easily hear the musical jokes as well as the foregrounding of the opera's principal conflict. The French authorities might well have banned the opera before the characters even began to sing if they had understood the overture in the way Sellars presents it.[9]

The opera unfolds inside the Trump Tower so emphatically announced, with the Count and Countess Almaviva as wealthy owners of a luxury penthouse suite, Figaro and Susanna as their liveried servants who occupy back rooms littered with brand-name cleaning products. The transfer from noble Spanish palace to Manhattan took very little effort. But it does ask that we see some of those busy shoppers of the overture as going home to cramped quarters and humiliating conditions, while the abusive Count enjoys the pleasures identified with Gucci, the Rolls Royce, and the Tower.

Because Sellars's *Figaro* contains so many brilliant buffa moments to enumerate, I will deal with only a couple of my favorites. Surely the most memorable comic episode in this production occurs when Susan Larson sings Cherubino's "Non sò più cosa son, cosa faccio" (I no longer know what I am, what I'm doing). A pants role, Cherubino often appears as a scarcely made-up woman, singing quite chastely of awakening sexual urges. By contrast, Larson takes advantage of Mozart's bouncy, off-beat rhythmic figures by joyously humping the bed and anything else in sight. This indeed is a horny teenage boy.[10]

Eighteenth-century audiences would have known that the third play of Beaumarchais's trilogy, following *Le barbier de Séville* and *La folle journée ou Le mariage de Figaro*, was *La mère coupable* (The guilty mother), in which Countess Almaviva has borne a child fathered by Cherubino.[11] In fact, Beaumarchais's Countess responds quite a bit more enthusiastically to Cherubino's flirtations than in the opera's deliberately cleaned-up version.[12] But in Sellars's production, the Count's jealous fury, which may seem a bit far-fetched in most productions, becomes entirely plausible. This kid, clad in hockey gear, is clearly on the make, and the Countess responds perhaps too willingly to her page's youthful advances.

My other favorite moment features Sanford Sylvan. Anyone who identifies this singer-actor with Leon Klinghoffer sinking slowly into the sea in his wheelchair or with a somber Chou En-lai needs to watch his performance of "Se vuol ballare." In this aria, Figaro imagines telling the Count that he'll reverse power roles with him, forcing him unwittingly to dance to his servant's tune. In his famously impudent subtitles, Sellars translates the opening line as "If you want to dance, Count baby!" (surely an apt rendering of "signor contino"), and Sylvan's exuberant physical comedy matches Mozart's perfectly.

I will start with the short recitative leading into the aria because Sellars choreographs these throwaway passages with such care. Susanna has left the room, having just informed her fiancé of the Count's designs on her. Sylvan turns toward the Count's closed door and addresses him in absentia. Mozart inserts little riffs in the continuo between Figaro's statements, and with each of these, Figaro becomes clearer about his strategy. Sellars knows how to manipulate silence particularly well, and long pauses occur between Figaro's statements, each of them showing greater self-awareness and potential aggression, with mercurial changes in attitude registering on the tight close-ups of Sylvan's face. After he has recalled the Count's plan of taking Susanna along on diplomatic trips, he rapidly puts an accusing finger on the door, shaking his head quietly as if threateningly. "Non sarà, non sarà" (it will not be!), he promises; "Figaro il dice" (Figaro says so). He pivots quickly for the aria but waits a moment while a knowing smirk crosses his face.

Mozart wraps Figaro's subversive text in the meter of the aristocratic minuet, thereby mimicking the Count's own idiom. When Sylvan refers to accompanying the Count's dance with a "chitarrino," he picks up and picks at a conveniently placed guitar. No real surprises yet. But when Mozart's melody waxes more belligerent on the threat of making the Count dance the "capriole," Sylvan brandishes the guitar like the weapon Da Ponte suggests it might become. A middle section marked Presto—what Allanbrook identifies as a contredanse, a type more appropriate to this working-class character—allows the singer to move into patter mode,[13] and here the rhythms get duplicated by insolent slaps on the Count's door and rapid-fire finger-snaps. A very long pause follows the end of this section before Sylvan returns to his starting material, now wiser and in firmer control of his scheme. He sits on the floor, apparently rehearsing his plan of action in his mind before singing the reprise of "Se vuol ballare." When an orchestral tag reprises the Presto, Sylvan leaps to his feet and marks the tag's conclusion by slamming the door behind him.

As we shall see, Sellars thinks a great deal about the purposes of all those formal repetitions in eighteenth-century music—one of the most serious obstacles to the realist dramaturgy modern audiences expect. "Se vuol ballare" does not pose enormous difficulty: it is relatively short in duration, and the highly contrasting middle section seems to require a recap of the opening. But when Sylvan sings "Se vuol ballare" the second time, it has taken on new, enhanced meanings. One lovely alteration in the staging of the reprise involves Sylvan's "just come and get it" gesture with his index finger. The finger that had earlier pointed in accusation now invites; righteous anger has turned to confident defiance.[14]

I mentioned the use of close-ups in the DVD of "Se vuol ballare." This technique matters enormously in all of Sellars's video work, even if a live audience might miss some of the nuances the camera picks up in the filmed versions. Sellars demands weeks of strenuous rehearsals with his principal singers, translating harmonic details into facial expression, rhythmic figures into kinetic activity, and formal structures into blocking. For the Mozart Trilogy, he relies on conductor Craig Smith, who worked out decisions concerning timing and musical emphasis together with Sellars and the singers.[15]

Before I leave my discussion of the comedic elements in *Figaro*, I want to consider one more Sellars trademark: synchronized gesturing by multiple characters. Sellars developed his use and repertory of gestures from many sources, including Asian (Chinese, Japanese, Indonesian) theatrical practices and his experience working with the National Theatre of the Deaf, for which he learned to work with actors who used sign language. Often mentioned by critics as an annoyance (as "semaphoring"), this strategy features ever more heavily in Sellars's work up to the present. Because it shows up first in his Mozart Trilogy, I will discuss it briefly here, in part to lay the groundwork for my examinations of later pieces. If these gestures register as slapstick in *Figaro* and in *Così fan tutte*, they will serve radically different ends in, say, *Theodora* or the *St. John Passion*. But even in *Figaro* they operate on several important levels.

The celebrated finale to act 2 finds all characters onstage, singing together, albeit to several disparate purposes. In a typical opera buffa finale, the action begins with a couple of characters, then expands gradually to include the entire cast. Mozart's multisectional finales maintain continuity without any breaks for recitative, though with changing time and key signatures to punctuate the dramatic situation as it evolves. His skill at working in purely instrumental idioms assisted him greatly in sustaining formal unity even as he stretched the bounds of coherence through his many interpolations and interruptions. Allanbrook has explained at length how Mozart structures this particular finale like an extended dance suite, with each new episode marking its autonomy with a characteristic rhythm. In the terms of her analysis, we pass through the opening march (the confrontation between the Count and Countess discussed below), a minuet, a passepied, a gavotte, and a gigue before returning to the opening key for another march: the ensemble that will bring down the curtain on act 2.[16]

As the finale begins, the Count, the Countess, Susanna, and Figaro are already on stage, the latter three characters having flummoxed the Count once again. Suddenly, three other characters—Marcellina, Bartolo, Basilio, all supporters of the Count—burst into the room. Marcellina presents a document in which Figaro promises to marry her if he fails to pay a debt; if her argument holds, Susanna will not be able to proceed with her wedding and the Count will win. The tables have turned: whereas before the Count faced three opponents, those three now have to confront the Count and his three sycophants. Although at times each of these seven characters sings alone, at others they all jabber simultaneously. Again, our elevated conception of Mozart's music can make this chaos seem smooth and harmonious, even as he juggles all those unruly sentiments. But the composer would have wanted us to hear the chaos rather than a glossy surface.

It is here that Sellars draws on stylized gestures: funny in and of themselves, of course, but also crucial for visualizing Mozart's counterpoint. As the antagonists present their positions individually to the Count, Susanna, the Countess, and Figaro cower in synchronized horror at the other side of the stage, reduced by the circumstances to a single comic unit. When they attempt to raise objections, the Count shuts them up with an imperious "Silenzio!" At tempo-marking Più allegro (the sign for the bum's rush part of the act), Marcellina, Bartolo, and Basilio line up behind the Count, congratulating themselves on having offered such a perfect case, on having hit the nail on the nose, and thanking whatever god allowed them to grasp the situation. Each of these warrants not just a single gesture but an array of different ones as the words keep repeating in Mozart's drive for the long-delayed cadence. Despite the fact that seven singers participate, Sellars makes sure we keep track of who's with whom as well as their particular arguments.

The opera's more serious moments might not withstand this cartoonish Mickey Mousing between music and actions, though it works perfectly in the context of this finale, in which a series of ever-more-ridiculous plot twists demands a powerful send-off.[17] Indeed, gesturing of this sort also appears in comic stagings by many other directors, and we could well regard this element as a relatively conventional (if brilliantly realized) solution in Sellars's *Figaro* finale. But, as we shall see, this device develops over the course of Sellars's career until it appears even in the most dire of dramatic situations, where it points to the complexities of the music's many layers, to the coordinated chaos of contrapuntal singing, to the externalization of emotional intensity.

Like the other Mozart–Da Ponte operas, *Figaro* has a dark side, and Sellars's filming of the overture hints at this dimension in advance. At about four minutes in, Mozart's harmonies swerve temporarily toward the minor. We might not even notice this: it does not stand out as unusual in the context of eighteenth-century practice (just a slight melodramatic hint of the ominous—what Allanbrook calls the "ombra"—before all returns to normal), and its parallel appearance earlier in the overture passes unmarked in the video.[18] But this second occurrence conjures a lingering shot of St. Patrick's Cathedral, briefly casting a strange shadow over the proceedings before the return of the unclouded major mode and footage of department store Santas. Only that enigmatic shot calls our attention to what Sellars sometimes calls wounded or bruised chords, and it suggests that this opera buffa may not all be fun and games.

Indeed, Sellars will reveal several dark patches in *Le nozze di Figaro* over the course of his production, all of them signaled explicitly in the libretto but not usually pursued quite so far as in this staging. We know already early in act 1 that the Count pressures his female servants to deliver sexual favors. In the recitative leading into "Se vuol ballare," Sellars has his Figaro cross from the side of the stage from which Susanna has just exited and stomp in proprietary fashion across the marriage bed in question (here a foldout couch) to the Count's door. The threat of sexual abuse fuels the entire plot: it ignites Figaro's explosive demand for vengeance, provokes the Countess's grief, and leads the other characters to make common cause against the Count. If class privilege in general lies behind Beaumarchais's play, it manifests itself in the opera most clearly in the Count's plan to resurrect the medieval droit du seigneur, whereby a feudal lord claimed the right to deflower the young women in his estate. Historians have sometimes argued that the droit du seigneur counted as an anachronism by the eighteenth century and have even questioned whether it ever existed at all. The recent revelation that prominent men in politics, journalism, education, music, and the entertainment industry still wield their power and authority in expectation of sexual payback demonstrates that this practice is alive and well, making this production all the more pertinent.[19]

But the opera addresses another dark issue that permeates relationships, sometimes even among individuals of the same class: namely, domestic violence. As dissimilar as Figaro may be from his boss, both lash out against their partners when they feel themselves disrespected. As we shall see, Sellars often homes in on scenes involving violence against women in his productions and, later, in his own libretti, making this one of his signature themes.

The most intensely disturbing scene in Sellars's *Figaro* occurs in act 2, which opens with "Porgi, amor," the Countess's lament over the loss of her husband's affections. Mozart's contemporaries would have known how tenderly Count Almaviva wooed her in *Le barbier*, and we see here the devastating ruins of that love affair. Just as she finishes her cavatina, Susanna and Cherubino burst in, and we seem to have returned to high jinks as usual. Suddenly the Count pounds on the door.

When the Countess (Jayne West) finally opens the door, the Count (James Maddalena) enters, dressed in hunting garb, as indicated in the libretto. Maddalena's costume, however, resembles that of Elmer Fudd in his deerstalker hat chasing the elusive Wabbit, thus inviting a chuckle from the audience. But his clothing also indicates that he seeks some kind of prey, and we quickly pivot from the cartoonish wink to a potentially deadly encounter.

Since the Count participated himself in the closet-hopping scenario characteristic of bedroom farces in the previous act, he naturally suspects hidden lovers, and the Countess's locked door incites his fury. That she is lying or covering up something is quite evident from her evasive answers. In this staging, their physical interactions suggest that he has threatened her before and that she has worked to develop coping mechanisms, as has Susanna—the hidden witness to and commentator during this scene. When the Countess stalls during their dialogue, her husband glowers and strokes her face sadistically as warning signals; occasionally the Countess taunts her husband by hinting that she knows of his attempted dalliances with her maid. The entire exchange during the recitative leading into the following ensemble contains long dramatic pauses, gaps that bristle with danger.

The Count kicks off the trio commanding "Susanna, or via sortite!" (Come out now, Susanna!). Although the triple meter recalls a stately minuet, the Count's melody and the drum-like flourishes in the orchestra sound

militant. The women sing defensively, trying to calm him as well as themselves, and for a while they manage to deflect the affect away from the Count's
imperiousness. Some of those vagrant minor-key harmonies that Sellars
highlighted in the overture appear as the Countess describes the situation as
brutal ("bruttissima"), the Count as all too clear ("chiarissima"). The three
singers move toward closure on the dominant key, toward which the Countess has tried to steer the proceedings, all of them halting briefly on a questioning, deceptive cadence. But the violence the Count has suggested
throughout now explodes, as he pushes the Countess roughly to the floor.
Over the course of this number, he will repeatedly shove her, though sometimes looking guiltily down at his hands. At the number's recapitulation (at
"Dunque parlate almeno"), the Count drags the Countess by the hair back to
the tonic key area, once more claiming his turf. The wrath and cowering become more pronounced toward the end of the trio when each spouse sings
"Giudizio" (I warn you), with no accompaniment. The threat here lies bare,
and the orchestra waits a very long time before Susanna's cry of horror brings
them back for a push toward the trio's closure.

Beautifully crafted as Mozart's ensemble writing always is, we sometimes
fail to notice the tensions among these characters; they fit together so perfectly! Some commentators seem not to notice the implied violence of this
scene; others describe it politely as nothing more than bullying or bluster.
But Sellars takes his cues from the harmonic tensions, the interruptions, the
sudden outbursts, the rhythmic aggression in the music. Each time we might
be inclined to write off something in the staging as gratuitous, Sellars asks us
to listen more carefully; it's all there in the score.

Maddalena's tyrannical Count, who looked so silly in his silk nightshirt
in the first act (or as Elmer Fudd earlier in this scene) and whose fear of cuck-
oldry will bear the brunt of the opera's joke, is no laughing matter here. When
he and the Countess return after a brief absence (during which Susanna and
Cherubino try to tidy things up), Maddalena brandishes a revolver in the
Countess's face. Even when he vows in his text to kill Cherubino, he aims his
murderous rage toward his wife. Only Susanna's surprise entrance interrupts
what risks becoming a homicide. Note that this horrifying scene initiates
that same finale that culminates in the goofy ending we examined earlier.

Sellars wants his viewers to notice not only the Count's sexual malfea-
sance but also his penchant for physical violence. That he has assaulted his
spouse before seems clear from Countess's frantic attempts at defusing him
and from his own facial expressions of guilt. In the minutes that follow, he
begs her forgiveness, as he will do again, of course, at the conclusion of the
opera. No one imagines—least of all the Countess—that he will actually re-

form. Despite the lesson she and their servants teach him, he will continue to philander and to respond to opposition with rage.

As we have seen, Sellars presents the buffoonish and the bullying sides of the Count, both widely recognized in productions even if Sellars goes further into comedy and violence. But he also humanizes the Count in act 3, asking us to grant him a bit of sympathy. This moment occurs just when the Count has behaved perhaps at his worst as he sets up his assignation with Susanna. During their duet, "Crudel! perchè finor farmi languir così?" (Cruel one, why do you still make me languish like this?), Maddalena actually thrusts his head up under the apron of Susanna's maid costume, peeking out only when she calls out the wrong answers to his questions. His obscene advance clearly reveals his sense that he owns the bodies of his female servants (his celebrity allows him to "grab them by the pussy," as the real Trump boasted later), and it also allows Susanna to register her disgust plainly, as she could not if they actually faced one another.

But, of course, Susanna has tolerated this physical humiliation because she is trying to entrap the Count, who overhears her conspiratorial whispers with Figaro. He explodes with fury in a recitative protesting his victimhood and plotting revenge, then in an extended rage aria, "Vedrò mentr'io sospiro" (Shall I see while I sigh), attended by the flourishes of the royal French overture, complete with trumpets and drums in D major. He draws, in other words, on all the aristocratic paraphernalia he can garner in order to shore himself up. He ends his monologue boasting that his vendetta will console his soul and make him jubilate.

Sellars's staging of this scene tells a somewhat different story, though always drawing on the harmonic details of Mozart's score, which careen abruptly from key to key as the Count attempts to find a solution. Moreover, Almaviva brings his hectoring habits with him, even in his interior monologues, his thoughts punctuated by emphatic, stomping octaves and fanfares in the orchestra. Sellars makes full use of exaggerated gestures in this scene. The more realistic stagecraft recalling Stanislavski method that Sellars deploys for scenes of social interaction here gives way to extreme physical contortion. No longer comic, the gestures serve to render visible the tumultuous emotions wracking this character as he reflects alone on his situation.

Maddalena begins his aria pouting with hurt (C major), then abruptly switches to rage (E major), wipes his mouth with disgust as he thinks of punishing his adversaries, then sadistically announces that their downfall will give him pleasure (F♯ minor). In his anger, he starts to ascend the staircase. But suddenly he turns, as he begins to contemplate potential schemes, one involving Marcellina, the other Susanna's Uncle Antonio, the gardener. As the strings churn up more and more suspense, he grasps the back of his neck, writhing with the tension he suffers. Maddalena has followed Mozart's harmonic and rhythmic nuances perfectly. Just watch his eyes as Mozart's chords begin to meander or his posture when his thoughts change direction.

But whereas the aria's introduction bristles with aristocratic arrogance, Sellars takes advantage of Mozart's downward-swooping ornaments to bring the Count to his knees as if with karate chops and then flat to the floor, trumpets and drums notwithstanding. As he starts to sing, he tries to rise, then, struck with the pain of the situation (as well as those swooping ornaments), collapses facedown again. He continues, caught between ranting and grieving, this affective mixture relying on Mozart's vacillation between major and minor, between his military instruments and the retreat into whiny strings and winds. Maddalena bucks up, standing to full height, when the trumpets accompany his protest, but then (with Mozart's sinister minor chords) flops forward, stroking his face in self-pity when he recalls Susanna's preference for Figaro. Once more, the timpani pull him out of this slump, as he exclaims over rising ornaments that he will not allow this situation to transpire.

Now the music switches gears in an Allegro assai as an apparent push to a triumph finish. Yet here too, Mozart continues to oscillate between major and minor, and Maddalena either shouts in defiance or falls to the floor in abjection. Indeed, he is lying on his side when he first sings about the joy his revenge will bring. Some jubilation! Even during his cadenza, Maddalena's face switches mercurially between wrath and pain. At the end, although he clenches his fists, pounding the floor in frustration, he ultimately collapses, rolling into the corner to lie in fetal position as his rightful trumpets and drums taunt him in their affective distance from his desperate state. These are, of course, wounds the Count has inflicted upon himself. But at this moment when he might have celebrated his manhood unambiguously, Sellars presents someone as deeply damaged as anyone else on the stage.[20]

We may well remember this when, in the final scene of *Figaro*, the Count is shamed in front of his whole community and is once again brought to his knees, this time begging his wife's forgiveness. That he richly deserves this humiliation is clear. Yet we have seen him emotionally naked, and surely he too deserves some modicum of compassion.

Sellars also offers a strong reading of the Countess through his staging. Her monologues, for instance, take place in sets that reveal her as radically isolated. In *Destination Mozart*, set designer Adrianne Lobel comments that she understands this character to be as vulnerable as a piece of fish laid out on ice at a sushi bar, and during "Porgi amor" (Pour, oh Love) the Countess lies curled up in anguish on a cold marble bench. The recitative of her second monologue, in which she bemoans the humiliation of having to exchange clothing with her maidservant, finds her on the upper level of the stark minimalist architecture of the penthouse suite, while Cherubino and Barbarina exhibit their mutual puppy love on the level below her. She goes on in "Dove sono i bei momenti" (Where are the lovely moments) to reminisce about the time when she and the Count shared such episodes of "sweetness and pleasure." In the middle section of her aria she asks why, given the pain her marriage now causes her, those memories will not go away. At this point she nearly leaves the stage; only her hand remains visible, lingering on the railing. But those memories tug her back into view as she sings the reprise and the fantasy of reconciliation that follows. To be sure, when the Countess is in the company of Susanna and Cherubino, she freely participates in their comic antics. But these two scenes in which Mozart invites us to witness her interiority take her into a vastly different realm.

At the end of the opera, the Count begs for forgiveness, and the Countess relents—apparently not for the first or last time—at which point the entire cast comes together to echo her merciful sentiments. In this production, they all face the audience, no longer interacting with each other and, indeed, dropping the facade of character altogether. We have witnessed each of these individuals engage in deceit, inflicting pain on one another as a result. They all have contributed to the erosion of trust that makes civil society possible; all have sinned and stand unworthy. But in this united thanksgiving for unearned clemency, barriers of class, gender, age, and even the gap between stage and audience drop away momentarily, as Sellars's staging makes clear. This still moment lifts Beaumarchais's farce to a very different affective plane, surely one of the great expressions of hope in music—all the more so for the fact that it operates on such a very human scale. As the ensemble addresses the audience, they bring the listeners into a communal moment of spiritual redemption and renewal, much as do the choruses in Bach's sacred works.

After this hushed prayer, the cast erupts into the curtain-closer in which they express the wish to make merry in the face of the traumatic day all have survived.[21] Here again those shades of the minor key drift by, on the words describing the day's events as "di capricci e di follia" (of deceits and madness), finally chased away by the characters' will to forget until tomorrow the injuries they have inflicted on one another. Only here does Sellars return to his signature impishness as cast members form a conga line around the Christmas tree, then display the wave formation fashionable at the time at sports events. But the utter seriousness of the request for and granting of forgiveness in the penultimate moment hovers still over the proceedings.

Between the extremes of slapstick and bad behavior and this transcendent moment, there exists yet another plane in this opera: the community of women. At first only Susanna and Countess come together for mutual support and comfort, but later Marcellina will join them in solidary against the men who so often mistreat them. Sellars stages these moments with great tenderness, as for instance in the scene in which the Countess dictates the letter to Susanna that will ensnare the Count, the Countess clearly recoiling in grief at this strategem, Susanna drifting off into a fantasy of her own wedding night.

Of course, these moments originate with Beaumarchais; recall also that the scenario of a maid who outsmarts her jealous, autocratic master was fundamental to opera buffa as a genre, beginning with its inception in Pergolesi's *La serva padrona* (1733) and, before that, in the standard shticks of commedia dell'arte. Mozart and Da Ponte emphasize these elements even more, in part to deflect away from the class-based tensions that drew down the wrath of the censors.[22] But I emphasize the woman-centered dimension of this production of *Figaro* because it will become crucial to Sellars in his choice of operas (*Theodora, Iolanta*), in the ways he shapes his own libretti (*Doctor Atomic, El Niño, The Gospel According to the Other Mary, The Indian Queen*), and even in his staging of the Bach passions. Compare this impulse with the explosion of misogynist operas—for example, *Powder Her Face, Anna Nicole*—that have emerged recently in our post-political-correctness era.[23] If Sellars learned feminism at Mozart's feet, he has carried it as a necessity throughout the rest of his career.[24]

In a short but perceptive discussion, Richard Dellamora points to another gender-related issue in Sellars's *Figaro*.[25] Always a stickler for setting complete texts, Sellars includes two arias—by Marcellina and Don Basilio respectively—that rarely appear in productions of this already overlong opera. Sue Ellen Kuzma, as Marcellina, sings about how men abuse women, and Don Bartolo (father of her child, now known as Figaro) has to pull her back from suicide. Her plaint, however dispensable for most productions, makes perfect sense within Beaumarchais's, Da Ponte's, and Sellars's scenarios.

But Don Basilio's aria—a bizarre narrative featuring a fairy godmother who bequeaths a horribly stinking ass's skin—seems to come out of nowhere. Since Basilio counts otherwise as a very minor character, most directors cut this enigmatic aria. Dellamora, however, reads this moment as deeply queer, especially in Frank Kelley's splendidly grotesque performance. What is this stigma to which he suddenly confesses? To be sure, he functions as the Count's butt-boy, carrying out the dirty work that not even Figaro will touch. But why the extreme abjection? Following Dellamora, I read this staging as extending humanity to those who harbor dark secrets in their core identities, sympathy to those who suffer from having to hide shameful truths. Perhaps Basilio's secret concerns his sexuality, perhaps not. But Sellars and Kelley present a searing image of unhealed wounds resulting from the disparity between the private self and the public veneer.

## Don Giovanni

Some opera fans may well object to the intrusion of explicit violence into the buffa world of *Le nozze di Figaro*, but no one would try to deny the collisions between comic antics and criminal misconduct in *Don Giovanni*. Heady with the tremendous success of *Figaro*, which premiered only a year earlier, Mozart and Da Ponte chose to take on an already-antiquated morality tale concerning a libertine aristocrat who meets his just deserts at the hand of one of his slain victims. Long a staple of street theater, this story scarcely seemed to offer the topical opportunities and sophistication of Beaumarchais's still scandal-associated play. But Mozart and Da Ponte transferred many of the themes already dramatized in *Figaro*—foremost among them, abuses of class privilege and gender inequality—into the creaky vessel of *The Stone Guest*. Following Carlo Goldoni, who worked to produce plays residing between the mutually exclusive extremes of opera seria and opera buffa, they labeled this opera a *dramma giocoso*.[26]

In the 1960s, *Mad* Magazine published a satire of this opera in response to a televised performance. Central to their satire was precisely the *giocoso* label, which promises jokes and tomfoolery—only to display a rape and a murder in the very first scene. "Isn't this hilarious?" the satire asks the reader. For those not inured to this classic, the opera clearly retained its shock value nearly two hundred years later.

In the discussion concerning the overture to *Figaro*, we saw that Sellars took advantage of a brief minor-mode inflection to foreshadow the sometimes painful scenes that would appear later in the opera. But Mozart himself announces the queasy admixture of affects in *Don Giovanni* with the extensive opening Sturm und Drang portion of the overture and then with that horrendous opening scene. Sellars doesn't have to present a special plea to explore the dark side this time, though we may not be prepared for how very deeply he goes into this brutal, cynical world.

The urban blight of Harlem takes the place of nocturnal Seville in Sellars's production. Indeed, the opening shots resemble those of many hip-hop videos at the time, some of which sought to engage in social criticism by indicting the destruction of neighborhoods by elite projects such as Robert Moses's Cross-Bronx Expressway.[27] As the ominous strains of the overture sound, the camera pans a bombed-out cityscape, lingering on the fronts of abandoned buildings, boarded-up windows, graffiti-laden walls, and trash heaps containing relics of families that have had to vacate. Images of churches figure heavily in this montage, for this *Don Giovanni* trades on tensions between religious faith and the unholy supernatural; in the stage set, a neon cross hovers over the proceedings. No trace of the bustling human society of the *Figaro* overture appears here. Because the footage insists on the nightmare locales of our own time, it deprives the viewer of the cheap thrills of Mozart's creepy-crawly gothic.

Without warning, Mozart's overture suddenly pivots to the gestural world of buffa, with the kinds of musical jokes and energies displayed in *Figaro*. But Sellars's camera remains in the ruins of Harlem, and the greater musical vigor of this section is reflected only in the stray dogs roaming the landscape in search of scraps and homeless individuals warming themselves by fires they have made in rusted-out oil barrels. A close-up of a dead rat signals that not even vermin can survive in this environment. In the middle of this jolly Moderato, the camera switches to rows of hardscrabble storefronts and to the struggling, disaffected humans who inhabit these mean streets—a long distance from the midtown shoppers we saw in *Figaro*. As the opening montage proceeds, daylight fades, and the last images plunge us into the sinister nighttime setting that lighting designer James Ingalls sustains for the entire opera. Yet here too it seems to be Christmas, and as Mozart's overture winds down, we catch a glimpse of flickering Christmas tree lights in the window of a tenement. We get no further comfort.

When the curtain rises, we see Leporello, played here by Herbert Perry. In a stroke of luck that would have turned Mozart green with envy, Eugene Perry, his identical twin, fills the role of Giovanni. Da Ponte often strives to make servant and master indistinguishable, as they swap clothing and impersonate each other repeatedly. In Sellars's production, these extraordinarily talented singer-actors create a fulcrum of hilarity, deceit, violence, and horror not easily forgotten, however one might try to erase certain images from one's memory.

The Perry twins are African American, which further affects the mise-en-scène. When I first saw this film in the early 1990s, I found it deeply troubling that black performers—however talented—had been cast as the miscreants Giovanni and Leporello, especially when the first scene features the attempted rape of a white woman, Donna Anna. Moreover, it seemed to me then that Sellars had sacrificed the dimension of class privilege so central to the original script in order to feature these two singers.

But within the social universe presented in this production, Giovanni indeed wields power over his neighbors. He reigns here as a kingpin, perhaps a drug lord (he, Donna Anna, and Don Ottavio are all portrayed as addicts). This topsy-turvy world of urban crime pays scant attention to the usual privileges of race.[28] It is also a world in which no one dares to state openly what they witness: neither Giovanni in the rape scene nor the three "masquere" (maskers) in the act 1 finale actually wear masks, for self-deception and denial have ensured mutual silence. With his bling and his moves borrowed from still-novel hip-hop and blaxploitation movies, this Giovanni is a rap star with his roots in the underworld of drugs, sex trafficking, and guns.

It is Leporello who first alludes to pop-music stardom as he strikes poses reminiscent of Prince and Michael Jackson videos during "Notte e giorno" (Night and day), his complaint against his servile situation and class inequality in general. I have already discussed the extraordinary finale to act 2 in *Figaro*—the ways in which Mozart deploys his skills honed in symphonic composition to create and unbroken series of interdependent musical numbers. In the *Figaro* finale, he moves from the disturbing confrontation between the Count and Countess to a chaotic conclusion with all characters at comical odds with one another: a modulation from domestic discord to silliness. In *Don Giovanni*, he and Da Ponte open act 1 with a similar unbroken chain, but this time they move from Leporello's comic banter to attempted rape to homicide—all within a single tonal trajectory.[29] No other opera whipsaws its audience from chuckles to such horror, from one emotional extreme to the other, in a single extended shot.

We like to think of Mozart's musical perfection as evidence of Enlightenment humanism.[30] But in *Don Giovanni* and *Così fan tutte*, he deploys his skills in the service of dubious ethical positions. What precisely does it mean to package together a patter song, a sexual assault, and a murder as if fulfilling universal rules of balance and order? Or, in *Così*, to stage a philosophe's experiment that leaves everyone severely damaged? Recall that the Marquis de Sade worked at this same time; the Enlightenment had many faces.

Nineteenth-century critics liked to regard the character Don Giovanni as a Romantic hero. Seduced themselves like Zerlina by "La ci darem la mano" or by the powerful virility of the Champagne Aria, many directors presented him as elegant and sensual, greatly preferable to his uptight foes. We may forget that male protagonists in Italian opera before this time were sung by tenors or, more frequently, castrati (Mozart still wrote for castrati in his last opera, *La clemenza di Tito*). Casting Giovanni as a baritone confounded genre as well as gender boundaries. Such voices might perform the parts of servants, villains, fathers, or monarchs, but not leading roles.[31] When

Giovanni comes spilling out of Donna Anna's apartment, wrestling to subdue her, then cracking jokes over the Commendatore's death, contemporary audiences would not have known whether to regard him as a villain or a comedian or something entirely new and unclassifiable. He is, of course, all of these things and much more.

Despite Eugene Perry's handsome appearance, Sellars works to make his antagonist as repugnant as he can. His performance of the Champagne Aria shows him as dangerously manic. At the start of the finale to act 2, Giovanni gorges messily on takeout from McDonald's, reacting to Leporello's comments concerning his gluttony by letting his half-chewed food dribble from his mouth. Anyone fond of, say, Cesare Siepi's urbane performance or who persists, like Kierkegaard, in celebrating him as primal energy may well resist this interpretation.[32] But, as always, Sellars takes his cues from the libretto and score. And in the years since Sellars premiered his version, others have vied to make their protagonist even more repellent and sociopathic.[33]

Sellars's Giovanni displays his viciousness with particular cold-bloodedness. In the opening scene, after he has shot Donna Anna's father, Perry stares defiantly into the camera, calmly lighting a cigarette, as the Commendatore—visible over Giovanni's shoulder—droops to his death. Mozart punctuates the Commendatore final breath with a deceptive harmony, matched by Perry's grinding out of his cigarette butt and the commencement of shockingly vulgar banter between Giovanni and Leporello. At the end of the opera, as the Commendatore intones Giovanni's death sentence, Perry again faces us in that same defiant pose, his judge (the Commendatore's living statue) hovering behind him. Even when singing his seductive duet with Zerlina, Perry casts his cruel gaze toward the camera. He presents no commendable traits in this production. Even Leporello finds him repulsive (as he does, of course, throughout Da Ponte's libretto).

The cadre of women we saw in *Figaro* also appears here, as Donna Elvira steps in to save Zerlina and Donna Anna, even though she cannot save herself from her own obsession with Giovanni. Of the three women, Zerlina (Ai Lan Zhu) emerges as having the most inner strength. Donna Elvira, sung here by Lorraine Hunt in 1980s Madonna wannabe gear, continues to the end to crave her treacherous lover, allowing herself to be tricked over and over again. Donna Anna (Dominique Labelle) is consumed with bloodlust, made most explicit in her duet with Don Ottavio (Carroll Freeman) in which she forces his hand down into the Commendatore's gore as she demands his oath of vengeance.

However reluctantly, Don Ottavio operates as an honorary member of this women's group. Mozart gave this character two unusually beautiful arias, perhaps underscoring his ineffectuality. But Sellars's Ottavio is wracked with ambivalence and self-hatred, and although Freeman sings both "Dalla sua pace" (On her peace) and "Il mio tesoro" (My treasure) gorgeously, he flirts with suicide in his stage actions. Presented here as a police officer, Ottavio vacillates between supporting and doubting Anna, becoming abusive when she holds onto her attachment to her father. His resentment of this emotional commitment even leads him after an extraordinarily bitter performance of "Il mio tesoro" to topple the Commendatore's statue. Eventually we witness Anna during "Non mi dir" (Do not call me) shooting up to relieve her anguish, and Ottavio trails after her with her drug paraphernalia, prepared to follow her in this mode of escape.

A telling feature of their relationship is the way Ottavio constantly attempts to stifle Anna's vehement appeals for justice by forcing her arms down, as if suppressing these gestures of righteous indignation will subdue her; he does so in their opening duet in which he tries to distract her from her dire D minor to an F major of forgetfulness, and again in her heroic "Or sai chi l'onore" (Now I know), and yet again in the trio in the act 1 finale. He wants not so much to help her as to silence her agency, to make her a submissive spouse. Her rage terrifies him.[34]

The people who inhabit this bleak landscape have all been corrupted, with little hope of redemption. In Sellars's words in *Destination Mozart*: "These people are in hell; they're in hell from the very beginning; they live in hell," and Da Ponte records that he was reading Dante when he penned this libretto. The closing chorus, in which everyone celebrates Giovanni's demise, presents the members of the cast in a Bosch-like purgatory, standing in hospital gowns in holes; the Boschian symbolism is even clearer when the Infernal Spirits pop up from under the streets, holding pavement tiles above their heads. Perhaps because none of the actual characters has emerged with any moral authority, Sellars has a young girl—maybe one of the targeted "beginners" Leporello mentions in his Catalogue Aria—take Giovanni's hand to drag him into hell, the gaping construction site with blinking warning lights onstage from the outset.

As he does in *Figaro*, Sellars strives in *Don Giovanni* to make Mozart's musical strategies visible, and he does this nowhere more brilliantly than in the ballroom scene in the act 1 finale. In a near miraculous feat of counterpoint, Mozart here superimposes three different dances in three different meters representing three different classes: the minuet (3/4 time), the contredanse (2/4 time), and the German dance (3/8 time). Anna, Elvira, and Ottavio lead out with their courtly dance, Giovanni entices Zerlina to perform her characteristic dance with him, and Leporello pressures Masetto to join him in a quasi jig. We usually notice this extraordinary achievement only when following the score, so deftly does the composer make these fit; the minuet seems to override everything else. The balancing act of meters and social strata finally topples only when Giovanni tries to rape Zerlina, who screams for help.

Sellars updates the dance steps in keeping with his concept, but he manages in doing so to reveal to us how precarious Mozart's house of cards truly is. Our aristocrats present a highly stylized, Spanish-flavored dance in which they snap their fingers on the last eighth note of every two bars (six beats, or 2 × 3). This set of motions maintains the principal metameasure, with the finger snaps resetting the clock each time. Giovanni (who had stripped to his briefs during his homage to liberty) compels Zerlina to do a slow boogie with him, and his lascivious pelvic thrusts articulate the duple meter of the contredanse; three of his measures fits into each metameasure (3 × 2). Finally, Leporello winds up the unwilling Masetto and sends him spinning wildly across the stage in his rustic German dance, with six of his 3/8 measures coinciding with each metameasure. And this last layer breaks the camel's back. If Zerlina did not scream, the viewer might do so at the sensory overload. We cannot just hum along serenely with the minuet, for Sellars insists that we see, hear, and feel these conflicting meters and register their incongruous, ideologically incompatible impulses.[35]

## Così fan tutte

The third of the Mozart–Da Ponte collaborations, *Così fan tutte*, seems at first glance to lack the political and ethical seriousness of the first two. Like its predecessor, it bears the label *dramma giocoso*, though it appears to uphold the "giocoso" designation rather more honestly: no rapes or murders or apparitions from hell here, but instead just ordinary people hanging out in a coffee shop chatting about their relationships. Yet nineteenth-century critics found it the most immoral, the most offensive, of the three. Based on a cynical wager, the plot traces a pair of young lovers lured into a game of switching partners and demonstrates the utter destruction of their souls.

Sellars sets his *Così* in a tacky beach-town diner, Despina's. The characters wear vacation clothes, as if on leave from their real lives. The older, presumably wiser Don Alfonso is a permanent fixture in Despina's establishment, apparently a business partner with his sometime girlfriend. The liner notes identify him as a Vietnam vet as a way of explaining his own damaged condition, and his existential malaise casts a pall over the entire production, even in the otherwise slapstick sequences.[36]

Our two idle louts, Fernando and Guglielmo, are engaged to two sisters, Fiordaligi and Dorabella, who seem equally trivial. In order to prove that women cannot remain faithful, Don Alfonso proposes to the men that they disguise themselves and seduce the other sister. When this scheme works all too well, it leaves everyone—Alfonso and Despina included—devastated. As Sellars puts it in *Destination Mozart*: "*Così* just burrows down to the root of these deceptions that people live with and force people around them to live with. And the tyranny of these deceptions and the ultimate quality that these deceptions have of eroding every piece of happiness you've ever known in your life."[37]

The opening montage to this DVD presents footage of a seaside resort, the opening Andante paired with images of people fishing or sunning, the Presto shot from a vehicle speeding toward the beach. As a sudden forte blast in the orchestra erupts, the camera pauses on a mansion, rather the way outbursts in the *Figaro* overture zeroed in on swanky stores. But this opera does not dwell on class issues, and as the car proceeds, we next scan a row of tourist shops. When a minor-key inflection pops up, it signals nothing more ominous than a traffic cop aiding vacationing pedestrians to cross the intersection; we are encouraged to notice the scary *ombra* topic and then chuckle when it coincides with the most innocuous manifestation of the police force. We reach the marina, and no clouds mar the pastoral landscape.

Yet toward the end of the overture, where Mozart presents his "Così fan tutte" motto for the second time, we find ourselves inside Despina's diner. Alfonso—Sanford Sylvan, again, our erstwhile Figaro—enters looking world-weary and grim in contrast to the frolicking music. With the last fortissimo outburst, he plants himself behind the cash register and opens his newspaper.

The entire opera will unfold within this cramped space. At first cheerful and homey, the diner will increasingly come to seem like a trap with no exit—worse, in fact, than the mansion in which Thomas Adès's aristocrats find themselves in *The Exterminating Angel*. There is a sense in which all three stage designs for Sellars's Mozart Trilogy offer visual metaphors of confinement: the strict hierarchical class structure of *Figaro*'s upstairs/downstairs configuration, the sinister back alley of *Giovanni*'s ghetto. But only in *Così* do the characters themselves conspire to construct their own prison.

When Fernando and Guglielmo burst in with their boastful opening number, they already behave violently, fulminating at Alfonso rather than at each other for having bad-mouthed their girlfriends. They pound on the counter, brandish plastic butter knives as if demanding a duel, and mime cutting their own throats (the women will soon seize the same weapons to threaten suicide). All quite silly histrionics accompanied by bouncy rhythms. But Alfonso's warnings resonate more here than in most productions. On a regular basis, Sellars has Sylvan address the audience/camera, as when he asks how one knows one's lover is faithful. In this production, Alfonso does not want to play this game, the consequences of which he knows all too well.

Most musicologists classify *Così*'s roles through eighteenth-century conventions, according to which Fiordiligi and Fernando qualify as closer to the ideals of opera seria, Dorabella and Guglielmo to those of buffa. Indeed, Fernando is wont to sing of lofty ideals rather than his lower body functions (Guglielmo's often-mentioned gut and sexual apparatus), and Fiordiligi broaches a higher style than Dorabella with her extended arias. To some extent, Sellars acknowledges these differences, especially in Fernando, whom he identifies with Mozart (it helps that tenor Frank Kelley bears a passing resemblance to the composer). But he largely subsumes those differences in tone for the sake of his larger argument, in which all four lovers behave foolishly and with devastating consequences. It is especially difficult to think of seria/buffa distinctions in this production because the Fiordiligi of Susan Larson (previously Cherubino) is so irrepressibly funny and the Guglielmo of James Maddalena (the Count in *Figaro*) has such enormous affective range as an actor, allowing him to embody pathos more compellingly than anyone else on stage.

For most of this production, Sellars presents the sisters as duplicates, and he does much the same with their suitors. In this he follows Mozart's penchant for having the two women and the two men sing so often in parallel thirds, declaiming the same words at the same time—a concept Sellars underscores in the synchronized gestures executed by each pair. Audiences seem to have questioned this strategy, for Susan Larson comments in *Destination Mozart* about what she calls the cast's reliance on "opera semaphore," which she explains away as just a different kind of stylization for the always-already artificial world of music theater. Earlier in this chapter, I discussed some of the ways Sellars uses this device in *Figaro*. But nothing prepares us for its ubiquity in his staging of *Così*.

For most of the first act, the identical motions and exaggerated facial expressions of the women and those of the men contribute to the humor. Similarly, in keeping with the rhetorical effects of the music, characters often execute gestures associated with melodrama: mock surprise or horror, for instance. Their actions appear cartoonish, making them seem all the more like marionettes. Whose puppets are they? Alfonso's? Mozart's and Da Ponte's? Or simply captives of social convention and unexamined feelings?

Eighteenth-century plots often proceed by setting up a standard situation and then blasting it apart. Handel's oratorio *Jephthah*, for instance, introduces us to a sitcom nuclear family—slightly pompous dad, adoring wife, pert teenage daughter, lustful boyfriend—then plunks them down in an untenable Old Testament story: the dad has promised to make a living sacrifice of his little girl, the mom goes ballistic, and so on.

Sellars knows the Handel operas and oratorios well, and he often draws on them for his own dramaturgy. The more mechanical the lovers appear in act 1 of *Così* the more devastating their downfall when everything unravels. Whereas most of the duets and trios in the first half feature only the men or only the women, the pairs have been split apart in the second. Now we get soliloquies and duets between the "wrong" lovers—as Susan Larson puts it in *Destination Mozart*, "people taking their guts out and staring at them." The former solidarity that had obtained between the sisters or between the men has been demolished, replaced by pairings they know to be based on deceit. If eighteenth-century conventions might find the new couples more appropriate—serious with serious, comic with comic—Sellars allows no such comfort. All four previously cartoonish characters have entered into a post-Edenic world of loss, distrust, and isolation, with no possible reprieve. When they do have to sing together, as in the finale to act 2, they do so as if against their wills, slumping and dragging their feet, registering on their faces their shattered conditions.[38]

And what of the puppeteers? David Cairns refers to Da Ponte's Don Alfonso as a "seaside Mephistopheles,"[39] and most productions present him as performing his mischief out of boredom. The trio he sings with the two women after their lovers have left, "Soave sia il vento," has always seemed to me Mozart's cruelest trick, as Alfonso joins in celestial harmony with the two women he is working to deceive. To the extent that we fall for the absolute beauty of this number, we also fall for the Mozart effect.

As mentioned above, Sellars shows this character from his first entrance as already damaged. But in his staging of "Soave sia il vento" he subtly pries Alfonso apart from the women. At first, all three engage in what seems a ritual of farewell, their gestures synchronized. On the words "nostri desir," however, as the women cross their hands across their breasts in an embracing motion, Alfonso covers his eyes as if in shame. Note that Mozart keeps harmonizing the word "desir" deceptively, his chord progressions warning the women to be careful what they wish for. Toward the end of the number, Sylvan wanders away, his solo riffs splitting off from the trio formation, inviting us to hear him as ruminating on something quite unconnected with the others; in short, Sellars introduces visual fissures into the sonic image of false harmony. Sylvan covers his heart with both hands in the age-old pose of supplication. When he returns to the lineup with the women, the camera favors him—he steps out in front of them as they recede into the background, even though they move together in a kind of dance with the repeating cadential pattern. As the ritornello moves toward its conclusion, the camera remains fixed on Sylvan's prayerful profile, lit with a golden glow like the halo around a penitent in a baroque painting.

This trio, which too often appears as a bad joke, becomes a moment of the utmost remorse, pointing backward to painful memories and also anticipating the devastation Alfonso knows his prank will bring about. As if to throw off the spell, Sellars has Sylvan burst into violence and reach for his whiskey bottle to drown out this moment of vulnerability. But his Alfonso becomes not only the agent who instigates the plot but also the emotional focal point of the opera. We will watch helplessly as the other characters spiral down to his level of cynical despair.

Despina (Sue Ellen Kuzma), who is ordinarily portrayed as a saucy maid dispensing sex tips and executing odd jobs, is presented here as a hard-bitten woman of experience. We first see her in this production—long before she appears in the score—wearily mopping up the beer the men have carelessly slopped onto the floor in the exuberant toasting that seals their bet. Although Alfonso and Despina seem to be off-and-on lovers, they base their attacks on the opposite sex on their mutual failures, and both often end their witty diatribes in tears. Recall that Da Ponte himself has Despina express her deep shame at having participated in the trickery that has destroyed these young people, and this production suggests that she and Alfonso have also inflicted injury on each other. As Mary Hunter suggests, Despina becomes a fully developed agent in Sellars's production rather than the stock comic figure of most stagings. "It took Sellars's sense of Despina as a subject to bring to my consciousness the idea that she is normally an object, which in turn raises fascinating questions about the historical and social/political responsibilities and obligations of performance and about the relations between those obligations."[40] This concern, of course, lies at the heart of Sellars's lifelong agenda.

Sellars has the six characters line up as equals to deliver the final chorus. No one belongs with anyone else any longer. In their reading of Mozart's last line, "bella calma troverà" (the lovely calm to be enjoyed after one has learned of life's adversities), they run madly around the diner, spinning out of control, collapsing, and twitching like broken mechanical dolls. Sylvan has pointed to the musical cues that led to this interpretation: against the words promising serenity, Mozart has put a scurrying figure, and the vocalists receive an oddly asymmetrical rhythm, with the first syllable of "calma" drawn out too long and "troverà" stomped out (Sylvan demonstrates this in *Destination Mozart* with the same virtuoso finger snaps he rendered in "Se vuol ballare"). Of course, others might render these details differently. But this cast derives its ideas from strong readings of score and libretto. Nothing is merely imposed.

Like Mozart and Da Ponte, Sellars begins each of these operas with lighthearted comedy and ends with much more equivocal affects. Even in the bouncy codas to all three operas, Sellars finds a darker hue that allows for more troubling meanings. In all three, the whole cast lines up and addresses the audience, thereby pulling us into the unsolved dilemmas raised over the course of these dramas.

But this does not make Sellars a pessimist. Rather he sees his job as awakening our sensibilities and leaving us with something greater than an amusing night at the opera. In *Destination Mozart* he states:

> These operas are about ensemble and the notion that people can do more working together, this idea of how to work with others—is it possible to work with others and exist with other human beings without killing them? Can you not only exist without killing them but can you exist without being indifferent to them? Can you exist in fact with them in a way that you are working together with them with a degree of fineness, nuance, and delicacy, that says that human interaction can be the most refined and exquisite part of life? Well, that's the Mozart operas.

In his productions, Sellars traces the ways Mozart's characters—not only the villains but even those who merely deceive those closest to them or themselves—participate in the disintegration of social unity. He reveals to us the fragility of community and yet its necessity. If these individuals can stand together and still sing at the final curtain, they extend a ray of hope to those of us struggling with such issues in our own lives.

# 2 • Ritualizing

## *Saint François* and *Theodora*

In his comments concerning his productions of the Bach passions, Sellars refers to his stagings as a process of ritualizing. Indeed, many of his productions incorporate elements of religious ceremony. But he does not thereby abandon his commitment to social activism; he has linked the spiritual with political awareness throughout his entire career, beginning with his affiliation with Emmanuel Church in Boston in 1978 when he was twenty-one. In an interview included with the DVD of his *St. Matthew Passion*, Sellars recalls that

> Emmanuel Church at that era had a homeless shelter, a shelter for battered women, a Salvadoran refugee program, because Salvadorans were escaping the death squads through an underground railroad. . . . So there were safe houses, there were three chapters of Alcoholics Anonymous, there was drug counseling, and of course there was a suicide prevention center.[1]

It was in this context that Sellars started experimenting with the staging of works by Bach and Handel, which he regarded as properly part of the social welfare program of Emmanuel as well as its worship services. As he explains:

> When you hear Bach's Cantata 199 [*Mein Herze schwimmt im Blut*; My heart swims in blood] after convincing someone not to kill themselves, you get that this music is deeply practical, and like Alcoholics Anonymous, it's a twelve-step program: you take each step with Bach, and Bach takes you and guides you through the next steps of your life.

Put simply, the social activism in Sellars work springs from the same sources as his deep concern with spirituality.

While at Emmanuel he staged several Bach cantatas, as well as Handel's *Saul* (1981), conducted by Craig Smith, then director of music at Emmanuel. Drawing on musicians in the Boston area, they assembled the repertory group featured in the Mozart Trilogy and elsewhere. As his work has continued to develop, Sellars's investment in communal expressions of spirituality has become ever more pronounced, though significant traces of this commitment occur already in his secular work: recall, for instance, the chorus that concludes *Le nozze di Figaro* (chapter 1).

But his grounding in ritual reaches far beyond his settings of European sacred music. Sellars teaches in the Department of World Arts and Cultures at UCLA. Originally a dance program, the unit morphed under the leadership of Judy Mitoma, who initiated an annual festival of performances by the many ethnic groups residing in Los Angeles. Sellars himself directed the Los Angeles Festival from 1986 to 1994,[2] and he brought this multicultural agenda with him in 2006 when he curated the New Crowned Hope Festival in Vienna. Although the event in Vienna was designed to celebrate Mozart's 250th birthday, Sellars insisted on using it as a platform for showcasing dance, theater, and music from Asia, Africa, and Latin America together with European and American fare expected at such an occasion.[3]

These disparate performance practices have deeply influenced Sellars. For example, he used Cambodian dancers in his production of Stravinsky's *Perséphone*, recreated the sixteenth-century Chinese classic *The Peony Pavilion* with Tan Dun, worked with John Adams on the South Asian–based *A Flowering Tree*, and collaborated with Kaija Saariaho on an opera based on Noh plays, *Only the Sound Remains* (see chapter 5).[4] Moreover, his libretti regularly incorporate texts in Spanish, Hindi, and other languages.

The most lasting manifestation of his exposure to other cultural practices, however, involves his idiosyncratic vocabulary of physical gestures. We can write some of those off in the Mozart productions as comic effects. But they become a constant feature in his work, not only in opera buffa but also in moments of psychological distress. Sellars honed this kinetic language from his contact with ceremonial customs and performance practices of many other cultures, from his work with deaf-mute actors, and from his own translation of musical energies into motion.

The two of the pieces discussed in this chapter, Olivier Messiaen's *Saint François d'Assise* and Handel's *Theodora*, present explicitly religious topics. Because Franciscan friars and early Christian sects both practiced sacred rites on a regular basis, simulations of ecstatic spirituality and the presence of stylized gesture seem consistent with the characters and dramatic situations in these works. As we shall see over the course of later chapters, some of the strategies Sellars hones for *Saint François* and *Theodora* will affect the rest of his career.

## Saint François d'Assise

Olivier Messiaen wrote the music and libretto for his only opera late in his career. A deeply personal endeavor, *Saint François* required eight years for completion (1975–83). It traces the life of the saint through a series of tableaux, each of which centers on an event: the encounter with a leper, the interactions with birds, the receiving of the stigmata, and so on. By eschewing conventional dramatic action, Messiaen could focus his music on his personal expressions of spirituality, as he had long done in his instrumental works (in, for instance, *Vingt régards sur l'enfant Jésus* or *Quartet for the End of Time*).

Sellars staged *Saint François* at the Salzburg Music Festival in 1992. Salzburg had offered Sellars a major international platform for the first time, and he reports that he was terrified; he even cut his hair for the occasion, hoping thereby to appear a bit more like a grown-up. As he prepared his production, he consulted with and received the blessing of the composer, who died in April of that year, then continued working with his widow, Yvonne Loriod.

A full video of Sellars's 1992 production does not exist, though one can view parts of it in a documentary by Jean-Pierre Gorin concerning its conception, along with footage of rehearsals and interviews, on YouTube.[5] It was this production that convinced Kaija Saariaho to collaborate with Sellars in writing her own operas. It also left a deep impression on Sellars: after this project, he greatly expanded his earlier experiments with the staging of oratorios, cantatas, and the passions, and traces of this swerve back into religious ritual mark his collaborations with John Adams and Saariaho. Moreover, Sellars adopted for his own libretti Messiaen's strategy of shaping his text through a series of tableaux, with very little by way of conventional dramatic action. *Saint François*, in short, stands as a pivotal moment not only in Sellars's career but also in the history of opera in the last twenty-five years.

If in his Mozart Trilogy Sellars sought powerful tropes that would translate eighteenth-century works to late twentieth-century Americans, he strives in *Saint François* to bring experiences of the spiritual to largely secular audiences. Sellars comments:

I love that Messiaen was not interested in documentary in this opera. He was interested in what does the life of Saint Francis *mean*. What did it mean to Saint Francis, and what does it mean to us? . . . You're dealing with religious topics, and religious topics can't be spoken of in human terms. Because they're not human—they're spiritual, they're divine. And the only way we can talk about them is as metaphor. . . . And at the same time, the need to render it useful in people's lives; if these spiritual truths stay as metaphor, we have violated the life of Saint Francis. Because for Saint Francis the huge innovation that he proposed was that the life of Christ wasn't metaphoric; it was meant to be lived in your own body, not as something that you know, but as something that you feel, you live—and has something to do with the fact that you don't wear shoes.

In his production, Sellars does allow the saint and his companions to dress in Franciscan robes (and without shoes).[6] But two major elements of his staging bring the contemporary world to bear on the opera.

The most obvious is his extensive use of multiple video screens, planted all over the stage, hovering overhead, or looking out from George Tsypin's gigantic set. Sellars's sets usually tend toward the ascetic; most of his productions after the relatively realistic Mozart settings rely on a few abstract objects and lighting. But the Salzburg Festival underwrote the construction of a massive structure, the building of which may be seen in *Lettera a Peter*. Tsypin's apparatus helps to explain why this production did not travel as easily to different venues as most of Sellars's stagings.[7] As the opera proceeds, the video monitors flicker with footage shot by Sellars himself. They present a visual counterpoint to the tableaux, reminding us constantly of Saint Francis's (and Messiaen's) obsessions with birds, nature, and the stigmata. Sellars compares these images with those of the stained-glass windows of ancient churches, especially with respect to the ways they infuse light directly into otherwise darkened interiors.

But he also designed this element with an ear toward Messiaen's compositional style. He says:

> That sense of movement which, I think, characterized Messiaen's music so profoundly meant that in the videos I could obtain that quality where nothing sits still. Everything in the world is in the process being birthed all over again through these vibrations, and every moment is a moment that is coming to you with the greatest possible intensity and at the same time is in the process of becoming, . . . is always becoming but never arrives at a fixed image, is always an attempt to become the next image of itself, which is what we think of as predestination.[8]

Conductor Esa-Pekka Salonen corroborates this understanding of the composer's strategies: "Messiaen's music never changes, ever. Every element remains the same throughout the piece."[9] Messiaen builds his score like a kind of mosaic from recurring melodic fragments, simulations of birdsong, patterns of irregular-sounding (non-retrogradable) rhythms, palindromic structures that refuse the convention of linear progression, monumental orchestral chords that punctuate without articulating evident meanings. Harmonic progressions as such rarely occur. It is this mosaic quality that Sellars, Salonen, and the singers grapple to present, and Sellars intended for the flickering video monitors to assist in providing a visual analogue.

In *Lettera a Peter*, Sellars confessed he had become painfully aware of the contradiction between this enormously expensive production (each of the forty-some monitors, he admits, could feed a Somali family for two years) and Saint Francis's—or, indeed, his own—ideals. He also worried that the videos would not work in the Salzburg space but would come across as flickering annoyances. He saw the project through to completion but never ventured again into overwhelming the stage with elaborate, costly sets. After *Saint François*, Sellars almost seems to have taken a Franciscan vow of austerity after this uncharacteristic binge, even when he works with Tsypin.

Far more characteristic of his modus operandi was the second element he designed to reach contemporary audiences: the presentation of the angel who appears first to the friars and then in Francis's apocalyptic visions. In the original staging under Messiaen's direction, the angel had spectacular, multi-colored wings—modeled directly after images in Giotto. But although Sellars dressed his angel, Dawn Upshaw, in drab contemporary garb, he also harkens back to Giotto for justification:

> If one charts the progress of the angel in this opera, I think the angel is introduced as a hospital worker, as someone who has devoted their life to serving in this hospice for lepers. A volunteer, probably. And who then reappears mysteriously in act 5 in Francis's dream. In this production [she] is either Saint Clare or just a girl who helps out. And every time you see her you say, "Now, was that an angel?" And, of course, that is what each of those tableaux ends with, is that question: "Is that an angel?" The leper says, "Who is that?" and Francis says, "Maybe it was an angel that came here to console you." Nobody knows. . . . So I have to stage it that way. It might have been an angel, but we're not telling. So she can't have wings, she can't arrive in a laser show. She has to walk in the door, and she has to open the door like anyone else to get in, and then she has to shut it behind her. There's no

magic carpet, there's no dissolving through walls—like the angels in Giotto, who are amazingly substantial and have to lean over things. What's important to me is that the angel is not a serene presence, but the angel is in anguish, the angel has doubts, the angel doesn't know what to do next, the angel has to think of new things. Because you look at those angels in Giotto and you see a full range from utter despair and weeping to expression of the highest joy. And you realize that angels are not flat cardboard figures.

During his discussion, Sellars mentions Dorothy Day of the Catholic Worker movement. Day qualifies as a real-life saint for Sellars, who draws extensively upon her writing in his libretto to Adams's *Gospel According to the Other Mary*. Upshaw's angel in ordinary clothing, who administers to lepers, becomes a Day-like figure in this production. Sellars did insert a second angel into his production: a red-clad, winged dancer (Sara Rudner of the Twyla Tharp Company) who enhances the gestural dimension of certain scenes.[10] But the character who sings retains that ambiguous identity between the human and the divine throughout, thereby making her a figure we might emulate in our own lives—always the most crucial point in any of Sellars's works.

The gestures Sellars had already used in the Mozart Trilogy undergo a transformation in his *Saint François*. Although only a few acted scenes appear in *Lettera a Peter*, they shed considerable light on the ways he works with his singers and the importance he places on their physical motions. In one sequence, we see José von Dam (as Saint François) practicing his gestures by himself. Sellars then joins him with the score and guides his understanding of two particularly significant actions: that of reaching up toward the heavens (prayer and supplication), then swiftly drawing inward (introspection, abjection). Not only do these two gestures correspond to crucial attitudes of Saint François, but they also call the viewer's attention to the waxing and waning impulses in Messiaen's score, to the alternation between a kind of fanfare (what Sellars calls the elevation of the Spirit) and a "crash" inward for graver moments (Sellars collapses down and utters something like "khrshh" when he demonstrates this to von Dam). After the footage of that coaching session, we view the scene as it appeared in performance.[11]

A clip of act 2, scene 4, offers further insights into Sellars's gestural strategies. Here we see the angel speaking about predestination to an abject Frère Bernard (29:33). As she encourages him to put away his former self, Upshaw caresses Bernard's left cheek and then quickly—together with a sudden high note—casts this imaginary self away and stares down at her empty hand. But with her advice that he take up "the new man," she caresses his other cheek and holds her palm up to him as if it were a mirror; with Messiaen's vacillating melody, she gestures back and forth between Bernard and her upheld hand, becoming more ecstatic with each higher iteration. When she explains that God has predetermined this, she raises the mirror-hand upward to heaven. Next, she praises justice on the one hand and sanctity on the other, and after she has plucked them from on high, she holds her hands outward as if holding the two virtues in a balance. She then brings her cupped hands together tenderly, one atop the other, as if sheltering a small animal. As Messiaen lingers on "santité" (sanctity), she makes a caressing movement between her hands, as if finding that word particularly precious. When she refers to truth, her fingers rise to her lips then flair outward, as if sending that word forth into the world, before holding her palms upward as if displaying those immense concepts as a sacrament. Messiaen sets the last syllable of "verité" (truth) very low, as if relaxing into the absolute.[12]

Over the course of this sequence, Frère Bernard (Tom Krause) undergoes a visible transfiguration. At first he slumps abjectly with his arms hanging limply at his sides. But as the angel reveals to him the key to salvation, his face lifts upward, and he accompanies her vision of justice and sanctity with slowly rising hands until, at the highest iteration of "santité," he performs the gesture Sellars calls elevation of the Spirit. On the angel's last pitch, he too relaxes back into human time but with a sense that he has changed forever. Sellars makes us aware here of two temporal streams occurring simultaneously: the angel's mystic utterance with its intensifications and Bernard's single motion that takes place over the course of those two minutes. Both are grounded in Messiaen's music, even if Bernard experiences his vision of the timeless state the composer always sought to capture by means of the necessarily shifting medium of music.

That same sense of Messiaen's phrasing and its meanings also manifests itself in the synchronized gestures Sellars asks of the chorus. In footage that begins at 5:54, we see the chorus members standing or kneeling with their arms folded across their breasts in prayer-like fashion as they sing Christ's invitation to "take up your cross and follow me."[13] At the words "and follow me," each raises a single arm toward heaven. (This moment in *Lettera a Peter* gives perhaps the best idea of the set, with its enormous backdrop of lights and video monitors arranged at various places. The choristers wear street clothing, all beige but ranging multiculturally from backward baseball caps to turbans.)

I want to mention one more feature of this documentary: Sellars's own self-presentation in the interviews. In addition to his extraordinary ability to articulate difficult ideas compellingly, he gesticulates almost without pause. Many of the hand motions and facial expressions he exhibits in his everyday speech become the building blocks to the motions he asks for onstage. To be sure, he refines and systematizes them as he transmits them to his performers. But this is an individual who cannot think, talk, or hear music without engaging his entire body. When he grapples with a score, he lets it determine how he breathes, feels, and moves. The gestures are designed to impart to the viewer something of that same experience. In Ruth Walz's photograph on the book cover, Sellars demonstrates to his performers both the gesture of protective cupping and the reach for transcendence.[14]

In an astute review of the live performances of the Mozart Trilogy at PepsiCo, the late Edward Said (celebrated literary theorist and classical music critic for *The Nation*) complained that Sellars's directorial brilliance often outstripped the capabilities of his performers.[15] He praised the work of James Maddalena, Sanford Sylvan, and the Perry twins, but he found the women in the troupe wanting in both singing and acting. I would quibble with this assessment, noting in particular Lorraine Hunt's extraordinary Donna Elvira and Susan Larson's hilarious Cherubino (less so, perhaps, her Fiordiligi and Cleopatra).

But some of the performers in the Mozart operas fail to embody the qualities Sellars apparently asked of them, and the results fall short, satisfying neither his concept nor the conventions of standard operatic deportment. As a coach of several decades experience, I know firsthand the difficulty of working with performers who can execute virtuoso vocal passages but who have no idea what it means to express the music through their bodies. Indeed, many performers have been taught *not* to engage their bodies, which still count somehow as vulgar.[16] Even when watching on screen I can sense what must have been Sellars's frustration with singers who would execute what he told them but who may as well be flashing a poster reading, "I have no idea why I'm doing this." It is when that gap between intention and execution becomes visible that Sellars's gestural vocabulary can seem ludicrous, unhinged either from the real world or from the musical energies they were meant to enhance.

Said longed to see what Sellars would do if he had conductors and singers worthy of his talents. Beginning with *Saint François*, he finally had access to internationally acclaimed conductors—Salonen for *Saint François*, William Christie for *Theodora*, and so on—and he incorporated Upshaw and Hunt into his central core of singers. Sellars managed to convince these artists to work with him in part because of the potential they saw in the Mozart Trilogy. Without that much-discussed (and much-decried) work to his credit, he would not have had the status or credibility to tell such seasoned artists how to do their jobs during collaborations. When working on Sellars's projects, they clearly follow his lead in decisions concerning timing, affect, and the channeling of energies.

## Theodora

Many important productions occurred in the four years following *Saint François*, including Debussy's *Pelléas et Mélisande* (1993), Hindemith's *Mathis der Maler* (1995), and Stravinsky's *L'histoire du soldat* (1992), *Oedipus Rex* and *Symphony of Psalms* (both in 1994), and *The Rake's Progress* (1996). In increasing demand worldwide, Sellars produced performances during these four years in Brussels, Lyon, Berlin, Amsterdam, Paris, Edinburgh, Helsinki, London, and Montreal. None of these, alas, made it onto film.

Consequently, I will move next to his 1996 Glyndebourne production of Handel's *Theodora*: a staging that convinced many longtime skeptics of his talents. Explaining this skepticism, Edward Seckerson's review in the *Independent* begins:

> "The Jews will not come to it because it is a Christian story, and the ladies will not come because it is a virtuous one" (Handel on *Theodora*, 1750). Time was when nobody would come because it was a Peter Sellars production. Times change. Sellars' powerful new staging of Handel's penultimate oratorio could seriously damage your prejudices.[17]

The reviewer goes on to identify certain American referents as "so very Sellars," but he appears astonished by the emotional depth of the performance as it unfolds.

For his production of *Theodora* Sellars had a genuine dream team: William Christie and his Orchestra of the Age of Enlightenment in the pit, Dawn Upshaw, Lorraine Hunt, David Daniels, and Richard Croft on stage. Even Frode Olsen as the villainous tyrant turns in an extraordinary performance. George Tsypin, who had designed the gargantuan set for *Saint François*, here offers the kind of abstract minimalist arrangement that he continues to deliver for Sellars. As always, James Ingalls controlled the extraordinary lighting.

Handel's oratorio concerning a third-century martyr flopped when it premiered in 1750. In contrast to his other dramatic oratorios, most of which featured stories from the Old Testament, *Theodora* drew on obscure Catholic hagiography, even if librettist Thomas Morell redirected the tensions of the plot in a Protestant or even deist direction. Only once does a character use the word "Christian" in reference to the persecuted sect. Otherwise the libretto emphasizes a nonspecific spirituality, making it palatable to the humanist inclinations of both Handel and Sellars.

In the original, Valens, the Roman governor of Antioch, announces to a throng that the emperor's birthday calls for celebration, and he demands that all inhabitants participate in the revels. Two of his soldiers, Didymus and Septimius, hesitate to enforce the decree: Didymus because Theodora has converted him to her religion, Septimius because of his fundamental decency. Scenes alternate between those featuring the brutal, lascivious Romans and those focused on the sect presided over by Irene and Theodora. When the sect refuses to comply with the decree, Valens has the soldiers arrest Theodora, condemning her to service in a brothel. Didymus rescues her but at the cost of his own death sentence. Theodora arrives to share his fate, and both are executed.

For his production, Sellars relocates the action to the contemporary United States, and he developed his concept in the aftermath of the FBI's 1983 massacre of seventy-six members of the Branch Davidians (including many children) in Waco, Texas. Although few supported the extremist precepts of the Branch Davidians, the incommensurate force shown by federal agents during this siege and its fiery conclusion shocked the nation. In a report highly critical of the government's actions, Alan A. Stone wrote that the Branch Davidians were "desperate religious fanatics expecting an apocalyptic ending, in which they were destined to die defending their sacred ground and destined to achieve salvation."[18] Members of the cult held their beliefs so deeply that they would gladly face death—as they ultimately did.

The spiritual fervor manifested in these followers makes them self-conscious twentieth-century analogues to those who sacrificed their lives for early Christianity. Not surprisingly, Sellars casts a callous US government in the place of the pagan Romans. Once again, as in the Mozart Trilogy, he holds up a mirror and suggests that "we" often stand on the side of an intolerant, hedonistic society that crushes small groups attempting to hold onto what they experience as the spiritual.[19]

But when Sellars speaks of this production, he emphasizes another point of social critique: capital punishment. Among advanced nations in the West today, only the United States clings to this barbaric custom, reinstated (after a moratorium) in 1976 by the Supreme Court. Lethal injection has now mostly supplanted earlier forms of capital punishment (e.g. hanging, firing squad, or electric chair) on the grounds that it is more humane. But recent botched injections have called the lie to that argument. In 2017, the governor of Arkansas quickly ordered a rash of executions as the date of expiration for the necessary toxins approached.

In preparation for this production, Sellars researched the process by means of which penitentiaries actually administer lethal injection, and he presents it in his final scene in full detail. Prison personnel strap Theodora and Didymus onto gurneys that feature extensions for their outstretched arms, so that when the gurneys are put upright, the two characters appear to be hanging on crosses. One might imagine that this arrangement originated with Sellars himself for the sake of symbolism. But no: that's what this apparatus actually looks like. Moreover, Sellars installs monitors that display the heartbeats of each victim, and the audience witnesses their weakening pulses and discerns when the two die. Valens demands that Septimius himself start the flow of the poison that will kill his friend and Theodora.

In an interview in 2012, conductor William Christie recalls his response to Sellars's production and this scene:

> I had not met Peter before although of course I knew of him: he's a fellow of great notoriety, in the best sense of the word. You knew that he wasn't going to give you anything other than a controversial, or at least a very personal, sense of the drama. The fact that this Christian woman and her converted lover find themselves on a gurney in a Texas military hospital awaiting execution was incredibly shocking, but I found it horribly moving. . . . Peter was hellbent on making a political statement, registering his dismay and revulsions about aspects of America, but also making music that was written several hundreds of years ago more relevant.[20]

Concerning the impact of this scene, in which we follow the countdown to the termination of two lives, Sellars reports:

> The effect was profound. During most performances, people had to be carried from the auditorium; there were emergency medical services standing by. I am not proud of putting people into an emergency medical van, of course, but I do think that's why the Greeks invented theatre: to put these things in front of citizens and say, how do we feel about them?[21]

When the curtain first opens, we see Valens as a demagogic politician, churning up hostilities against a religious minority group. Tall, blond, and charismatic, Frode Olsen bears a striking resemblance to the Donald Trump of thirty years ago, also the model for Sellars's Count Almaviva in *Figaro*. Valens knows well how to work his crowd, a press conference of adoring journalists. Two-thirds of the way through his vengeance aria, "Racks, gibbets, sword, and fire," he feigns a heart attack, prompting a crew of medical practitioners to rush in on cue; he sings the last section of the aria lying on a stretcher—only to pop up after his cadenza to show that he was just joshing. This choreography recalls James Brown, who would collapse during performances, signal to assistants to wrap him in his cape as he limped off, then rebound with renewed energy. Audiences loved Brown when he pulled this shtick in nearly every show, and it works on Valens's Romans, too.

Act 2 opens with a drunken Valens and his followers expressing their libidinous pleasure in "Venus laughing." Suddenly the festivities turn ugly as the men assault their female companions, rather like a fraternity party spinning out of control after hours of beer pong—or just the back room at Fox News.[22] Here again the referent is America, and it isn't flattering. Recall once more that Donald Trump had yet to emerge as the improbable and frightening political figure he became during and after the 2016 election, complete with his vows to exile Mexicans, boasts of sexual predation, and bans against Muslims.

Sellars makes extensive use of his codified hand gestures in his staging of *Theodora*. In his review in the *Independent*, Edward Seckerson associates these with baroque performance practices, and eighteenth-century stagecraft may well factor into Sellars's strategies here. As we shall see, however, those gestures appear in everything from *Saint François* to *Doctor Atomic*, and they clearly signify differently depending on the particular context.

As an oratorio, *Theodora* features many choruses, both Roman and Christian, and Sellars gives the two groups radically different kinetic vocabularies, assigning different purposes to their synchronized behaviors. The Romans exhibit extremely militant moves, in part because the aggressiveness of Handel's melodic motives in those contexts demand them. In their second chorus, "Forever thus stands fixed the doom," they may call to mind the Nazi salute—but recall that the Nazis appropriated this gesture from imperial Rome; it's right at home here in *Theodora*, as (alas) it has become at recent alt-right rallies.

Yet another important element in these physical signs is their function in demarcating the imitative entries of the different voice parts. In his scores, Handel carefully distinguishes between the passages in which his chorus acts as a group of individuals, each speaking separately, and those where they join forces to present a unified front. Sellars's choreography makes the contrapuntal interactions crystal clear, and when they all sing together, they congeal into a horrific mob.

For the scenes involving Theodora's sect, the chorus deploys many of the gestures Sellars developed for Messiaen's *Saint François*, gestures that attempt to simulate visually through bodily motions the inner feelings such as rapture and supplication. In "Come, mighty Father" (act 1), for instance, the group seeks to draw the Spirit down upon their beleaguered community, and the upraised arms and prayerful poses we saw Sellars ask of Saint François and his flock reappear. Of course, he also uses gestures to delineate this group's contrapuntal entrances, as he did with the Romans—or, for that matter, with his Mozart finales. But now they take on the added weight of sacred ritual.

The most brilliant staging of the chorus occurs at the end. Most of the choruses in *Theodora* divide neatly between the Romans and the Christians. In a standard oratorio (i.e., unstaged) performance, the same choral ensemble would voice both the Romans and the Christians without dramatic difficulty, just as the chorus in the Bach passions sometimes represent the Jews and sometimes Bach's Lutheran congregation. But in this production, Sellars has consistently distinguished the two with costuming, and he has to decide who offers up "O love divine," the hymn of thanksgiving that concludes the oratorio. He might well have had the Christians onstage to witness the execution; after all, Irene herself enters at the end to sing. Instead he has his chorus don their Roman costumes to back up Valens, as in the opening scene.

And this specific use of costuming allows for another interpretive transformation. As the guards prepare for the lethal injection, with the two lovers gladly welcoming their martyrdom, the chorus sings a haunting number, "How strange their ends, and yet how glorious." They ponder together the mystery of this transcendent sacrifice. By the time the ecstatic duet has ended and Irene has announced their glorious end, the Romans have changed—something like the Roman soldier at the foot of the cross who utters: "Surely this man was the son of God." Now themselves converts, Valens's troops face the audience to sing "O love divine," the tribute to communal spirituality so crucial to Sellars's agenda. Deprived now of their support, their leader falls lifeless onto the desk from which he had passed judgment.

But the oratorio as a whole belongs to the more introspective characters, who spend much of their time expressing spiritual joy. Handel posed a tremendous problem for himself—and Sellars—in dwelling unrelentingly on affects that lack obvious dramatic appeal. The music itself has to carry the burden of the proceedings. Fortunately, both Handel and Sellars rise to the challenge.

In my discussion of Figaro's "Se vuol ballare," I dealt to some extent with the problem of formal musical repetition in contemporary stagings. Mozart sometimes composed full-blown da capo arias, in which the first part of piece comes back for a full repetition after a contrasting middle section. Some arias last for several minutes, during which the dramatic action halts. So antithetical is this procedure to nineteenth-century assumptions concerning drama that a scholar of opera seria, Robert Freeman, titled his long-definitive book on this genre *Opera without Drama*.[23] More recently, however, musicologists have returned to precisely the ritualistic dimension of opera seria, to explain why this convention made sense to discerning eighteenth-century audiences, why it stood as the dominant musical genre for over a hundred years.[24]

Yet this historical contextualization does not solve the practical problem of what to do on stage during those extensive bouts of repetition, however much the singer may add virtuosic ornamentation to the reiterations. When twentieth-century musicians started attempting to revive these pieces, they often cut sections of arias or even whole arias in the interest of time and of preserving some sense of realistic action for audiences accustomed to linear plots.

But Sellars insists on retaining the entirety of the scores he performs and on making us hear the whole length of every aria. He does so not out of a dogmatic appeal to period authenticity (about which he cares relatively little) but rather because he relishes the potential of the da capo aria to shed light on the psychology of his personae. In a talk he gave in Toronto before a performance of Handel's *Hercules*, he explained that a character will offer a first response to a situation in the opening A section, then move to something else—a deeper or contrasting reaction—in the B section, then reiterate A with a new understanding of the initial statement, now inflected by virtue of the entire process and intensified expressively through improvised ornamentation. As we shall see, his staging of da capo arias attempts to make that sequence of thought visible.

Handel presents other difficulties than just the large-scale repetition of his da capo arias. Within each A section, the orchestra presents the principal musical material at least twice and often three or more times. When the singer finally enters to place the words on the previously instrumental music, she or he has to repeat the same verbal phrases over and over and over again. Even in the eighteenth-century this approach to text setting often got lampooned. How does a director cope with such unapologetic redundancy?

Since I take this to be among Sellars's most ingenious techniques, I will examine a couple of arias from *Theodora* at some length. I will also have to mention key relationships (abstractly in my text, in fuller technical detail in my notes), because eighteenth-century composers calibrated their dramatic effects largely by means of their modulations and harmonic progressions. Sellars attends carefully to such matters because these articulate very precisely the nuances and changes in a character's inner feelings. Fortunately for those who have not studied music theory, Sellars translates all these moves into visual analogues, thereby inviting even nonspecialists in the audience to notice the intricacies of Handel's score as they occur.

The first of these occurs just after Valens has uttered his decree and left the stage. During this opening scene, Septimius and Didymus have stood on either side of Valens in riot gear, holding their machine guns at the ready. Only after the Roman mob has exited does Didymus begin to address Septimius in a recitative protesting the edict. At the end of his recitative, on his words, "Ought we not to leave the free-born mind of man still ever free?" he slowly removes his helmet, thereby revealing his face for the first time, then readies himself for his aria.

An opening ritornello of ten bars in the orchestra introduces two motives: a florid one Didymus will match with "The raptur'd soul" and a decisive one later paired with "defies the sword." But in the ritornello, the two flow one into another. It isn't until Didymus enters with the text that the two elements—the soul and defiance of the sword—become radically disassociated and then fused back together. But meanwhile, Sellars has had nearly half a minute of visuals to attend to while the ritornello proceeds.

Sellars understands full well the motivic repetitions in Handel's ritornello, and he uses them to convey a sense of ambivalence in Didymus. Note that neither Handel's music nor Morell's text suggest ambivalence. But by staging the opening in this way, Sellars allows for a process of psychological development that can span the entire duration of the aria. Three times during this instrumental introduction Didymus crosses the stage to speak to Septimius, always halting and then heading back as if not able to decide on a course of action. In the orchestral flourish leading toward the ritornello's conclusion, he puts down his assault rifle and faces front. But still Handel's motives continue to tumble out, as Didymus bunches his tension into his shoulders before relaxing for his entrance.

"The raptur'd soul" demonstrates Handel's, Sellars's, and countertenor David Daniel's prowess exceptionally well. The entire text reads:

[A] The raptur'd soul defies the sword, secure of virtue's claim,
And trusting heaven's unerring word, enjoys the circling flame.
[B] No engines can a tyrant find, to storm the truth-supported mind.
   [dal segno]

Handel setting draws this text out such that it lasts an astonishing ten minutes in performance. Like Bach, Handel had learned from studying Vivaldi's published scores how to build large-scale musical forms by means of a linear background structure that travels through a number of keys, each of them prolonged by a staggering variety of motivic and rhetorical devices.

"The raptur'd soul" reaches its first major cadence at the words "secure of virtue's claim." Handel next flirts with a number of possible resting points before landing (at "circling flame") in a relatively remote key, punctuated by a shortened instrumental ritornello. The text then begins all over again, this time with "raptur'd" in an even more remote key before returning to the tonic for the cadence and another iteration of the full ritornello. These journeys through distantly related keys allow Handel to present Didymus's words with two different affective colorings: what appeared in major in the first iteration appears the second time in minor, casting a new light on those lines. Moreover, because it takes longer to get to and back from the extreme key Handel posits as his midpoint, his modulations allow for a much more extended tonal trajectory than would a more typical background. In other words, this is already a hefty and complex apparatus, even before we get to the B section: a tempestuous interlude that maintains a single affect for its whole duration before the return to the A-complex.[25] In essence, Handel asks Didymus to sing an entire concerto movement plus a middle part and then the whole concerto movement yet again.

Handel has Didymus begin without accompaniment, merely singing "The raptur'd soul" in long notes in common time, breaking with the jaunty jig-like meter that preceded him; he effectively stops the action with this statement. The absence of accompaniment and the metrical freeze invite the singer to regard this moment as an opportunity for extended embellishment, and Daniels offers here, on the syllable "ra-," his first glimpse of vocal bliss—something he will offer with increasing intensity over the course of this aria. Arms raised, with head back and eyes closed, Daniels lavishes on this syllable ornaments, and then ornaments on those ornaments, as if unwilling to let it go. The performance of this single syllable constitutes the turning point of the entire oratorio: the visceral experience of eternal pleasure that will inspire the Christian community to defy the threats of the Romans.

Didymus then launches into the aria per se, with its motives and meter drawn from the ritornello. I am including here the text as Handel actually sets it, complete with all its internal repetitions so that the reader may see what a stage director has to confront. This is the opening A section alone (similar stammering occurs in the B section, to say nothing of the full-scale return of the entire A section after that):

The raptur'd soul, the raptur'd soul defies the sword, defies the sword, defies the sword, the raptur'd soul defies the sword, defies the sword, defies the sword, secure of virtue's claim, secure of virtue's claim, secure of virtue's claim, and trusting Heaven's unerring word, enjoys the circling flame, enjoys the circling flame, the circling flame, enjoys the circling flame. The raptur'd soul defies the sword, secure of virtue's claim, the raptur'd soul defies the sword, and trusting Heaven's unerring word, enjoys the circling flame, the circling flame, enjoys the circling flame, and trusting Heaven's unerring word, unerring word, enjoys, enjoys the circling flame.

What can one say?

In his staging of this aria, Sellars traces Didymus's transformation from radical inwardness as he reflects upon his experience of bliss (the first image of the opening line) to one of militancy (the second image of that same line). As already mentioned, Handel joins the two motives into a continuous line in the ritornello, and aspects of both appear throughout. The first time through, "rapture" receives the "elevation of the spirit" gesture familiar to us from *Saint François*. But when Daniels repeats his A section, he sings defiantly, often cradling his gun in his rapturous state. Throughout the aria, he interacts with Septimius, sometimes beseeching him, sometimes turning on him when his friend attempts to cool him down, sometimes leaning on him for support, sometimes possessed with an almost divine frenzy. As the next aria, sung by Septimius, reveals, he is nearly convinced by Didymus's evangelical appeal—almost (but not quite) persuaded, given that he administers, however unwillingly, the final coup de grace in the execution scene at the end.

These two crucial narrative arguments—Didymus's move from meditation to action and Septimius's near conversion—take place over the course of the aria. In other words, the plot scarcely stands still for these ten minutes, as critiques of opera seria often complain. We learn a great deal about both men individually and with respect to one another.

Sellars carefully clocks important structural events in his blocking to Handel's score. For instance, Septimius has ordered Didymus off the stage at the end of his first A section, which is sufficiently extended to seem like an entire exit aria (so called because some arias ended with the singer leaving the stage, eliciting thunderous applause). But Didymus suddenly rushes back in for his stormy B section, which makes full use of what Monteverdi had invented as the *stile concitato* (the agitated style) for the warlike madrigals of his Eighth Book. Even within this apparently unified line of text, Sellars exploits an inner contradiction: when he sings the word "mind" (in "truth-supported mind"), Didymus brings a hand up and shields one or both eyes, as if concentrating despite pain or as if forcing himself to think about his behavior and its possible consequences.[26] The conclusion of the B section finds Daniels draped over Septimius's gun, as if hanging from a cross, though energetic enough to produce an improvised high ending.

Most arias of this period would return to the opening ritornello at this point, but Handel has the singer go back directly from the B section to his initial cadenza on "raptured."[27] Daniels waits in silence after the aggressive cadence on "mind"; during this pause, his face slowly recomposes, preparing to turn his thoughts once again toward paradise. If his first presentation of "ra-" seemed ornate, his second defies belief as he spins it out and out. He then pauses again for a very long time before, as if suddenly awakening from a trance, he launches into the aria itself. We might have imagined that Sellars and Daniels had exhausted the gestures that could accompany those words, but the second presentation of the A section offers an entirely new range of possibilities, each of them calibrated to fit Handel's rhythms and harmonic strategies as well as the dramatic and emotional progression he wishes to trace in his staging. As Sellars has explained, we need to hear the A section again to find out what has transpired within the character as a consequence of the journey through the entire aria. It can never ever be just a repetition.

The second moment I wish to discuss is Theodora's extended soliloquy near the beginning of act 2. Her scene follows the orgiastic Romans singing, "Venus laughing from the skies, will applaud her votaries; while seizing the treasure, we revel in pleasure, revenge sweet love supplies" (it is this chorus that presents the simulated rape mentioned above). From that drunken jollity, we move to a near-dark stage, with Theodora in orange prison-garb lying on a floor mat awaiting her transfer to the brothel to which Valens has condemned her. For this extraordinary twelve-minute scena, Handel eschews his usual alternation of recitatives and da capo arias to trace a complex psychological evolution through an unbroken sequence, something like what Mozart does later in his finales. Handel typically does this only for the most crucial of dramatic situations, and this one certainly qualifies.

He begins with one of his most stunning creations: a Largo in which the strings trudge in funereal lockstep punctuated by a flute, which plays a single note alone on the weak beat of each bar. Nothing could depict Theodora's woeful condition more perfectly than that isolated, tremulous sonority—a lament that can eke out only one pitch at a time. Eventually, as it must, the bassline limps down to an inconclusive cadence.

Sellars's staging of the Largo draws extensively on those lone pitches, which Theodora apparently hears. With each entrance of the flute, she responds as if she were a caged animal jabbed by a sharp object: in successive bars she looks up, half sits, flinches, rises to a crouch, flips onto her back then onto her side. At the end of this orchestral introduction, she sinks back down, gazing around in despair on the flute's cadential trill.

Theodora begins singing her recitative in major rather than the minor key of her lead-in, and a brief smile crosses her face on "sweet rays."

> Oh thou bright sun! how sweet thy rays
> To health and liberty! But here, alas!
> They swell the agonizing thought of shame
> And pierce my soul with sorrows yet unknown.

But her torment drives her through a series of twisted harmonies. In a mere eight bars, Handel yanks the key center up unceremoniously by two whole steps, thereby violating every eighteenth-century rule for rational harmonic behavior. Nor does he stop there: instead of continuing in the key he has so laboriously achieved, he pushes even beyond that for the exceedingly remote key of the aria that follows.[28] Whereas the modulations in Didymus's aria still operate within recognizable tonal practice (however unusual they may be), the moves in this recitative no longer qualify as functional; Handel simply lurches from place to place, in keeping with Theodora's tortured mind. Upshaw reflects each of these harmonic moves with her body and her face. Standing out in particular are her stricken grimace on "shame" and the descent of her upper body in incremental jerks, calibrated to fit the chords on "and pierce my soul."

> With darkness deep, as is my woe,
> Hide me, ye shades of Night!
> Your thickest veil around me throw,
> Conceal'd from human sight!
> Or come, thou Death, thy victim save,
> Kindly embosom'd in the grave!

The ritornello of this aria, "With darkness deep, as is my woe," at first recalls the Largo with its single pitch isolated from the lockstep rhythm that presents the harmonies. As the dirge unfolds, Upshaw lies facedown, pulling herself along with her arms. After two measures, this bleak figure yields to a lavishly orchestrated circling motive, the rocking symmetries of which induce Upshaw to writhe rhythmically. When she finally sings, she does so without even the scant comfort of orchestral accompaniment. Recall that Didymus also began his aria a cappella with a cadenza, but he did so in a radically different affective context. Ornaments would not suit Theodora's cell. As she begs for night to conceal her and for Death to take her, she shifts her poses (always in sync with Handel's phrases), sometimes kneeling, then collapsing back with arms outstretched as if on a cross. On the last iteration of the circling figure before the return of the closing ritornello, she pulls her knees up to her chest, as if awaiting burial. Handel brings Theodora's sense of futility up to the formal level by denying her even a contrasting B section. None of her pleas or attempts at modulation has any effect, and she ends up lying flat on her stomach in the key with which she began her aria. She has made no progress.

Once again ignoring harmonic protocol, Handel now brings back the opening Largo, but in a key that bears no rational relationship to the sonority we have just left.[29] And this time he cranks up the tension even more, expanding the material to nearly twice its previous length and introducing even more dissonances. As before, Upshaw responds to those isolated flute tones as if startled; they become a form of torture. About halfway through she begins to sob audibly. This iteration of the Largo, like the first one, limps down to conclude on a half cadence, apparently prompting the singer to continue in the same alien key. Upshaw lies on her side in fetal position as if lifeless.

Suddenly a gorgeous arpeggio in the theorbo awakens her, and she expresses a radical shift of attitude.

> But why art thou disquieted, my soul?
> Hark! Heaven invites thee in sweet rapt'rous strains
> To join the ever-singing, ever-loving choir
> Of saints and angels in the courts above.

Over the course of this recitative Theodora will reach upward, first with only one extended arm, then to her knees, and finally with both arms raised in supplication and praise. She will conclude this pivotal moment with a cadence that leads seamlessly forward to her extended aria, "Oh, that I on wings could rise."

> Oh that I on wings could rise,
> Swiftly sailing through the skies,
> As skims the silver dove!
> That I might rest,
> For ever blest
> With harmony and love. [da capo]

This soaring aria grants Theodora rational agency. Standing erect at the beginning of the ritornello, she paces in circles in rhythm with Handel's walking bass line. Morell's text presents several key words, all of which Handel and Upshaw exploit at one point or another: "rise," "sailing through the skies," and "the silver dove." Although it may appear a single image, "sailing" inspires a wide range of gestures, some smooth, some abrupt, depending on Handel's rhythmic choices. Perhaps most interesting in view of Upshaw's angel in Saint François is her imaginary dove, which she seems to pull down and caress in protective hands: exactly as she did with Frère Bernard when she mentioned Truth. Her A section finds her with arms outstretched in ecstasy.

In this aria, Theodora receives the B section her first one lacked. And while the lyrics deal with harmony and love, the second setting of this text becomes more fraught. Accordingly, Upshaw's gestures become desperate as if begging for these blessings. Moreover, she dives back to her repeat of the A section without the orchestra leading her there—and without even pausing to breathe. Ornamenting her lines far more elaborately this time through, she concludes with an extravagant, triumphant cadenza before falling back in exhaustion. She has embraced her martyrdom and thereby controls the meaning of her destiny; she has traveled a long emotional distance since the opening Largo.

Before leaving *Theodora*, I want to address one more issue: Sellars's interest in presenting the deep bonds of mutual support among women. We already saw evidence of this trait in the Mozart Trilogy, especially in his staging of *Figaro*. But it becomes even more pronounced in *Theodora* as well as in his own libretti and collaborations with Adams and Saariaho.

The extraordinary rapport between Theodora and Irene, her spiritual advisor, forms one of the emotional axes of this oratorio—at least as important in its own way as the love between Theodora and Didymus. But just as the cluster of women in *Figaro* originated with Beaumarchais, Da Ponte, and Mozart, so this pair of women arrived already fully constituted in Handel's and Morell's text. In other words, Sellars does not impose this feminist agenda on these eighteenth-century works; they were already there.

Although the jury is still out on this issue, I find convincing the arguments by Gary Thomas and Ellen Harris that Handel was probably inclined toward relationships with other men in his personal life.[30] Yet despite—or perhaps *because* of—this inclination, much of his work shows women in a particularly sympathetic light. In his *Jephthah* (libretto also by Morell), the mother and daughter voice the moral objections to Jephthah's arrogant acts. Whether because Handel felt similarly oppressed by patriarchal gender codes or just because he happened to like women as human beings (a frequent preference among gay men), he often appears in his theatrical works to identify with his female characters, granting them the moral authority and personal strength absent from many of his men.[31]

*Theodora* could have functioned perfectly well as the tale of the two tragic lovers. But Handel and Morell included the apparently extraneous figure of Irene—not a male priest (as became mandatory in Christian orthodoxy) but a woman who serves as the epicenter of this small, persecuted sect. We know nothing of her other than her gentle but powerful utterances, her ability to guide her flock and provide comfort in times of distress. Recall that Irene enters to pronounce the final benediction after the lovers' execution. She survives to prompt the healing chorus that concludes the oratorio.

Because scenes between women take on such significance in Sellars's later work, I want to look at their interactions in act 1. The two women do not sing together here (though they do in act 3 when Irene tries to dissuade Theodora from sacrificing herself), but Sellars presents their individual strengths and the dynamic between them particularly well in his staging of this opening sequence. That he has the supreme talents of Dawn Upshaw and Lorraine Hunt to work with here takes this scenario to a level he could only have imagined in his earlier productions; he will, of course, retain them both for *El Niño* (discussed in chapter 4), where they more or less reprise their turns as Irene and Theodora.

In this scene that introduces both women, Irene dominates. Theodora appears as a new convert, relinquishing to Irene the jewelry that marks her previous status as a wealthy noble. Even during Theodora's ritornello as she prepares to sing her first aria, "Fond flatt'ring world, adieu," Irene performs a laying-on-of-hands ceremony. With each of Handel's swooping gestures, she applies pressure to Theodora's forehead, then spins her hand away—much as Upshaw did in her scene with Frère Bernard. Although it is Theodora who sings, it is in response to Irene's prompting. When Upshaw approaches her da capo, she takes on those gestures Irene initiated and now exorcizes her old burdens herself.

Irene then officiates with an aria condemning riches, "Bane of virtue," which becomes a kind of offertory. Theodora has set the example, and the other members of the sect now follow. But although the aria's text addresses the entire group, Sellars punctuates the form with tender interactions between the two women. As the B section begins, the women have braided their hands together and both move into the rapturous state Irene describes.

Following "Bane of virtue," the two women kneel in front of the group (all facing the audience) and effectively lead the chorus "Come, mighty father." Because Upshaw sings the soprano part and Hunt the alto, they present their gestures at different times in keeping with the contrapuntal lines in

Handel's fugal prayer. As is typical of Sellars's stagings of such numbers, he draws the viewer's attention to the ways individual voices enter and the imitative fabric of the music. At this point, each woman has sung an extended aria, but with visual interaction throughout, and they now stand as twin pillars of the community. Moreover, the fact that the entire group faces front—as they did near the end of *Figaro* and elsewhere—invites the audience to feel part of the celebration.

But after a messenger interrupts the proceedings to issue a warning, Irene once again assumes her role as leader. An arpeggio in the theorbo introduces a recitative in which she strives to calm her flock, and the aria "As with rosy steps the dawn" allows her to pray and offer comfort. In this aria, Hunt's face becomes nothing less than luminous.[32] In Sellars's staging, Theodora stands now at the extreme edge of the group, and Ingalls's lighting keeps her in shadow. But the DVD keeps reminding us of her centrality despite her silence, as shots of her silhouette continually punctuate Irene's prayer. She serves as principal witness to this devotional service. When Irene begins her da capo, Theodora echoes the gestures Irene had deployed the first time through. Although a novice, she has learned the rituals quickly, and she sings the following chorus as just one of the group.

Soon, however, she finds her marginal position ruptured. Septimius enters with his riot police and selects Theodora as the sacrificial victim. With apparent reluctance, he tells her that she has been sentenced not to death but to a brothel. She sings her initial response, "O worse than death," collapsed over the back of a chair in shame and grief. But her faith revives, and she sings the poignant "Angels ever bright and fair." So powerful is the strength of her conviction that when she raises her arms in praise, the soldiers holding her find themselves drawn into those gestures to their evident amazement. When she sings "take me" to the angels, the soldiers respond obediently to her musical imperatives, so contagious is her belief. The guards arrest and start to lead her away during her B section, but Irene clasps her around the waist and supports her. Now teacher and pupil have exchanged places, as Irene echoes Theodora's movements. As Theodora completes her aria, Irene kneels in prayer before her as if acknowledging her sainthood.

None of the intersections between these characters is stipulated in Handel's score. The complex, developing relationship of the two women derives from Sellars's staging and—in the case of Theodora's silhouettes—from lighting and video editing. But the bonds developed over the course of this scene in act 1 give dramatic motivation to Irene's subsequent appearances in Theodora's prison cell and at the execution.

Irene's moral stature does not preclude her from experiencing anguish, doubt, and even anger. She opens act 3 with a prayer, "Lord to Thee, each night and day, strong in hope we sing and pray." Crumpled up on a vacant stage, she strives in her A section to summon up the courage she exhibits in front of her followers, though as she sings she sometimes falters, sometimes beseeches. But her fury erupts in the rapid-fire B section with the text: "Though convulsive rocks the ground, and Thy thunders roll around, still to Thee, each night and day, we sing and pray." Note the echo here, with "night and day" and "sing and pray" appearing in different affective guises in the two sections.

If the first part mostly focuses on humble supplication, this part comes very close to accusing God of the tribulations we suffer—curse God and die, as Job's friends tell him. In order to underscore this dark night of the soul, Ingalls kills the lights and puts a spot on Hunt alone so that she casts a huge shadow. She collapses by the end of this outburst and lies on the floor nearly unable to undertake her da capo. But then her white-clad disciples appear one by one out of the darkness, like guardian angels. They help her to her feet and sustain her physically. The stage lights gradually come back up, illuminating Irene and her flock, which now nourishes her. As a result of her having survived this nadir, Irene can stand as a pillar of strength throughout the ordeals that ensue. She takes the lead in the final chorus, "O love divine."

Although the tragic love story between Theodora and Didymus forms the core of this oratorio, it also features the confrontation between competing rituals—the worship of Venus by pagans versus the chaste devotions of the Christians. Valens stirs up the bloodlust and lechery of his mob, while Irene inspires the members of her congregation to fearless spirituality. Eventually, her position prevails, as the Romans cross over to her side at the end. If the specific plot concerning martyrdom ends with the execution, the broader scope offered by the choruses allows the oratorio to open up to include us all.

Handel turned to the oratorio genre in part because it invited the choral movements at which he excelled, even though these might seem to compromise dramatic progress. Sellars not only learned how to make these disruptions work on stage, but he brought what he gleaned from his productions of pieces such as *Saint François* and *Theodora* into his own ways of construing music theater in his collaborations with John Adams and Kaija Saariaho, to which we now turn.

# 3 • Inventing New Operas

## Collaborations with John Adams, Part I

The works examined up to this point have involved Sellars as stage director, but they all existed before he came to them. In other words, we have to see his artistry refracted through materials that already had performance histories, some of them dating back over two hundred years. Sellars never abandoned this sort of project: witness his recent productions of Mozart's *Zaide*, Handel's *Hercules*, and Tchaikovsky's *Iolanta*. All of these eschew the jokey qualities he sometimes brought to his Mozart Trilogy and Handel's *Giulio Cesare* to focus with the greatest urgency on social problems still rampant today. His *Zaide* concerns human trafficking and slavery, and his *Hercules* deals with the post-traumatic stress experienced by so many returning veterans. Setting Tchaikovsky's opera in an unmarked locale (i.e., not specifically North America), he grapples in *Iolanta* with issues of spiritual and moral blindness.

But in the early 1980s Sellars began to act on his desire to create his own operas. John Adams happened to be in the same vicinity in 1983, and Sellars proposed to him that they write an opera together. I imagine their first encounter as something like Mickey Rooney and Judy Garland shouting: "Hey kids! Let's put on a show!"[1]

It is hard to overestimate the importance of this moment for American music history. Although opera had flourished throughout previous eras, the postwar reign of post-tonal idioms had all but killed it as an acceptable enterprise. Most serious avant-garde composers avoided theatrical genres like the very plague. As Adams puts it, "Modernism, with its obsession for purity and rigor in musical rhetoric, had proven to be a debilitating artistic ground for effective music drama."[2] Of course, some British and American composers had refused to give up tonal procedures and their audiences. But graduate programs such as the one Adams and I attended at Harvard taught students

**61**

to sneer at the likes of Benjamin Britten or Gian Carlo Menotti. To succumb to Sellars's invitation to write an opera took a great deal of courage and professional confidence.

It also required an extraordinary leap of imagination for Sellars. Thirty-five years later, long after Adams has established himself as North America's preeminent opera composer, we might have trouble appreciating the foolhardiness of Sellars's quest. Adams had already begun to acquire a national reputation at this point, but he had written almost exclusively for instruments. Nor had he ever shown much interest in the component of melody—usually indispensable to composers of vocal music. Sellars had recently listened to Adams's *Shaker Loops*, which scarcely screams "opera." Before they could begin, Sellars had to persuade Adams that opera was a worthwhile endeavor and that he might bend his modus operandi to dramatic singing.

What drew Sellars to Adams? As we have seen in the previous two chapters, Sellars always homes in on crucial qualities of the music itself, particularly its phrasing and kinetic gestures but also its harmonic changes. Yet the eighteenth-century idioms of Mozart and Handel have little in common with the music Adams had produced, especially with respect to those crucial qualities. Starting out as a composer of abstract, complex structures, he had moved away from the Ivy League context that privileged serialist procedures to California, with its eclectic mix of media. The influences of Philip Glass and Steve Reich began to appear in his works, leading critics to lump him together with the minimalists—a term all three of them abhor. But although one can easily hear traces of those pioneering minimalists in Adams's music, he also departed from them in significant ways.

In the mid-1980s I became something of a firebrand for what we called the Downtown school: artists operating in that warren of lofts and studios located in Greenwich Village, as opposed to the Uptown composers located at Columbia, Princeton, and other elite universities. When I first heard Adams's *Harmonielehre*, I wrote quite disparagingly of what I called the gentrification of postmodernism. For Adams brought to his version of Glassian ostinatos and Reichian percussive effects many of narrative devices long the provenance of nineteenth-century symphonies, especially the drive for climax so rigorously eschewed by his experimentalist contemporaries. Moreover, Adams had always proved outrageously talented at writing for and conducting large-scale orchestras. And so, while Glass and Reich continued to work through their own ensembles, Adams suddenly became the darling of traditional concert subscribers. He was feeding them, I thought, what they wanted to hear.[3]

All those debates are now water under the bridge.[4] Like one of Bluebeard's former wives, serialism has taken its place in the succession of historical moments, and the ubiquity of work by Glass and others renders ideological differentiation quaint.[5] Yet Sellars heard some of the same qualities in Adams's music as I did. As he explains it (in far more generous terms than mine):

> The rhythmic impulse and physical motor under way in John's music is another thing that lifts it from university-composed academic art music into a field of thought and action in the world. That worldly imagery of John's music, coupled with its otherworldly, transcendental side, generates the tension that makes these pieces have long lives.[6]

> John's music has builds, it has tension. It's not just abstract, it's actually incredibly vivid and alive. It has—like Mozart—a lot of dance music, a lot of sharp changes. It's funny, then it's not, it's tender, then it's suddenly sharp.[7]

Both of us celebrated Adam's liberation from serialist tyranny. But Sellars heard operatic potential in the very elements, such as narrative drive, that I then found objectionable. And he was absolutely right in pursuing this improbable partnership.

Adams famously held out for a couple of years as Sellars kept up his courtship. But then he surrendered, relying heavily on Sellars's experience at first:

> I didn't know what I was doing in a lot of ways.... But luckily we had Peter Sellars, who was then maybe 30, and was already very, very experienced and skilled in opera, because he'd done the three Mozart-Da Ponte operas. And he was famous for those; they were very provocative and deeply thought and felt works.

> Peter had an innate dramaturgical sense. You know, a lot of operas are created these days by people—composers, librettists and directors—none of whom have a refined sense of the theater. And if you look at a career like Verdi's or Puccini's, you can see how it takes a long time to gain that knowledge and experience; these guys wrote dozens of operas before they got it right.... I was very, very lucky to be able to work from the start with Peter, because I'm sure I couldn't otherwise have created something with the staying power of *Nixon in China* without his extraordinary theatrical genius to guide me.[8]

In order for this collaboration to work, both men had to adjust radically their approaches to music: Adams to accommodate singers over his roiling orchestras, Sellars to devise a kinetic vocabulary that could translate this very new idiom into visual analogues. Although Sellars emphasizes other influences, I would posit Glass's operas as significant models. Only a few years before Sellars began to cajole Adams into writing for the stage, Robert Wilson had convinced a somewhat reluctant Philip Glass to collaborate on *Einstein on the Beach* (1977), which probably qualifies as ground zero for postmodernist opera.[9] Several of the strategies manifested in *Einstein*—as well as *Satyagraha* (1979) and *Akhnaten* (1982)—also show up in the first Adams-Sellars works, particularly an emphasis on extended rituals. Lucinda Childs even deploys similar choreographies in *Einstein* (see particularly "Dance 1") and *Doctor Atomic*.

But whereas Glass has continued to resist narrative structures, Adams and Sellars forged an amalgam between storytelling and Glass's austere tableaux orientation, just as Adams had already tilted Glass's process idiom toward teleological drive. In adapting Glass's and Wilson's innovations to quite different ends, they created a new kind of opera suited to both Adams's compositional style and Sellars's dramaturgical investments. I would say that they hit their stride with *El Niño*. But their first two operas, *Nixon in China* and *The Death of Klinghoffer*, reveal the remarkable strength of their liaison.

Sellars suggested the topics for *Nixon* and *Klinghoffer*. Anyone not familiar with the vast range of his interests might find implausible his claim: "Working on Haydn's *Armida*, trying to understand the Vietnam War, I got out the Kissinger memoirs and was rereading my Mao. In the middle of all of that, I thought, Oh, there's an opera waiting in there!"[10] Although the Adams operas may seem quite distant from the eighteenth-century classics Sellars was re-envisioning at the same time, they share a commitment to put American culture on stage for American audiences and to address the cultural dilemmas with which his contemporaries grappled. In an interview with Thomas May, Sellars says:

> The . . . thing that was important for me was constantly to make operas about Americans: it's *Nixon* in China. *The Death of Klinghoffer* deals with Palestinians, but is about Americans in the middle of the situation. . . . For me, it was important constantly to work as American artists and as Americans and not in a tradition of opera based on exoticism, writing about pearl fishers and so on. We wanted to create a way in which one of the key questions becomes "What are we doing in the middle of this?"[11]

If the Mozart Trilogy entailed translating eighteenth-century works into American terms, the collaborations with Adams required transforming the genre of opera itself in ways that could accommodate new musical idioms and stories drawn from American political life. Mussorgsky and Verdi wrote operas about czars and kings; why not feature presidents or nuclear physicists as protagonists? As Thomas May puts it: "In his stage works Adams, with his collaborators Peter Sellars and Alice Goodman, has been able to locate the power of myth in figures from contemporary history."[12]

At this early stage in their working relationship, Adams wanted a libretto by a "real poet," and he even requested rhyming couplets for *Nixon*. He hoped that "the artifice of verse might lift the story and its characters, so numbingly familiar to us from the news media, out of the ordinary and onto a more archetypal plane."[13] At Sellars's suggestion, he invited Alice Goodman—a college friend of Sellars's—to write the lyrics for *Nixon* and then *Klinghoffer*.

Beginning with *El Niño* in 2000, Sellars assumed the responsibility for developing the libretti along with Adams. In these works, in which Sellars served as Da Ponte to Adams's Mozart, we can see many of elements in Sellars's productions of repertory works coming unmistakably to the fore; now he could shape the scenarios himself and help to create an idiosyncratic genre of music theater (see chapter 4). But first I want to deal with those two previous operas with Goodman's libretti, in which Sellars and Adams first started to work together toward a new kind of music drama.

## Nixon in China

It cannot have been easy for Alice Goodman to collaborate with these two control freaks, and the addition of choreographer Mark Morris to the team seems to have exacerbated the situation. In an interview with Sellars presented during the HD broadcast of the Metropolitan Opera production of *Nixon in China*, host Thomas Hampson asks Sellars point-blank: "Did she mind you sitting on her shoulder?"—a question Sellars deflects by choosing to praise her contributions.[14] Goodman, however, has publicly expressed mixed feelings about her experience, even in her published program notes:

> There are places where the music goes against the grain of the libretto, and places where the staging goes against the grain of both. My Nixon is not quite the same character as John Adams's Nixon, and they both differ slightly from Peter Sellars's Nixon, not to mention James Mad-

dalena's [Nixon in both the original and Metropolitan Opera productions]. My view of the Cultural Revolution is not the same as theirs, and theirs are not the same. I suspect we disagree about peace and progress. This collaboration is polyphonic. We have done our best to make our disagreements counterpoints; not to drown each other out, but, like the characters in the opera, each to be as eloquent as possible.[15]

We know from other accounts that Goodman became quite bitter, especially with respect to Sellars.[16] This is a bit like Aesop's frog carrying the scorpion across the river and then protesting when stung; what else could one expect of someone who delighted in deconstructing sacrosanct texts by Mozart and Shakespeare?

Goodman eventually bailed out of a planned third project, *Doctor Atomic*, for which Adams and Sellars crafted their own libretto (see chapter 4). Adams has reported concerning her decision to withdraw:

We had major disputes, even some hard feelings with [*Nixon in China* and *The Death of Klinghoffer*]. I think some of it had to do with the fact that she was a literary person working in what's fundamentally a musical world, opera, always feeling that her value was never quite appreciated. Parts of the *Nixon* libretto were never set to music, something that puzzled and probably annoyed her. . . . I don't think she has any idea how much her work is beloved by people who know the opera.[17]

Whatever the conditions under which she worked, however, Goodman produced many brilliant poetic passages in *Nixon*: the Chinese chorus grimly chanting "The people are the heroes now, Behemoth pulls the peasant's plow"; Pat's lovely homespun soliloquy blessing Middle America; Nixon's excited "News, news, news"; the hyperbolic excess of "I am the wife of Mao Tse-tung!"; Chou En-lai's heartbreaking valediction that concludes the opera. Adams responded to each of these texts so perfectly that they remain— music and words—permanently etched in the cultural memory, joining the ranks of great operatic numbers, and he and Sellars continue to express the greatest respect for Goodman's libretto.[18]

We have two filmed versions of *Nixon in China*: the original production at the Houston Grand Opera in 1987 (broadcast on PBS) and, following myriad stagings in the intervening years, the production at the Metropolitan Opera in 2011, both directed by Sellars. I will deal with these at some length, teasing out features shared with the Mozart Trilogy stagings and those that continue to mark Sellars's work with Adams and others. But I will also discuss elements that seem to have required rethinking. This was the first stab at a new kind of opera for all involved, and although *Nixon* has now entered the canon in its own right, it has some areas of weakness. Sellars and Adams themselves seem to have been dissatisfied with certain aspects of the piece, for they transformed these in their later enterprises.

Which member of this four-way collaboration can claim credit for any given element of the work that finally reached the stage? Morris's choreography might seem most autonomous, though Sellars proposed the scenario for *The Red Detachment of Women*, based on his research into Chiang Ch'ing's [Madame Mao's] own productions; indeed, it was those vintage ballets (as well as his study of Kissinger and Mao) that first inspired Sellars to suggest the topic of Nixon's Chinese visit.[19] The complex intersections between the ballet, the Nixons' bafflement, Kissinger's surprise appearance as the entertainment's villain (thereby resonating with his role in the Vietnam War), and Chiang Ch'ing's violent overthrow of the performance may recall the comedic side of Sellars in the Mozart Trilogy. In addition, Sellars and his collaborators consulted and relied upon Cecilia Zung's *Secrets of the Chinese Drama*.[20]

Also included in Sellars's retinue of regulars was Adrianne Lobel (set design) and James F. Ingalls (lights). Lobel had produced the minimalist sets for the Mozart Trilogy at PepsiCo; with the much greater budgets of the Houston Grand Opera and the Metropolitan, she was able to expand to the monumental. Basing her sets on the many photographs taken during Nixon's historic trip, Lobel recreated in detail the scenarios already familiar to audiences from news reels. Her photorealist simulacrum of Mao's library astonished even attachés who had attended that eventful meeting, and her conjuring onstage of Air Force One surely counts as one of the great coups de théâtre of recent opera. For the televised performance in 1987, PBS brought in Walter Cronkite to ground the opera in archival reality. As he introduced the opera, he recalled his own impressions of the visit while news footage rolled behind him. The collaborators did everything they could to connect their American audiences with its recent history.

But many other features of this opera bear Sellars's idiosyncratic signature, and several of these remain will constant through his later work with Adams. When given license to shape his own narratives, Sellars turned to the ritualized conventions of the oratorios, cantatas, and passions he had encountered at Emmanuel Church, as well as to the non-Western performance traditions he had showcased in the Los Angeles Festival. Anticipating a central theme of this book, Michael Steinberg wrote:

Concerning the dramaturgy of *The Death of Klinghoffer*, John Adams has noted that one does better to seek a model in Johann Sebastian Bach's Passion settings than in any opera. Peter Sellars likewise cites three Bach *Passions* as points of comparison, along with Greek tragedy, Persian *Ta'ziyeh*, and Javanese *Wayang Wong*, all works made up of multiple layers and all religious.[21]

The strategy of *Nixon in China*'s oratorical opening, with the chorus facing front and reciting Maoist slogans, recurs in *The Death of Klinghoffer*, *El Niño*, *Doctor Atomic*, and elsewhere. We have already seen how Sellars in his stagings of Mozart and Handel makes use of ensembles to simulate community, thereby suturing the audience into the proceedings. As Steinberg reports, he and Adams took their inspiration for the choruses of *Klinghoffer* explicitly from the Bach passions, and this influence already resonates in the dramaturgy of *Nixon*'s first scene.

Another important influence with respect to the shaping of the piece in tableaux must come from the operas of Philip Glass. *Akhnaten* (1982) in particular features many sequences in which the chorus presents ritualistic pageantry: for instance, the opening funeral of Amenhotep III and Akhnaten's coronation. Moreover, Glass fashioned his own libretto for *Akhnaten* from found texts, and Sellars would soon adopt that as his own modus operandi when he began to assemble his own libretti with Adams. As we shall see, Adams drew extensively on Glass's idiom as he composed his first opera. But Adams and Sellars would attempt to take the extreme austerity of Glass's works and meld them with more traditional temporal, theatrical, and musical modes. If postmodernist opera kicked off with *Einstein on the Beach*, Adams and Sellars took many of those elements in quite different directions.

Surely the prominence of Sellars's regular sidekicks James Maddalena and Sanford Sylvan—also appearing in *Cosi fan tutte* that very same season, *Figaro* the next—identifies both *Nixon* and *Klinghoffer* with his larger opus. Viewing Maddalena's Guglielmo or Sylvan's Figaro up against their roles in *Nixon* (Maddalena's Nixon or Sylvan's Chou En-lai and Klinghoffer) demonstrates why Sellars and Adams would want to retain these virtuoso singer-actors, regardless of the composition at hand.[22]

Who watching Sylvan's comic capering as Figaro could predict the gravitas of his Chou En-lai? But as his almost unbearably intimate performance of Chou's final aria reveals, Sylvan had already established himself as a master interpreter of art song as well as opera buffa. Maddalena's ability to pivot between Count Almaviva's ridiculous buffa moments and his poignant self-doubt shows up repeatedly in his portrayal of Nixon. As critic Tim Page observed, Maddalena "doesn't really look all that much like Nixon,"[23] but he so perfectly channels the tics and postures of the fallen president that he *becomes* Nixon. So much does he own that role that he reprised it twenty-five years later for the Met production, even though his voice had lost its former strength and luster. In a sense, the fact that he had to exert tension and sometimes failed to meet the challenges of this part in the latter performance resonates with the ways Nixon so often seemed to strain to inhabit his own self-manufactured persona.

Just as Maddalena brought empathy to his versions of the Count and Guglielmo, he (along with Adams, Sellars, and Goodman) saves Nixon from what might have appeared as a cartoon and grants him a touching humanity—not an easy task given the way he had fallen into disgrace with Vietnam, Watergate, and the impeachment. But we get a glimpse of Nixon's inner demons in the first act when he interrupts his self-congratulatory "News" with "The rats begin to chew the sheets!"—an outburst that remains enigmatic until act 3, when he returns explicitly to ruminating on the horrors of his wartime experiences. Pat, who has heard these stories many times before and knows how deeply wounded her husband truly is, assumes the task of pulling him back from that dark recess in his psyche; in this opera at least, Pat proves herself the stronger of the two. Yet this rescue of Nixon's image is only plausible dramatically because of Maddalena's uncanny ability to display masculine vulnerability.[24]

Much of *Nixon in China*'s libretto dwells on dialogue, on conversations between the Nixons and on actual transcriptions of diplomatic conversations. Within these contexts, Sellars could not easily use the stylized stagecraft he deploys so well with Mozart and Handel. The famous semaphores do show up, however, in his direction of the Maoettes, as the team (alluding to Ray Charles's backup singers, the Raylettes) called the trio of female interpreters hovering around Mao in scene 2.

Sellars reported in an interview that he drew the gestures for the Maoettes from the stagecraft of Chinese opera.[25] Yet they resemble quite closely the movements he used in the final of *Figaro*'s second act. Recall that Sellars was working on both productions at the same time. Did traces of Chinese opera make their way into his staging of Mozart and Handel? Or did his simultaneous immersion in both repertories lead to cross-fertilization? In any case, the Maoettes' gestures keep us attached to the literal meanings of Mao's images, amplifying his words and turning them into Red Book mottos right before our eyes: see in particular their animated miming of Mao's "Founders come first, then profiteers" and "We no longer need Confucius." They also lend a spark of visual humor to what otherwise might sink into turgid philosophical to-and-fro. But more than anything, they point to Adams's complex rhythmic impulses—just as they had Mozart's in the *Figaro* finale.

Many have read *Nixon in China* as perpetrating orientalist or "yellow-face" stereotypes. In his interview with Thomas May, Sellars seeks to explain:

> The way culture works is never "pure"—everything is cross-pollinating all the time. That is the energy of our period, which is by definition multicultural and multileveled, where everything comes from a surprising place. *Nixon in China*, for example, has no overt Chinese reference in it musically, but sets up a world which you regard as Chinese—in some amazing way that goes beyond *The Mikado*. [laughs] Instead of using a kind of musical orientalism, it's quite the opposite: what is the *shared* world here? One of the most important things about John's music is that it's not a colonialist viewpoint tapping into someone else's music. It presents the texture of a world we are actually sharing, in which this interpenetration of influence and aspiration from all sides is creating something that is a new culture.[26]

Adams's music, as Sellars claims, never seeks to reveal how these cultural Others really are, the way Bizet does with his pseudoflamenco or Puccini with his Japonaiserie; all his characters sing in an idiom far removed from that of either the Nixons or the Maos.

The staging itself, however, sometimes seems to cross the line: seeing Sylvan's Chou En-lai in makeup that resembles that of Charlie Chan movies, Mao's three translators ("three little maids from school"), or Chiang Ch'ing's Dragon Lady might give one pause. I am not convinced that casting is the real problem here. Does it help having Kathleen Kim, a Korean American coloratura, sing Chiang Ch'ing's rants in the Metropolitan Opera production? Isn't this still a caricature?[27]

As one of the first musicologists to raise the issue of orientalism, I would point back to Edward Said's work, which posits that Western portrayals of the East often have had the effect of stacking the political deck.[28] Those who learned to view Arabic people as lascivious and indolent could more easily justify appropriating their resources while indulging in a sensuality invented for that purpose by artists, novelists, and musicians. Carmen needs to be killed because she's a scheming, promiscuous Gypsy; ask the Roma about the consequences of this opera that comprises all most listeners know (or think they know) about Spain.[29]

For all the stereotyping in *Nixon*, I doubt that anyone takes them as the way the Chinese people truly are. Even at the time of the historic meeting the opera presents, China had become a major player in international relations, with Mao, Chou En-lai, and Chiang Ch'ing as formidable powers on the world stage. Although parodied in the opera (as are the Americans), they do not get flattened into geisha girls or opium-smoking coolies; they come across as brilliant, well-read individuals, thereby shattering the orientalist images the Nixons might have presupposed before they arrived. I do not read this as exoticism.

Critics have also sometimes complained of the static quality of *Nixon*'s dramaturgy. The opening sequence, for instance, seems positively glacial until after the landing of Air Force One. When the lights first come up, the chorus members face forward, stock still, and they remain absolutely expressionless as they chant their slogans. Yet Sellars has the camera home in closely on these faces, one after the other: for all that they sing in lockstep and according to doctrine, he strives to shows them as unique individuals.[30] This is not, in other words, an undifferentiated conglomerate but rather a group of persons, all of them entrained to conform and to suppress their emotion. If Sellars usually celebrates community, he here demonstrates—as in the scenes of Romans in *Theodora* or the murderous crowds in the passions—the dangers of mass-think.

Throughout this scene, Sellars offers visual cues to mark shifts in Adams's musical figuration: the full chorus appears on screen only when they reach "The peasants are the heroes now"; now and then, Sellars has one of the singers pivot and walk toward the back; during a kind of da capo of "The peasants," they all step forward in unison, conveying a sense of encroaching menace; then, to articulate another change in the music, banners with Chinese characters descend slowly in the back of the stage. But the stage remains otherwise motionless, thereby creating a strong visual counterweight to the sonic momentum: if we hear growing excitement in the orchestra, the choristers show no evidence whatsoever of affect. When a sudden stroke low in the piano establishes a pedal point, Chou En-lai strides officiously onto the stage to greet the plane, though he too retains a poker face.

As a stage director, Sellars risks a great deal in withholding motion throughout this extended sequence. He does so in part so that we might attend without distraction to the structural procedures of Adams's music. The opera's introduction begins with slowly ascending scales (inspired particularly by Glass),[31] moves through the rigid chorus's "The people are the peasants now," then drives in a thrilling crescendo (punctuated with urgent pushes toward climax) to the descent of the plane, and finally (with hilarious allusions to the brandishing of the sword in Wagner's *Ring*), to the triumphant emergence of the Nixons. This surely qualifies as the most exciting buildup to a protagonist since Verdi's Otello strides onstage having quelled the storm. Adams pulls out every desire-generating trick in the nineteenth-century symphonic playbook here, as he deftly modulates from the cool stasis of minimalism to the overheated teleologies of late romanticism. Recall that I had heard those sorts of stylistic modulations as selling out.[32] Sellars sought out Adams as a collaborator precisely for the dynamic effect he creates in the opening segments of *Nixon*.

But Sellars also delays visual action for dramatic purposes. As Adams's music intensifies and accelerates, the tension between what we hear and the paralysis we see on stage becomes nearly unbearable. After Nixon has landed, Maddalena's manic aria "News!" kicks the motion into high gear, and the stasis of Sellars's opening suddenly shatters into frenetic motion. He has presented us with a frozen China soon to be blasted apart by brash Americans. Indeed, the riots that break out at the ends of acts 1 and 2 demonstrate that these alien energies have the potential to disrupt the regimented discipline we witness at the opera's outset.

"News" sets up much more than the cultural collision we will witness. As Nixon moves mechanically down a receiving line of Chinese dignitaries, he sings not to them but to the camera, his face and body both displaying in exaggerated fashion the expressiveness denied the Chinese onstage. Adams's setting of Goodman's lyrics allows Maddalena to glory in the scattershot delivery, redundant tics, self-aggrandizement, and loony tropes characteristic of Nixon's speech patterns; for the latter, note in particular the weird yodeling on "mystery" and the arpeggiation on "quietly." Sellars had worked extensively in eighteenth-century opera and oratorio in which lines in the libretto get chopped up, with small segments or individual words repeated endlessly (see the discussion of Didymus's "The raptur'd soul" in chapter 2). As Adams suggests, Sellars brought his dramaturgical proclivities with him to this and other collaborations.

We might anticipate this aria to maintain its exuberant tone throughout, but Goodman inserts several other key elements, including Nixon's longing to uphold American ideals and traces of his recurring paranoia. When Maddalena reaches the middle of the aria, a curtain lowers, indicating that he has moved from the public arena into the private sphere. Pat (Carolyn Page in Houston, Janis Kelly at the Met), who has had much experience with her husband's mood swings, invites him to lie down to rest. But he proves too excited to nap and pops back up, first with a reprise of "News," then more disturbingly with his chronic nightmare, "The rats begin to chew the sheets." Over the course of this scene, Maddalena delivers a panorama of the various Nixons: diplomat, braggart, beleaguered president, damaged veteran, vulnerable spouse. Pat utters not a syllable during this sequence, yet she comes to be seen as a tower of strength, effectively stage-managing her husband's volatile affective life.

Sellars and Adams have spoken about the risk of letting the too-familiar figures of Nixon and Kissinger slide over into caricature, into (in Adams words) "the subject of late-night comedian jokes."[33] When a shambling Kissinger descends from Air Force One in the premiere production, it might appear that they had fallen into that trap; the Metropolitan production offers a somewhat more dignified secretary of state. But the collaborators save their Nixon from ridicule, allowing him to veer in his opening sequence from comic chatter to much deeper psychological concerns. Although Nixon may seem foolish on occasions during the opera (especially during the ballet sequence), he emerges unexpectedly as a sympathetic and sometimes even heroic character. Witness his moving appeal for peace during the negotiations with Mao, "Fathers and sons, let us join hands, History's our mother," to which Mao responds with the hostile rejoinder, "History is a dirty sow!"[34]

Winston Lord, Kissinger's special assistant on the trip, reports that much of the libretto came verbatim from transcriptions, and he describes Mao during this historic session as "either being brilliantly subtle or senile, you're not sure which."[35] The two productions differ considerably in their portrait of the Chairman (John Duykers in Houston, Robert Brubaker at the Met). For Mao's initial entrance to meet with the Americans at the Imperial City, Adams's score offers repetitive figuration with heavy downbeats. Although the Maoettes have to assist the ailing Mao in walking in both performances, Sellars chooses to have Duykers rock from foot to foot on those powerful pulses, delivering an impression of monstrous power. In the Metropolitan Opera production, however, Robert Brubaker's palsied legs respond to the much shorter rhythmic values within the metric hierarchy. These qualities of motion differ hugely, in part because the collaborators had come to understand the grave deterioration in Mao's physical condition. Adams's music may lead the way, but Sellars parses his patterns in ways that reinterpret the Mao we see and hear.

Yet as if to compensate for his greater physical infirmity, Brubaker's face radiates malice far more than does Duykers's. If his body has diminished in strength, the Chairman still comes across as a very dangerous figure: witness his emphatic hand motions on "We more than once led the right wing forward." Observe also how Duykers rises triumphantly to his feet to deliver his Heldentenor description of the Revolution, "It is duration"; by contrast, Brubaker scarcely can rise, but totters (picking up again on the rapid pitches in Adams's figuration), extending his arms in what must once have seemed a threatening pose. Duykers seems smug when he makes his points, whereas Brubaker continually collapses from exertion. Maddalena reacts differently to these two characterizations: he continues with his stilted diplomatic banter in the Houston production, but he registers shock and dismay in his demeanor in the Met; this is not the legendary, larger-than-life Mao he had expected. Yet Nixon remains wary, as if encountering a wounded beast.

For most of the first act, Chou En-lai remains visible but reserved; he intervenes occasionally during the meeting between Mao and Nixon, but just looks on for the most part. He first moves into the spotlight for his toast in the banquet of scene 3. Sanford Sylvan's Chou holds a mask of what seems like oriental inscrutability until this moment, when his dream of a future for China and the United States lights up his face. He breaks off after "From vision to inheritance," and Sellars has the camera train on individuals during the instrumental interlude—something that once again encourages us to see this not as just a mass of people. In the Met production, Russell Braun's Chou communicates much more openly whenever he speaks. But both men stand and sing in recital style with no bodily gestures, as does Nixon when he returns the toast. In other words, Sellars exercises a more realistic mode of representation for these documented moments.

As mentioned above, Pat Nixon shoulders the burdens of maintaining her husband's public veneer and presenting a viable face of mainstream America. During her husband's administration, Pat remained in the background, mostly silent even during his painful scandals—an easy target for second-wave feminists, who saw her as a dutiful wife, sacrificing her life and integrity for the sake of her corrupt spouse's career. Goodman not only gives Pat voice but she bestows upon her a low-key eloquence not out of line with the First Lady's middle-American values.

The collaborators devoted act 2 of *Nixon in China* largely to the women: scene 1 features Pat's tour of Peking and her private reflections, scene 2 Chiang Ch'ing's ballet. In an interview included in the PBS broadcast of the Houston production, Adams explains:

> Act 2 is about the women. In an event like this . . . everyone in the media seems to assume that the important events that are happening are happening with the men. And women are almost always treated in a rather offhanded way. The press always discusses what the First Lady was wearing and how she went and met with the children and so on and so forth. We feel that what's going on the minds of these women is in a certain sense every bit as important as what's going on in the minds of the men. And I think . . . that this opera is just as much about

the role of women—sexual oppression or whatever—as it is about politics or culture or whatever.

And what makes it interesting is that we have two women who typify different kinds of sexual oppression. Pat is the classic case of the Republican women; she's the model of the woman who always stays in the background, who stands by her man. And we know that she hated politics throughout her life but that she learned to grin and bear it. And I was always interested when I saw this stoic woman standing in the background, what was going on in her mind?

So on the one hand we have this American ideal of womanhood and on the other we have Chiang Ch'ing, Madame Mao, who was another case of an oppressed woman. Most Americans don't know that this person was during the 1930s a movie actress. And she sort of scratched and clawed her way up the power structure, moving from Shanghai to Yan'an, meeting Mao, hitching her wagon to his star. And then when Mao began to lose his own control in the sixties, she rose to the front and became in a sense the most powerful person in China. And this is a case of a person who was oppressed to begin with and then whose power triumphed in a rather shocking way.[36]

I have included this very long quotation not only because it encapsulates so well the intentions of the *Nixon* collaborators but also because it offers insight into the emphasis on women in nearly all of Sellars's work, whether designed with Adams or not. Indeed, we already have seen how he focuses on Mozart's and Handel's women, asking us to comprehend the world from their vantage points. Adams's words here resonate very strongly with statements by Sellars in his interviews. Whether he brought this sensibility to Adams or whether they found a common bond in this commitment, feminism became a cornerstone of their work together.

Act 2 opens with Pat asleep on her bed, her famous red coat already on, her purse at the ready. Although Adams's music percolates along in a sprightly manner, she has difficulty rising to the challenge: she wolfs down two palms full of pills and continually flops back in exhaustion. As she prepares to meet the women's delegation that will guide her tour, she tries to brace herself: "I treat each day like Christmas," "Trivial things are not for me," "I come from a poor family." In the Houston production, Carolyn Page appears to be speaking inwardly as she dutifully makes up the hotel bed; Janis Kelly shows more animation, as if in her imagination she is reciting these apparently well-worn sayings to her daughters. In essence, she is donning armor to help her survive the ordeal she faces.

The next sequence counts as a great tours de force in staging, as Pat moves through the stops—a faculty, a clinic, a pig farm, a classroom—documented during the actual visit. Lobel's representations of the tour's stations slide easily in and out of view as the chorus excitedly pulls Pat along. Despite the fatigue from which she has just roused herself, Pat smiles with delight at each activity, displaying the tireless graciousness expected of her as First Lady. Adam concocts a kind of "pictures at an exhibition" for the duration of the tour: the perky music we heard when she awoke continues throughout, broken occasionally with more particular references: the stop-off at the pig farm, for instance, features a folklike dance as the chorus chants, "Pig, pig, pig . . ." over alternating tonic and subdominant chords. But Adams embeds such eclectic moments within the bustling soundscape that represents the treadmill of Pat's daily existence. Because we first hear that figuration when she is cringing in bed, we know that she does not entirely identify with the perkiness she has to feign.

At last the adoring children vanish and Adams's frenetic patterning subsides, leaving Pat alone with her thoughts. Her extended soliloquy, "This is prophetic," presents her vision of the future, far removed from those already painted by Chou En-lai and her husband in their respective toasts at the act 1 banquet. Standing alone on an empty stage, she files through images of families having dinner, of Gypsy Rose Lee, of travelers, of town-square bands, offering a benediction for all their homely activities. In concluding, Pat conjures a bride and groom: "Bless this union, let it remain inviolate." This comes very close to home, for she implicitly reflects here on her own marriage that has brought her to this distant land.

During this aria, Adam's score unfolds through slow, Glass-like ostinatos, his melody rising acutely at the ends of most lines as if Pat were launching her wishes into the air like doves, one after the other. Although her face reflects the impact these images have on her, she moves naturally: Sellars allows her voice and Adams's music to carry the burden of the monologue. The quiet stillness of this profoundly lonely woman, standing alone on a dark stage rehearsing her memories and dreams, haunts the rest of the opera.

A group of children interrupts her reverie, and a cluster of workers drags in a huge statue of an elephant, which she identifies as the emblem of her husband's political party, and a chorus sings of past hardships. In the Houston production, Pat walks off the stage with her guides as the lights fade. But in the Metropolitan version, she wanders back in by herself and gazes silently at the elephant—the Republican Party that has usurped her marriage and her life.

In the following scene, Mark Morris's version of *The Red Detachment of*

*Women* dominates the proceedings. Recall that the entire opera project sprang from Sellars's watching a film of Chiang Ch'ing's own ballet, and he and Morris drew extensively on that footage.[37] Ch'ing's ballet—based in turn on a movie by Chou En-lai—traces the trials and conversion of a young woman, Wu Qinghua, who appears first in red pajamas, chained and tortured by an evil landlord, Nanbatian. A dashing young man, Hong Changqing, rescues her and takes her to the Red Detachment for which he serves as commissar. Wu learns of the enlightened world her new comrades inhabit, and she quickly rises in their ranks. Eventually they mount an attack; although Hong sacrifices his life (as an unseen chorus croons "The Internationale"!), Wu manages to shoot Nanbatian and ascend to the position of commissar.

In their adaptation for *Nixon in China*, the collaborators retained many elements from the ballet: Wu appears exactly as she did in Ch'ing's film, and the scenes in which Nanbatian (now played by the singer in the role of Kissinger) and his lackey's whip her remain mostly intact; Wang makes his heroic entrance, saves her, and instills in her his vision of a glorious future; a group of young recruits sit under a palm tree receiving instruction on Communist principles. Mme. Mao sits with Nixons, egging her performers on.

But Pat becomes appalled at the abuse inflicted on Wu and seeks to intervene. At first the president tries to calm her, to remind her that this is just a play. But eventually he too gets drawn into the action, handing Wu a gun and offering her a glass of juice. References to subsequent scenes in the ballet appear—Hong shows up (escorted by Nixon himself) to attend Nanbatian's gala disguised as a Southeast Asian businessman; colorfully clad servant girls bring in baskets of fruit; recruits attend the makeshift indoctrination classroom. The Nixons effectively capsize the performance, and most of these references become unintelligible in the mayhem. Mme. Mao attempts to put the production back on track by ushering in the Red Detachment, who carry out their precision military drills as the chorus sings the hilarious "Flesh rebéls."

Throughout this scene, Adams's brilliant score offers a highly eclectic smorgasbord, alluding to sources as disparate as the threatening pulses borrowed from Stravinsky's *Le sacre du printemps*, Romantic climaxes in Wagner and Strauss, and rousing patriotic marches developed in Soviet film scores such as Prokofiev's *Alexander Nevsky*. Adams knows his music history, and he does not hesitate to draw upon the styles and tropes that seem appropriate to the moment.

For the most part, the original Houston choreography remains intact in the Metropolitan performance. But the productions diverge substantially in the presentation of Chiang Ch'ing herself. The extent of the tyranny she exercised over China in Mao's waning years and afterward had come to light, and this deeper understanding shaped the latter portrayal. At least as important, however, was the decision to cast coloratura Kathleen Kim in the role premiered by Trudy Ellen Craney. With her standard-issue eyeglasses (the same worn by the Maoettes), Craney appears somewhat mousy. She stands on her chair for the first part of "I am the wife of Mao Tse-Tung," and she brandishes her copy of the Red Book from that static position.

Kim, on the other hand, looks as if she might dive down off the stage and devour everyone in the front row. As the Nixons wreak havoc on her performance, she leaves her seat in the audience and begins shoving her dancers around. Her demented whoops on "the Book, the Book" leave no doubt about her potential ruthlessness. Finally, she incites a full-blown riot: a terrifying monster, especially contrasted with the infirm Mao, the tenderhearted Pat, and even Nixon. Only one figure stands up to her: at the end of the act, as chaos roils the stage, Chou En-lai silently confronts her.[38]

As discussed in chapter 1, Mozart often organized his finales—those concluding segments in which all characters appear—as dance suites. Doing so allowed him continuous music over which he could present action and multiple, often contradictory voices. Adams and Sellars brought their experience with Mozart's dramaturgy to bear on the last act of *Nixon in China*. The original libretto had set the last scene as yet another public banquet, and while working on *Nixon*, Adams composed an instrumental piece titled "The Chairman Dances," a quasi fox-trot played by big-band instruments, intended to evoke the kinds of music both the Nixons and the Maos would have heard during their respective courtships. This would have fit perfectly well in a banquet setting.

But Sellars argued (despite considerable pushback from his colleagues) that the opera already had a sufficient number of banquets.

> I just said, "forget it. Get rid of the party scene. Get the band offstage." The way it had originally been designed we had a big party scene. The tables were supposed to come back—the whole thing. We removed everything and I had them make those beds. That night I called Adrianne from Houston and said "we need six beds that look like coffins." ... The beds were exactly like coffins. ... That night is such a nocturnal scene, the music is so nocturnal, the kind of sense of the sex, of going to bed and at the same time of being laid to rest—those images.[39]

Turning from actions and orations played out in the public sphere, Sellars wished to devote this final scene to the private thoughts of the participants in this historical occasion. As they retire to their sleeping quarters, they reflect not only on the events of the last few days but also on the life experiences that have brought them to this point. They express themselves sometimes separately, sometimes all at the same time, together weaving a contrapuntal web of shared humanity.

In choosing to stage the scene in this way, Sellars courted serious risks. First, a string of beds with six people hovering around or lying on them scarcely qualifies as visually scintillating theater. Second, the interplay of six singers simultaneously presenting complex reminiscences invites confusion, even with the aid of supertitles. Mozart always introduced each strand at a time before combining them. Moreover, Da Ponte did not give his characters complications such as Nixon's hallucinations concerning his wartime experiences in the South Pacific or the Maos' reflections on politics and seduction. Any one of these threads would have posed sufficient challenges; together they prove nearly insurmountable.

At one crucial moment, for instance, Chou En-lai and Mao sing the following dense, elliptical lyrics at the same time:

CHOU: I have no offspring—In my dreams the peasants with their hundred names, unnamed children and nameless wives deaden my footsteps like dead leaves; No one I killed, but those I saw starved to death. Only they can tell how the land lies, where the pitfall was excavated, the mines laid.

MAO: Your few subjectivist mistakes only confirm mythology's eternal charm; Roused from a state of seeming rest its landscape offers up the ghost, an ancient tactical retreat retrenched in the inanimate. Saved from our decay. Admire that perfect skeleton, those veins, that skin like cellophane. Take them and press them in a book. Dare we behave as if the meek will mark the places of the wise? The instant before the bomb explodes intricate struggles coexist within an entity, embraced till they ignite.

If this were not enough, Chiang Ch'ing enters over Mao's final sentence ("The instant . . .") to sing "The masses stride ahead of us. We follow." In the DVD of the Houston Grand Opera production, Chou and Mao sing side by side on a split screen, and Chiang Ch'ing later appears behind them—a strategy that helps a bit. But the DVD of the Metropolitan production trains the camera on one character and then another. Especially frustrating is the enigmatic moment when Mao seems to be throttling Chiang Ch'ing, and we might have difficulty hearing his words or grasping his motivation. I am not entirely convinced that the collaborators solved this problem. Armed with a score, a copy of the libretto, and the possibility of multiple viewings, the layering presented in this scene becomes dazzlingly brilliant. Without those, however, Goodman's poetry gets lost in the shuffle. Adams and Sellars would avoid doing anything like this again.

But Sellars does strive to bring much-needed visual activity into the scene by way of a pair of dancers held over from the previous act. Although they still wear the ballet costumes they wore when portraying Wu and Hong, their motions resemble familiar ballroom genres, thereby resonating with the recollections of the courtships of the Nixons and the Maos. Even if "The Chairman Dances" does not appear intact in the opera, Adams's first entry into the opera's subject matter does receive some acknowledgment here. More important, the dancers invite us to follow Adams's ever-changing rhythmic patterns. Without these apparently extraneous figures, this scene with its superimposed narrations and wordy reminiscences might be intolerably static. Sellars will make this device of including dancers a central strategy in subsequent work.

Although most of the original 1987 staging of *Nixon in China* remains in place in the Metropolitan production of 2011, the last scene contains some striking revisions. After *Nixon*'s premiere, a good deal of previously unavailable information concerning Mao's China came to light, including the fact that Chou En-lai was dying of pancreatic cancer at the time of the visit and that Mao was withholding treatment. In response to this knowledge, Sellars now made Chou's bed a literal coffin. While he lies in state, the choristers file in, placing funeral lilies around his bier. Fragments of Goodman's text, such as Chou's inability to sleep, take on a new significance, as the singer keeps arising as if from the dead to sing his prophetic lines and his final farewell. Similarly, we now know that Mao himself was then experiencing severe health problems. Whereas John Duykers in the Houston production appears relatively robust during this last scene, Robert Brubaker in the Metropolitan version can scarcely haul himself down the ramp that previously served for Nixon triumphant entrance. As a result, Mao's relationship with Chiang Ch'ing also undergoes revision.

Indeed, the opera now subjects both couples to intense scrutiny. The men who had gloried in the limelight now become dependent on their spouses, whom they alternately insult ("Your lipstick is crooked," "Your few subjectivist mistakes") and cling to as children to their nursemaids. Clearly accustomed to both kinds of treatment, Pat and Chiang Ch'ing flinch from this abuse yet step forward nonetheless to coddle their adult babies. Most painful perhaps is the scene in which Nixon persists in reliving his military glory days, miming how he flipped burgers for homesick GIs as Pat tries desperately to pull him back into some kind of grown-up relationship. He finally whimpers the sad apology, "This is my way of saying thanks." Sellars's Countess and Despina observe from the wings.

It falls finally to Chou En-lai to offer the final benediction. In both productions, Chou stands alone on a darkened stage, singing of his onetime hopes and his terror of dying as the others slumber around him. He becomes Christ in the Garden of Gethsemane when the disciples all abandon him in his hour of need. Both Sanford Sylvan and Russell Braun perform this scene exquisitely. The tomfoolery of the arrival, the negotiations, and the ballet now retreat into history, and we are left with Chou's pessimistic prognosis of the future and of human existence in general. Adams's beautiful solo violin line grants scant comfort and support at this moment as the premier looks toward the grave and beyond.

## The Death of Klinghoffer

Following hard on the heels of their first effort, the same collaborators moved on to a new project, again suggested and developed by Sellars. The increasing tensions between Israelis and Palestinians had attracted Sellars's attention, and—given his proclivity for making operas relevant to Americans—he decided to focus on the murder of an American tourist, Leon Klinghoffer, at the hands of Palestinian terrorists who had hijacked the cruise ship *Achille Lauro* in 1985.

This incident resonated powerfully with one of Sellars's permanent interests: the roots and psychology of terrorism. His interpretation of Handel's *Giulio Cesare* pushes the Emperor and his Egyptian mistress to the side to concentrate instead on the gradual transformation of Sesto, Pompey's son, from dutiful teenage boy to blood-soaked avenger. Lorraine Hunt always invites identification because of her glorious voice and charismatic acting, but her performance of Sesto is so horrifying that you might find yourself averting your eyes. I can only compare it to Fritz Lang's film *Kriemhilds Rache*: the saga of how Siegfried's widow moves from sympathetic victim to mass murderer; although Lang's original German audience started out cheering Kriemhild as she took on their traditional foes, they recoiled midway through and begged the projectionist to turn the film off. Hunt's series of rage arias become almost unbearable, but watch them we must. Sellars wants us to grasp how even the most justifiable of grievances can metamorphize into murderous fanaticism.

Sellars has returned to the issue of terrorism repeatedly over the course of his career: in Saariaho's *Adriana Mater*, in Mozart's *Zaide* and *La clemenza di Tito* (with another Sesto turning radical), in his portrayal of Judas in the *St. Matthew Passion*. Although none of these productions defends such acts, they all seek to understand why extreme violence takes root and erupts as it does. At the time *Klinghoffer* premiered, no one would have imagined that children of immigrants to the United States could be so easily recruited by ISIS: as the soprano sings in the *St. Matthew*, "Ah, a child whom you raised, who suckled at your breast, threatens to murder its guardian for it has become a serpent" (see chapter 7). We all need to contemplate these issues from as many angles as possible.

At every turn since its premiere in Brussels in 1991, *The Death of Klinghoffer* has met with virulent hatred and, not infrequently, outright censorship. Two of the houses involved in the original commission, the Los Angeles Opera and Glyndebourne, declined to stage it. After the events of September 11, 2001, the Boston Symphony withdrew a scheduled performance of excerpts from the opera. Defending the BSO's decision, musicologist Richard Taruskin mounted an extended attack on *Klinghoffer* in the *New York Times*:

> If terrorism—specifically, the commission or advocacy of deliberate acts of deadly violence directed randomly at the innocent—is to be defeated, world public opinion has to be turned on the acts rather than their claimed (or conjectured) motivations, and to characterize all such acts, whatever their motivation, as crimes. This means no longer romanticizing terrorists as Robin Hoods and no longer idealizing their deeds as rough poetic justice.
>
> Censorship is always deplorable, but the exercise of forbearance can be noble. Not to be able to distinguish the noble from the deplorable is morally obtuse. In the wake of September 11, we might want, finally, to get beyond sentimental complacency about art. Art is not blameless. Art can inflect harm. The Taliban know that. It's about time we learned.[40]

Most recently, the Metropolitan Opera bowed to complaints and pulled *Klinghoffer* from its *Live in HD* series in 2014.

I had had dealings with some of those who led the charge against the Met. I served for a few years as associate vice provost of UCLA's International Institute, and also as cochair of the Center for Islamic Studies. In the wake of the Gaza War of 2008–9, the Institute's Center for Middle Eastern Studies sponsored a panel comprising Israeli, Palestinian, and Jewish American academics. Not only did protesters disrupt the panel repeatedly, but they reported to the press that the panelists had coerced the audience into chanting "Zionism is Nazism." Although nothing of the sort had transpired during this dignified exchange of views, the report went viral, and some of my colleagues almost lost their tenured positions as a result. I recognized the names of the leaders of this made-up scandal in the protests over the Met's production of *Klinghoffer*.

I bring this up because we still live in a society in which mentioning the plight of the Palestinians counts as anathema, as anti-Semitism (even though the Palestinians are also Semitic people, descendants of Abraham, as the Hagar chorus in *Klinghoffer* reminds us).[41] So long as we insist on reducing terrorists to voiceless criminals, we will never begin to engage in serious diplomacy. And that is precisely the impasse the *Klinghoffer*'s collaborators sought to break through. As Adams puts it: "The opera . . . gives voice to the other side. We look into the minds and souls of the Palestinians and see what might have driven them to produce a generation of young men easily willing to give up their lives to make their grievances known."[42] In a similar vein, Mark Swed wrote, in one of the rare defenses of the opera:

> As a profoundly disturbing meditation on the tragic death of an innocent man, *Klinghoffer* hardly supports or apologizes for terrorism. But it does require, in the way that only opera can, that we identify with the emotions that drive actions we despise. And by presenting the terrorist act from all points of view, it becomes not just a study in suffering, a painting in the simple strokes of the banality of evil, but a wrenching panoramic expression of the complex interaction of motives and actions, all against a background of the biblical imperatives that both enliven the Middle East and tear it apart.[43]

As Adams and his collaborators attest, they modeled *The Death of Klinghoffer* on the Bach passions; indeed, Sellars wanted at one point to title it *Klinghoffers Tod*. Like the passions, *Klinghoffer* unfolds in extended choruses, tableaux, and long stretches of reflection. The chorus, characters, and Mark Morris's dancers interact ritualistically on bare scaffolding. Sellars describes his production as "creating a ceremony, a ritual of remembrance that was a million miles away from television and cheap documentaries."[44]

Alas, we do not have video footage of Sellars's original production.[45] Most people become acquainted with the opera through a filmed version by British director Penny Woolcock, which adheres to action-thriller conventions within realistic settings. Taking the narrative of the events as her guide, Woolcock fashioned a linear plot with flashes to backstories, and she adopted the imperative forward thrust of contemporary cinema.

As a result of this adaptation, Adams's score retreats to the status of background music. The opening choruses take place up against period and newly shot footage of the displacements of both European Jews and Palestinian villagers.[46] Not even Klinghoffer's posthumous aria, the extraordinary "Gymnopédie," receives the stillness its music suggests but rather is subjected to crosscutting to the arrest of the hijackers and other strands of plot.[47] Goodman and Adams's structure of symmetrical choral odes cannot fit within the linear story now foregrounded, and, with Adams's blessing, Woolcock cut the brooding Chorus of the Sea and the Chorus of the Desert. Adams has written that the film

> was more provocative than the Sellars stage version. Instead of allusive uses of dance and ritualized gesture, Penny employed graphic cinematic reenactments of the events. There was nothing at all symbolic about this murder, and little left to the imagination. She elicited a disturbing intensity from the singers. Watching them on-screen one forgets that they are opera singers at all.[48]

Before I leave *Klinghoffer*, I want to offer some observations concerning large-scale rhythmic design, which the stark contrast between Sellars's conception and Woolcock's film invites. As we have seen in previous chapters, Sellars cut his teeth on works by Handel and Mozart in the context of which he developed the patience necessary for staging lengthy choruses and da capo arias. In films of his productions, he concentrates either on the big picture that embraces the entire community or on tight close-ups of individual singers. As in the eighteenth-century dramaturgy that serves as his model, linear action per se rarely emerges. Adams, who came to opera by way of Sellars, has adopted those rhythms in the music he writes for their collaborations.

Needless to say, action films operate according to radically different principles, and they have taught viewers to expect constant change and nervous excitement. Few of us have the attention spans of our forebears who gladly immersed themselves in multivolume novels or five-hour-long plays. We often label movies that indulge in lengthy monologues or nature shots as "operatic" (the films of Terrence Malick come to mind here), and they stand at the opposite end of the spectrum from those that feature car chases and explosions.

For all that the violence of *Klinghoffer*'s story may suggest this latter mode of cinema, the translation falters on the fact that Woolcock committed her-self to bringing Adams's music along for the ride. A soundtrack designed spe-cifically for this movie—created to match the exigencies of the final edit after it was already in the can—would display very different characteristics. To my mind, the visual and sonic components of this film work continually at cross-purposes, satisfying neither the listener who strains to hear Adams's score nor the viewer who expects the adrenalin rush of cinematic mayhem.

I did not see the production by director Tom Morris at the Met, though reviews indicate that he tried for a middle ground between Sellars's medi-tative concept and Woolcock's realism. For a change, the critics celebrated the opera, rising uniformly to defend both *Klinghoffer* and the Metropoli-tan, which did at last go ahead with its scheduled staging (if not the broad-cast), despite the protests outside and inside the hall.[49] Perhaps this quali-fies as a turning point in the reception history of an important and consequential opera.

Woolcock and Tom Morris responded admirably to what they saw as dif-ferent kinds of dramatic potential for this opera, and their efforts have made it possible for a wide range of viewers to listen and think about *Klinghoffer*, which critics had reduced to a cultural brouhaha. But it is hard to discern in newer productions the meditative oratorio Sellars and choreographer Mark Morris first envisioned and staged. In any case, by the time Alice Goodman pulled out of the *Doctor Atomic* project, Sellars and Adams had already left *Klinghoffer* far behind. Now they embarked on a series of works for which they themselves cobbled together their own libretti, their own scenarios, their own ways of matching music and stage action.

# 4 • A Libretto of One's Own

## Collaborations with John Adams, Part II

A director with extensive experience animating the dialogue and arias written by others, Sellars developed a sense over the years of what does and does not work as music drama, at least for his purposes. Some of the struggles with Alice Goodman documented in the previous chapter involve their different notions of how to choose words for musical settings. The last scene of *Nixon*, for instance, has the characters all singing complex, independent texts simultaneously. As beautiful as Goodman's poetry may be, it does not always serve effectively as the verbal basis for sung drama.

In the late 1990s, Sellars began to conceive of creating his own libretti—as Glass had done for *Akhnaten*. More recently, he has also taken to piecing together new scores (see the discussion of *The Indian Queen* in chapter 6). Yet he does not presume to produce his own poetry or music but rather relies on "found" sources: he culls materials from a wide range of historical and international sources and patches them together to create his music-theater pieces in keeping with his particular aesthetic and critical priorities.

We might call his creative genre assemblage.[1] To a certain extent, this process emerges quite naturally from the ways he always has brought together singing, dance, instrumental music, gesture, and striking visual settings for the sake of social awareness. But in his stagings of operas that already existed, he often had to tease out (many would say impose) the kinds of points he wanted to make through his performances. Mozart and Handel could scarcely rise from the dead to argue with his decisions, of course, though critics happily have done so in their stead. In any case, Sellars's collaborations with Adams and Goodman gave him a taste for hands-on development.

As we have seen, the Bach passions have preoccupied Sellars throughout his career, and both *Nixon in China* and *The Death of Klinghoffer* bear unmistakable traces of this influence. When he turned to devising his own libretti, he adopted even more overtly the dramaturgical procedures characteristic of the eighteenth-century passions and oratorios that had long informed him. In chapter 5, I will discuss the *La passion de Simone*: a collaboration with Kaija Saariaho and Amin Maalouf based on the writing of Simone Weil. His passion of Federico García Lorca, *Ainadamar*, with a score by Osvaldo Golijov, premiered in 2000, the same year that saw the first performances of both *El Niño* and *Simone*. And we might well regard *Doctor Atomic* as *The Passion of J. Robert Oppenheimer*.

As was the practice of poets and composers who compiled eighteenth-century cantatas and passions, Sellars supplements the plot-oriented components of his libretti with reflective verse. For *El Niño* (2000), he fashioned a libretto that comprised excerpts from canonic scriptures and apocryphal gospels, as well as poetry by Rosario Castellanos (Mexico, 1925–74), Gabriela Mistral (Chile, 1889–1957; Nobel Prize, 1945), Hildegard von Bingen (Germany, 1098–1179), Sor Juana Inés de la Cruz (Mexico, 1651–95), Rubén Darío (Nicaragua, 1867–1916), and Vicente Huidobro (Chile, 1893–1948). Fourteen years later, Sellars returned to this format for *The Gospel of the Other Mary*, a work that similarly intersperses scriptural narration with texts by Castellanos, Darío, Dorothy Day (United States, 1897–1980), June Jordan (United States / Jamaica, 1936–2002), Louise Erdrich (Ojibwe, 1954–), and Primo Levi (Italy, 1919–87). *Doctor Atomic* draws on documentation from Los Alamos, parts of the Bhagavad Gita, and poetry by Muriel Rukeyser (United States, 1913–80), Charles Baudelaire (France, 1821–67), and John Donne (England, 1572–1631). His version of *The Indian Queen* presents a narrative thread based on a novel by Rosario Aguilar (Nicaragua, 1938–), with music assembled from Henry Purcell's entire oeuvre.

Just as Bach designed his cantatas and passions to speak to his own eighteenth-century congregation, so Sellars chooses materials that address today's social injustices. We have already witnessed the ways he relocates the Mozart-Da Ponte operas and Handel oratorios in the United States of the 1980s so that they might speak variously to income inequality, domestic violence, drug abuse, persecution of religious minorities, and capital punishment. Ligeti objected to Sellars's concept for *Le grand macabre* precisely because it read what the composer intended as an absurdist spectacle through the lens of social critique. When Sellars and Adams began to consider topics for operas, they gravitated toward events and crises in American culture: Nixon's historic trip to China, Klinghoffer's execution by terrorists, Oppenheimer's development of the atomic bomb. And even when they turned to biblical subjects, they permeated their versions with references to contemporary issues and controversies.

Sellars had suggested the subjects for their earlier collaborations, but Adams came up with the idea of composing a Christmas oratorio. The father of two children, he found himself profoundly altered by the phenomenon of birth: "The birth of a child can be an event of such intense psychic power that it will cause the most insurmountable walls of psychic resistance to come tumbling down. The birth of both of our children had this kind of numinous power for me, so much so that I returned to this primal event fifteen years later and made it the theme of the Nativity oratorio, *El Niño*."[2] Like Handel's *Messiah*, which served as a model of sorts, *El Niño* proceeds through Luke's story of the birth of Christ, and it also includes excerpts from Old Testament prophecies. *The Gospel According to the Other Mary* brings together scriptures concerning what may be one or several women named "Mary," besides the one designated specifically as the mother of Jesus: Mary the sister of Martha and Lazarus, Mary Magdalene, the Mary who bathes Christ's feet.

Sellars's libretti situate these stories within contemporary contexts. Drawing on the experiences of Dorothy Day, he casts Martha and Mary as social workers who tend to the needy and even risk imprisonment when they participate in protest demonstrations. We have already seen Day held up as a model in Sellars's conception of Messiaen's angel in his production of *Saint François* and in his recollections of the outreach efforts of Emmanuel Church. If the Gospels present Martha and Mary as homebodies, Sellars makes them activists following—or possibly even anticipating—Christ's teachings in their defiant deeds.

In *El Niño*, Sellars refracts the Nativity story so that it concerns not only a mythical birth two thousand years ago but also the pregnancy and delivery of a young Latina in present-day Los Angeles. Gold-incrusted paintings of the Holy Family can make us forget their destitution and desperation, but Mary and Joseph qualified as outcasts from their society. Watching the familiar story unfold up against video projections of a young immigrant couple asks us to remember Jesus's humble origins, the anguish of his impoverished parents as they sought shelter; it asks us to regard the childbirth experienced by this adolescent girl also as wondrous, as a holy event. In Adams's words: "The miracle to which I reacted most profoundly was the initial one, that of birth. I did not require a 'virgin' birth in order to make evident the miraculous nature of the event, an event that repeats itself thousands of times every minute throughout the planet and that is never any the less astonishing and inexplicable."[3]

When the gospel account turns to the Slaughter of the Innocents by King Herod, Sellars patches in Castellanos's "Memorial de Tlatelolco": a long poem mourning the 1968 massacre of protesting students by the Mexican armed forces. Thousands died or "were disappeared" in the aftermath of this event. As student protests escalated in the next few years, governments turned repeatedly to violent responses. In 1970, the Ohio National Guard gunned down kids protesting the Vietnam War on the campus of Kent State University, and both John Adams and I were injured in one of the ensuing police riots in Harvard Square. These attempts at suppressing young people at any expense have left an indelible mark on individuals of our generation. Sellars and Adams want to remind us that we will always have Herods who resort to slaughter in order to protect power and privilege.[4]

Another hallmark of Sellars's libretti is his emphasis on sexuality and the body. Although he never plays to prurience, his pieces explicitly celebrate the erotic. Through his incorporation of poetry by Castellanos, Hildegard, and Erdrich, he has both Mary Magdalene and the Blessed Virgin Mary sing ecstatically of Divine Love, an ardent desire for physical and spiritual union with the godhead. This concern will also lead him to offer a vision of Christ as the lover of Mary Magdalene in Bach's *St. John Passion* (see chapter 7).

Given the cult of celibacy and virginity that dominates Christianity, these intrusions of the sexual into the most sacred of moments in scriptural narratives may seem offensive to some. But Sellars draws on a strand of Judeo-Christian thought that descends at least as far back as the Song of Songs. We do not know why that batch of hedonistic love poems was included in the Hebrew Bible. But its presence there has allowed for countless meditations on direct corporeal contact between believers and God. In the twelfth century, Saint Hildegard von Bingen and Saint Bernard of Clairvaux wrote extensively on this theme, and sixteenth-century Spanish mystics Saint Teresa of Ávila and Saint John of the Cross set off an avalanche of sacred-erotic poetry, paintings, statues, and music. Seventeenth-century baroque culture— both Reformation and Counter-Reformation—relied heavily on these images that promised unmediated fusion with Jesus. Think, for instance, of Bernini's swooning statues or Heinrich Schütz's sacred concerti or John Donne's still-shocking "Batter my heart, three-person'd God": Oppenheimer's favorite poem and, not coincidentally, the text of the climatic aria that concludes the first act of *Doctor Atomic*.[5]

As he takes over the controls, Sellars draws our attention more and more to the complex physical and emotional duress of birthing. In *El Niño*, when it comes time for Mary to be delivered (to quote Luke's pain-free description), the footage shows a woman holding her belly and doubling over with labor pangs in a desolate kitchenette. Saariaho's *Adriana Mater* concerns a woman who becomes pregnant as a result of a rape and who struggles with whether or not to bring the child to term. Although *Doctor Atomic* does not include pregnancy, the long nursery scene in act 2 does focus on childcare and, by extension, an attachment to the environment expressed through the Native American nanny. Even his stagings of the Bach passions will focus on pregnancy and motherhood. Sellars invites us repeatedly to contemplate the joys and terrors of women in travail.

## El Niño

Because *El Niño* marks a new phase in Sellars's creative oeuvre, I will spend some time examining the ways he assembles materials for this work. We have already discerned many of these elements in his stagings of classic operas, though they take on greater significance when they become part of his own modus operandi. When he writes the script, how does he manage to interweave scripture, Latin American feminist poetry, singing, dance, and video, all in the service of social action?

Adams begins his score for *El Niño* with motoric rhythms—much closer in tone to Stravinsky than to the usual sentimental syrup parodied so wickedly in the opening sequence of Monty Python's *The Life of Brian*. Accentuating Adams's syncopated patterns are flashing colored lights, abstract for a long while until the camera gradually pulls back to reveal them as Christmas tree lights. But this is no ordinary Christmas tree: it resonates with the star that guides visitors to the manger and also with the pillar that led the Israelites across the wilderness. A nearby palm tree signals that Southern California will serve as the setting for this Nativity, and those flashing lights will recur as a kind of motif throughout the piece in video footage of Los Angeles freeways.

Sellars had experimented with video in his Salzburg production of *Saint François*, with myriad monitors posted all over the set's elaborate scaffolding. Sometimes featuring Francis's beloved birds, at other times emblems of faith and martyrdom, the flickering images seemed to many viewers, as well as to some of the performers, to detract from the characters and stage action. In *El Niño*, by contrast, Sellars chose to project footage onto a space above the stage, so that the audience could easily attend to both the screen and the live performers.

Much of the power of *El Niño* emerges from the dialectic between screen and stage. If the live singers represent the principals of the Nativity story (Mary, Joseph, Elizabeth, Herod, the wise men), the video offers footage shot by handheld cameras in the Los Angeles area. On the screen we see the young Latino couple mentioned above, who present episodes analogous to the gospel accounts of Mary and Joseph. They drive around in their car, apparently their only home; when the narrative deals with Joseph's discovery of Mary's condition, Sellars shows the young man walking away from his girlfriend, crushed at the news she has just given him. Through this footage, he indicates that this is not just a story about women: it also deeply concerns male partners asked to overcome their distrust and to shoulder the burden of parenthood, however the pregnancy came about. After the young woman has delivered her baby, we see the new family on the beach surrounded by friends who celebrate the birth through native rituals.

Another figure in the video, an LAPD officer, is first shown weeping at work, sharing his distress with a colleague who tries to comfort him. But then he witnesses the star and eventually finds the young Latino couple on the beach, where the mother cradles their new infant. As an officer of the law, he ought to take these illegal immigrants into custody. By implication, however, he represents one of the Magi or a shepherd who leaves his flock behind in order to adore the birth of the child, miraculous regardless of its pedigree.

None of these individuals appears on the stage; they enter only through quasi-documentary footage. Yet this material allows Sellars to engage with issues such as homelessness, the patrolling of illegal immigrants, and unplanned pregnancies—all urgent issues in Los Angeles, where he lives and works. Nor have these issues subsided in the years since *El Niño* premiered: President Trump has promised to build a wall to keep Mexicans out of the United States and to round up Salvadorans for deportation. By fanning the resentments attached to immigrants (Muslim as well as Latin American) and their purported proclivity to reproduce, he has managed to galvanize a hoard of rabid supporters.

A second thread in the video footage features three dancers: Daniela Graça, Nora Kimball, and Michael Schumacher. In his footage and stage direction, Sellars usually identifies Schumacher as the angel Gabriel, Graça as Mary, and Kimball sometimes as Elizabeth but at other times as Mary. They all wear modern clothing and perform in Southern California settings, bringing yet other points of view to the Nativity story here enacted.

Throughout the production, we see the three dancers not only on the screen but also live on the stage, pulling together what might otherwise seem two disparate zones. For instance, Schumacher appears as Gabriel to Dawn Upshaw, the soprano singing the role of Mary, and Kimball shadows Upshaw during the episodes of the delivery and the flight from Herod. Sometimes all three dancers perform as a unit: when a tale from the apocryphal Gospel of Pseudo-Matthew has the infant Jesus calming a nest of dragons, the three represent the writhing monsters on stage as the story unfolds.

In addition to amplifying the Nativity narrative through multiple contemporary sites, the video footage and the onstage dancers animate visually what could become a too-static oratorio. Note that the libretto contains no actual dialogue; the collaborators eliminated in advance the strategy of having the singers act out the events. Sellars and videographer Bill Viola approached Wagner in much the same way in their *Tristan Project*, in which the singers move very little underneath a screen that presents allegorical imagery. If the video in *Saint François* seemed extraneous to many viewers, Sellars here makes full and productive use of his media.[6]

Sellars and Adams classify both *El Niño* and *The Gospel According to the Other Mary* as oratorios, and they follow oratorio convention in requiring narrators to present the scriptural portions of the texts. In his passions, Bach assigns this task to a tenor soloist, the Evangelist. Adams assigns the role to a trio of countertenors, who recite their lines together in tight harmony inspired, he claims, by sonorities in the music of fourteenth-century composer Guillaume de Machaut.[7] In his staging, Sellars has the trio interact with the principals, hailing Mary, protecting her when Joseph explodes in anger, and even reaching out in response to his threatening gesture. They also sing the parts of Gaspar, Melchior, and Balthazar: the three wise men. As we shall see in chapter 7, Sellars also involves his Evangelist in the action in his stagings of the Bach passions, a practice that dates at least as far back in his work to *El Niño*.

For his principals, Sellars returns to Dawn Upshaw and Lorraine Hunt Lieberson, who had starred so memorably together in his *Theodora*. Upshaw, dressed in a plaid flannel shirt, represents Mary, while Lieberson sings many of the poetic interpolations. Willard White makes for a forceful Joseph and Herod, seething over perceived challenges to patriarchal authority, whether as husband or as king. He also delivers the sections of the libretto taken from the apocalyptic prophecies of Haggai and Isaiah, making him something of a wrathful Old Testament deity, giving way for the gentler, more woman-centered reign of his son.

Part I of *El Niño* opens with a chorus singing the words of an old English carol, "I Sing a Maiden." Dressed in red jumpsuits, the seated choristers continue the motoric polyrhythms from the overture and accentuate Adams's stammering setting of "Mai-, mai-, mai-, maiden" with their stylized hand gestures. Upshaw listens and occasionally joins in with gestures of her own, as, for example, when she raises her arms in wonderment at the phrase "mother and maiden." At this point the Latina appears on the screen, alternating with footage of Graça meditating alone in her apartment. These, then, are our three manifestations of the Virgin Mary, whose experiences Sellars braids together visually.

Adams's rhythms gradually subside, giving way to a tingling tremolo that announce the advent of the angel Gabriel. Schumacher appears on stage with Upshaw, on the screen in Graça's apartment, and also outside in a desert landscape, backlit by a dazzling sun. As the angel announces her miraculous conception, Upshaw and Graça both cup their hands together, then open them like blossoming flowers or, of course, like their ready wombs. The countertenors sing "Hail, Mary," not the familiar version reported in Luke but rather a troped version from *The Wakefield Plays* in which Mary and Gabriel converse in rhyme. As Schumacher dances his news to Upshaw, the countertenors recite the parts of the text ascribed to Gabriel.

Sellars and Adams have only begun to explore the moment of the annunciation, however. Again, overfamiliarity has stripped away the utter bizarreness of this moment in the scriptural account in which an apparition informs a young woman who has not yet consummated her marriage with her older husband that the Holy Ghost has impregnated her with the Son of God. A very long tradition seeks to deny Mary's reproductive apparatus altogether, sometimes even suggesting that if the Spirit entered through her ear, she must have given birth through the same canal rather than the despised orifice typically deployed. The label of her as "ever-virgin" similarly refuses to acknowledge the children she later had with Joseph.

Sellars's annunciation combines existential isolation with explicitly carnal love, in part by means of an interpolated poem, "La anunciación," by Mexican author Rosario Castellanos. Although Castellanos is widely recognized in feminist circles, Adams (and most of his fans) had never heard of her before Sellars introduced her work into this and other libretti. The literary sources listed earlier in this chapter reveal Sellars's particular devotion to the poetry of Latin American women, and most often he retains the original Spanish in his productions, as he also insists on Italian for Mozart and Da Ponte.

The ten-minute aria based on "La anunciación" precedes even the recitation of the biblical part of the libretto, leading the viewer to hear the words of Luke through Castellanos's lens. Because this insertion concerning the annunciation matters so much to this piece and because it can tell us a great deal about Sellars's approach to the writing of libretti, I want to deal with it in some detail; here are some highlights in the translation that appeared in supertitles:

Because from the start you were fated as mine . . . when God had nothing more than horizons of unending blue . . . when everything lay in the divine lap, confused and intertwined, you and I lay there, complete, together. But then came the punishment of clay. It took me in its fingers, tore me from that absolute and ancient fullness. . . . Deprived of your sweet weight on my chest, nameless, so long as you did not descend, I languished in exile. . . . I couldn't die because I was still waiting.

Because you were come to break my bones, my bones, at your arrival, break. And here you are. Among contradictory angels you approach, pouring yourself like gentle music, like a glassful of unguents and aromas. You praise my humility. Your gaze, benevolent, turns my wounds to fiery splendors.[8]

Castellanos's Mary differs radically from the passive young girl typical of representations in that she identifies Mary as part of the divine plan from the beginning, as the designated Mother and Spouse of God. Just as Christ had to suffer the incarnation, so this Mary is cast out of heaven to await the fulfillment of her destiny. The first section concerns her memories of plenitude and her unbearable exile, the second the anticipated ordeal of childbirth, and the third her reunion with the Beloved. An eternal being, though subject to desire, pain, and exultation, she receives the announcement of her impending pregnancy not with puzzlement but as an event she had known of and longed for forever.

This Mary's erotic connection to her son also has a very long history. In the twelfth century, theologians eager to produce a model of the self that incorporated both soul and body understood Mary's conception as the quintessential locus of divine union for Christianity, and they turned to the Song of Songs for their imagery. For them, spirit met and intertwined with flesh in the Virgin's experience of childbirth. She became simultaneously the Bride of the Canticles and the Mother of God.[9] Adams clearly embraced the possibilities offered by Castellanos's vivid imagery, and he rose to the challenge with some of the most effective dramatic music he had ever composed. In keeping with the poem's speaker, he writes the aria not for a girlish soprano but rather for the mature mezzo-soprano voice of Lorraine Hunt Lieberson.[10]

Sellars stages the appearance of the angel Gabriel to the young Virgin Mary with every medium at his disposal. As she describes her Edenic past, Lieberson sings tenderly, smiling with each recalled detail. But her affect changes abruptly when she relates her forced incarnation, and she conveys the image of flagellation as if wracked in pain. Throughout this sequence, however, Graça and Schumacher enact the period of plenitude when the two bodies intertwine. It is Graça who first approaches Schumacher, who lies facedown in fetal position; she drapes herself over him, turning him toward her. Even when the text becomes bitter and Lieberson sings with wrath, the dancers continue their ever-changing embrace.

After Lieberson cries out in protest about not being allowed to die, Adams inserts an agitated instrumental interlude. Schumacher as Gabriel suddenly hovers over Graça, as Lieberson writhes in anguish on the stage. As the aria continues, the dancers return to their intertwinings, sometimes violently, sometimes as if attempting to become one body. Toward the end of the second verse, Adams builds in anticipation. Lieberson grasps her torso as if rending it in childbirth as she sings of her breaking bones, then raises her arms in bliss, for this experience—however painful—makes possible the longed-for reunion. Suddenly, all three dancers arrive onstage, leaping ecstatically around Lieberson. Adam's music now accelerates, and at its tingling climax Graça on screen throws Schumacher back as if their necessary interaction is now completed. During the final verse, the screen shows only flames; Lieberson sings joyously as the three angels amplify her embrace of the divine plan.

Through his interpolation of Castellanos and his video footage, Sellars's annunciation sequence seeks to introduce eros back into the account of Mary's pregnancy and childbirth. If centuries of interpretations have used this moment to promote shame over sexuality, El Niño celebrates the human body—more specifically, the *female* body—and its experiences associated with reproduction.

Sellars turns now to the scriptures with Luke 1:37, "For with God nothing shall be impossible." But Adams elides the seam between Castellanos and scriptural text by having the chorus enter with this text while Lieberson still holds her rapturous final pitch on "altas." The choristers gesture exuberantly, marking the impulses that animate a harmonically static holding position, rather the way Philip Glass and Lucinda Childs did in *Einstein on the Beach*. On the screen, the heavily edited video displays rhythmically spliced footage of the exultant three dancers, backlit against a dazzling sun. This serves as the culmination of the annunciation sequence, which began about fifteen minutes earlier.

The next sequence presents Mary's encounter with her cousin Elizabeth, who has also become pregnant (with the future John the Baptist) through the intervention of the Holy Spirit. During the episode with Elizabeth, the video presents Graça and Kimball together, sometimes dancing in Joshua Tree National Monument and sometimes interacting in the dingy laundry room of an apartment complex. The two display great physical affection toward one another, emphasizing particularly their shared experience of feeling new life stirring within them. Such scenes of mutual support between women occur often in Sellars's productions; in this instance, he could rely directly upon biblical authority and on Adams's decision to repeat the Elizabeth's line "the babe leapt in my womb" many times. Even the countertenors grasp their lower abdomens in sympathy.

This text leads in Luke into Mary's famous response, the Magnificat, and Upshaw walks onto the stage in preparation for this speech. But against expectations, Adams's music erupts percussively. On the screen the Latino couple appears, the young man storming away from the car as the girl stands alone. This footage may seem incongruous at the time, and the music soon subsides for Upshaw's Magnificat, albeit with continual close-ups of the young Latina's worried profile. Yet it foreshadows the next episode in which Joseph reacts with dismay to Mary's condition. Recall that Elizabeth also went into hiding to avoid gossip when she was pregnant. The secret these two women share holds potential danger, even as Mary performs her prayer of thanksgiving, and Sellars does not let us forget the threat that hangs over Mary, Elizabeth, and the Latina as they reveal their pregnancies to dubious male partners.

In addition to the canonic Gospels of Matthew and Luke, Sellars's libretto also draws on a cluster of so-called infancy gospels: second-century apocryphal texts that offer background information concerning the birth and childhood of Mary as well as stories involving miracles performed by the baby Jesus. These texts—the Gospel of James, the Gospel of Pseudo-Matthew—circulated widely in the years when Christianity was working aggressively to attract non-Jewish converts. All those cycles of medieval paintings that represent various episodes in the life of the Virgin stem from these sources.

Although the familiar New Testament account in Matthew, chapter 1, relates Joseph's misgivings over Mary's pregnancy, it does so quite briefly. The apocryphal Gospel of James, however, expands considerably upon this moment of marital tension:

13. It came to be the sixth month for her, and, behold, Joseph came from his buildings; and he came into his house, he found her pregnant. He struck his face, and threw himself on the ground. He wept bitterly, saying: "Who is this who has deceived me? Who did this evil thing in my house and defiled her? Mary, why did you do this? Who is he who deceived me?" She wept bitterly saying: "I am pure and I do not know a man." Joseph said to her: "Whence then is this in your womb?" She said, "As the Lord my God lives, I do not know whence it came to me."

In the following verse, as Joseph struggles with the option of putting Mary away, the angel appears to him, clarifying the situation. But meanwhile, he raves threateningly.

Sellars's inclusion of this text allows him to quote Joseph alongside the famed quotations in the scriptures of Mary and Elizabeth. And it introduces into this pastoral tableau dominated thus far by pregnant women the specter of domestic violence. Recall the foregrounding of such scenes in Sellars's Mozart Trilogy, especially the explicit attacks of Count Almaviva on his wife. Adams's score introduces the scene with percussive slashing, worthy of Stravinsky's *Sacre du printemps*. Onscreen, we see a close-up of the young Latina's face as her partner drives angrily. And even before Joseph comes onto the stage, we see the three countertenors huddling around Mary, protecting her from the angry strokes we hear. If neither woman is actually beaten, the music lashes away at them.

Dressed in a tight muscle shirt, baritone Willard White storms while he sings his lines. Adams has him and Upshaw repeat their quoted lines several times as husband and wife clash—he as aggressive as Stanley Kowalski, she begging and cowering. But the tempest passes. The angel assuages Joseph's fears but also foretells the hardships he and Mary must endure as they undertake their travel. Adams gives the words of the prophecy to White such that it is his voice that moves gradually toward epiphany. During the lingering trance state of Joseph's dream, Schumacher appears on stage to dance as the angel who has brought the tidings.

Yet after an instrumental interlude for the angel, Adams and Sellars return to rage mode with a setting of the text familiar from the great blustering moment in Handel's *Messiah*: "Thus saith the Lord of hosts; Yet once, it is a little while, and I will shake the heavens, and the earth, and the sea, and the dry land; And I will shake all nations, and the desire of all nations shall come: and I will fill this house with glory, and in this place, I will give peace, saith the Lord of hosts" (Haggai 2:6–7). Adams's bluster exceeds even Handel's in his extended settings of the word "shake." In Haggai, this speech comes as a warning, though it also forecasts that the necessary turmoil will result in a better world—the world ushered in by Jesus, according to Christian readings.

While White is delivering this scorching speech, the screen displays working-class police officers. As they lunch on fast food, one of them begins to weep as the other offers solace. But toward the end of the sequence, they stand outside gazing up into the night sky. They will eventually find their way to the newborn child. As the narrators present the remarkably beautiful account from the Gospel of James concerning Joseph's reconciliation with Mary, we see the young Latino couple reconciling and embracing tenderly.

Now the libretto returns to Mary. But it filters her experiences of pregnancy and childbirth through Castellanos's vivid account of her thoughts as she carried her own son, Gabriel, "Se habla de Gabriel":

> Like all guests my son got in the way, taking up a space, existing at all the wrong times, making me divide each bite in two. . . . His body begged for birth, to let him pass; to allot him his place in the world. . . . Through the wound of his departure, through the hemorrhage of his breaking free the last I ever felt of the solitude of myself. . . . I was left open, an offering to visitations, to the wind, to presence.[11]

If the first Castellanos interpolation, "La anunciación," referred explicitly to the Nativity story, "Se habla de Gabriel" relates directly to her own experiences. But Sellars includes this monologue to give voice to Mary's travail, which the canonic Gospels do not record. Indeed, few male poets attempt to describe what it feels like to carry a fetus and await delivery. As Adams explains:

> The intimate confessional style of these Castellanos poems, so intensely personal, so much a part of both the darkest as well as the most sublime experienced for a woman giving birth, is utterly absent from the canonical Nativity texts, all written by men. Those men, most presumably celibate, could only have abstractly imagined the experience. In Matthew and in Luke there are no detailed descriptions of Mary's emotional or physical state either before or after the birth.[12]

Because Sellars has already associated Upshaw, Lieberson, and Kimball with Mary, he easily leads us to perceive Castellanos's text as the Virgin's. Adams divides the poem up such that the two women sing the outer sections together, with the mezzo-soprano singing alone a section on her discomfort during pregnancy. At the beginning of the scena, Kimball appears on the screen in footage shot in the kitchenette of a small apartment. She moves as if already suffering pain, grasping her back to relieve it from the imagined weight of the unborn child. On the stage, Upshaw and Lieberson stand facing the audience, and Kimball stands with them. The three initially share the same gestures, lovingly stroking their bellies in anticipation. But Kimball's dance moves onstage go much further into the simulation of labor, which she simultaneously manifests in the video.

In the middle section, Lieberson and Kimball perform alone, the dancer reflecting or acting in counterpoint to the singer's sentiments. One especially lovely moment occurs with the words "lo sentía crecer a mis expansas" (I felt him grow at my expense), where both dip down and execute a cradling motion, first in sync then in opposite directions as mirror images of one another. At "Suo cuerpo" (his body), Adams's score—in which the orchestra had hovered in the background with a barely inflected drone—suddenly blossoms. He begins to move harmonically as if toward a goal but also with gorgeous chord changes marking the poignancy of lines such as "un sitio en el mundo" (a place in the world). Lieberson's voice conveys the abjection of Mary's condition and also the joy of imagining this new life.

With the word "Consentí" (I consented), the elation presented at the end of the previous section subsides. Upshaw joins the ensemble again, and once more all three women move in synchronized gestures. Both music and staging here recall the da capo structures familiar to Sellars through his work with Handel, with the middle section offering a contrasting viewpoint that illuminates the return. Here we do not have another rendition of the opening but rather a regrouping: the moment in the poem in which the mother in the poem comes to a rapprochement with the child inside her. No longer a troublesome guest, the baby now is understood to transform the parent, making a new creature of her. Now Upshaw takes the solo lead for the lines describing childbirth, and she sings lying on her back, simulating the throes of delivery.

Kimball shares her gestures, but at the word "desprendimiento" (breaking free), the footage of her suddenly moves from the claustrophobic kitchenette back to the open space and blazing sky of the desert. Throughout the rest of this scene, the footage toggles between inside and outside, between the oppressiveness of physical pain and the promise of the birth itself. All three women present the final two lines, their voices and arms both reaching out to future triumph.

I have emphasized Castellanos's words and Sellars's investment in them during this discussion. But I have also underscored Adams's participation—not as a composer who stands by waiting for texts to set but, as the quotations above reveal, as a man deeply affected by his own experiences as a father. He wrote some of his most beautiful passages for this extended sequence, which revealed a developing talent for lyrical expression not characteristic of much of his earlier work. Sellars's ear for singable texts and his interest in the da capo format for its dramatic potential seem to have inspired Adams to move in new directions.

At the conclusion of Part I, Adams simulates the birth itself by drawing on both the verse and music of twelfth-century Hildegard von Bingen. Hildegard received papal clearance to write and disseminate her theological insights, her poetry, and her music, which was set down in a large book, the

Riesenkodex: by far the largest compendium by a single composer at the time. Her work includes a handbook on medicine that contains the most accurate information on female anatomy and reproduction available until the last hundred years, and her deep dedication to women's bodies resonates throughout her meditations on Mary. Her responsory, "O quam preciosa est virginitas virginis," contemplates the virgin birth.

| | |
|---|---|
| O quam preciosa est | How precious is |
| Virginitas virginis huius | this virgin's sweet virginity, |
| Que clausam portam habet, | a closed gate |
| Et cuius viscera | and whose womb |
| Sancta divinitas | holy divinity |
| Calore suo infudit, ita | has flooded with its |
| Quod flos in ea crevit. | warmth, so that |
| | a flower sprung within it. |
| | |
| Et Filius Dei per secreta | The Son of God has come |
| Ipsius | forth from |
| Quasi aurora exivit. | her hidden chamber like the |
| | dawn. |
| | |
| Unde dulce germen, | And so the sweet, tender |
| Quod Filius ipsius est, | shoot— |
| Per clausuram ventris eius | her Son— |
| Paradisum aperuit. | has through her womb's |
| | enclosure |
| | opened Paradise. |

Seizing particularly on the line "que clausam portam habet" concerning the closed gate, Adams has the entire ensemble sing Hildegard's melody. He proceeds then to extend elements from the chant with choristers and soloists as the orchestra tingles expectantly behind them. He concludes with a series of amen cadences, over which Upshaw ecstatically sings the tonic pitch, as the chorus chants underneath, animating the static moment of arrival with cross rhythms. In Hildegard's words, Christ bursts forth like the dawn, and Adams seeks to render this image as viscerally as possible.

Sellars brings a wide range of visual effects to this climactic moment. As the music starts, the screen displays footage from a car driving through a tunnel, by implication a birth canal. This alternates with a dazzling light, at once the Star of Bethlehem and a baby's head crowning. Onstage, Upshaw and Lieberson create a ring with their arms, and Schumacher emerges up through the ring. Both on the screen and the stage, Kimball writhes in childbirth.

Part II of El Niño draws variously on the seventeenth-century Mexican mystic Sor Juana Inés de la Cruz, Castellanos's "Memorial de Tlatelolco," and scriptures—both canonical and apocryphal. The hell, fire, and brimstone of Part II's middle section slowly subsides by the end into the sweetness of a villancico by Castellanos. But the extensive exploration of catastrophe and violence in *El Niño* matters enormously to Sellars and Adams. If they decided to take on a story long trivialized by saccharine presentations, they also determined to make it their own—which meant finding ways of bringing contemporary social tensions into play.

### Doctor Atomic

The next Adams-Sellars collaboration, *Doctor Atomic*, would seem more closely related to *Nixon in China* and *The Death of Klinghoffer*. They label all three as operas, and all three focus on American social issues. Yet in many ways, *Doctor Atomic* emerges from the innovations of *El Niño*. Its libretto continues Sellars's commitment to the assemblage of found texts, though in place of scriptural quotation he now relies on documents gleaned from government archives and from the key players in Los Alamos.[13]

The project emerged from the San Francisco Opera suggestion that Adams might write an opera based on *Faust*. Turning aside from Goethe, Adams proposed to Sellars that they focus on an American Faust figure, J. Robert Oppenheimer: the father of the atomic bomb. Sellars mulled over the ethical problems of creating an opera based on such a horrendous device:

> What does it take to make something that *is* regenerative? Because the sheer horror by itself—art is not up to that. There is nothing you can put on a stage or in a painting that matches the suffering of those people. And therefore the art itself becomes, if it's sincere, strangely inadequate; and if it's insincere, really obscene. And so as Samuel Beckett said, in our century some things must remain unspeakable. And how do you begin to find something that's capable of bearing the weight and intensity of that experience?[14]

This very naked statement reveals the inner struggles of an artist who devotes so much of his life to engaging with social criticism. But whatever his misgivings, he does go forward—time and again—to address the unspeakable, even if the results fall short of his intended goals. In the end, he and Adams did take on this radioactive material.

Opera fans have accustomed themselves to hearing sung conversations. Indeed, the genre itself emerged from the desire of early seventeenth-century composers to get in on the sudden move from lyric poetry to the theatrical performances then sweeping all of Europe. Not content with simply inserting song-and-dance numbers here and there, Jacopo Peri, Monteverdi, and others worked to develop techniques that simulated natural speech. Still, that speech nearly always followed the mannerisms of poetry, with regularly parsed lines and even rhyme. Consequently, it may come as a shock to hear scientists quibbling in sung recitative over the threat of chain reactions and nuclear fallout. Even the opening passion-like chorus presents a text that appears lifted from official reports, its static quality mitigated by Lucinda Childs's dancers simulating (much as they did in *Einstein on the Beach*) the motions of subatomic particles.

Adams and Sellars wanted to get as close to authentic exchanges as they could for their dialogues.

> A lot of the libretto is made up of classified documents. I really wanted to see what the American people were not allowed to know or see or hear. And I'm very proud: superclassified documents that have been obtained through the Freedom of Information Act are now set for chorus and orchestra and are being broadcast out there—in a democracy, of course. And to me that's one of the great functions of opera, is to take people's secrets, and to take the secrets of civilization, and to take the secrets of entire swaths of history and not just whisper them, but sing them aloud with power and with some kind of grace and create something that you have a visceral reaction to—you "Oh, my God!"—something that's not allowed to be spoken, therefore has to be sung.[15]

When Oppenheimer (Gerald Finley), Edward Teller (Richard Paul Fink), and General Leslie Groves (Eric Owens) sing their technical and ethical debates, their statements rise from the exigencies of everyday speech to a mythic level; each word leading up to that incomparable benchmark in Western science—the testing of the atomic bomb—takes on the weight of unstoppable destiny. If their utterances necessarily lack the finesse of Da Ponte's or Boïto's or Alice Goodman's carefully crafted lines, they confront listeners with the brute arguments that have shaped our atomic world. Within this context, Groves's vacillation between his harsh commands and his love of chocolate bars puts a human face on a man who pushed the scientists at Los Alamos to override their own misgivings. Adams, Sellars, and I belong to the generation born in the shadow of the bomb; as schoolchildren we had to practice duck-and-cover drills in preparation for a nuclear explosion—an event expected on virtually a daily basis.[16] Returning to the primal scene just before the first test, Sellars reminds us of both the ruthlessness and the casual banality of this momentous decision. The very flatness of the language underscores this complex mixture of affects.

Into the materials drawn from historical sources, Sellars interpolates a wide range of poetry, as he did in *El Niño*. In a vitriolic review of *Doctor Atomic*, critic Ron Rosenbaum writes that Sellars "has a career as a curator of bad poetry." Well, in this opera those poems include those by Muriel Rukeyser, Charles Baudelaire, and John Donne—not bad poetry by a long shot (nor are those featured in *El Niño*). Acknowledging this, Rosenbaum continues: "His 'appropriations' sound fake-profound when not merely ridiculous (the way they might not sound in context). Even Donne's 'Holy Sonnet,' which is magnificent, is mangled."[17]

Rosenbaum's review throws down the gauntlet, attacking as it does the modus operandi of Sellars's approach to constructing libretti. Since *The Gospel According to the Other Mary*, *Girls of the Golden West*, and *The Indian Queen* follow in the same vein, Sellars clearly did not mend his ways in response to this criticism, just or not. And thanks to the fact that this "mangled" version of Donne's sonnet appears in all the anthologies used in music history surveys, thousands of undergraduates now know "Batter my heart." I have long begun my seminars on the phenomenon of Divine Love in seventeenth-century culture with this poem, and it used to be met with puzzlement; now if anything it seems overfamiliar. Similarly, this "curator of bad poetry" has introduced vast numbers of people to Rukeyser, Castellanos, and Sor Juana, just as Mozart and Da Ponte have kept Beaumarchais's name in wide circulation.

I doubt that I could change Rosenbaum's mind concerning the efficacy of Sellars's poetic interpolations, but I can offer a different perspective. For I happen to admire precisely those moments in *Doctor Atomic*—and in *El Niño*. Most libretti serve as vehicles onto which composers affix the music that animates them. With few exceptions, they do not qualify as literary works by themselves. Stripped of the scores and performances for which they are intended, they usually offer little of aesthetic value, though even quite mediocre ones can and often do supply the scaffolding for operatic masterpieces.

Sellars's assemblages allow him to do several things crucial to his vision. As we saw in the discussion of *El Niño*, the poetry he incorporates into his libretti give voice to subject positions he hesitates to simulate by himself. Foremost among these are those of women: women in love, women bearing and raising children, women suffering loss, women protesting social injustices. Many of us cringe at the words put into the mouths of female characters, their sentiments alien to our own experiences, less the utterances of recognizable women than the wishful projections of their male creators. Robert Schumann's *Frauenliebe und Leben*, settings of texts by Adelbert von Chamisso, comes to mind here as particularly infamous example. In choosing poetry by women, Sellars sidesteps this problem. He does not pretend to know how women feel but rather showcases instances of women's speech he finds unusually powerful and pertinent to the dramatic situation at hand.

The collaborations with Alice Goodman had already presented unusually strong wives. Pat Nixon's poignant reflections and her ability to shield her vulnerable husband raise her from what could have been a joke, and Marilyn Klinghoffer fearlessly addresses her adversaries, even at a moment when grief might well have overwhelmed her. Although Sellars no doubt had a hand in shaping these characters, they utter Goodman's texts. But he himself establishes what Kitty Oppenheimer will sing in *Doctor Atomic*.[18]

Kitty Oppenheimer (Jessica Rivera) appears first in act 1, scene 2. A 1940s housewife, Kitty has borne two children. But she struggles to get her preoccupied husband's attention, fears for her family's safety, and—as act 2 reveals—tries to drown her anxieties in alcohol. In the opening scene, we have seen Oppenheimer working with colleagues as they attempt to face the technological and ethical challenges raised by the bomb. Under the strain of severe intellectual and psychological pressures, he paces nervously and smokes compulsively. But he is clearly in charge, always dominating the proceedings. He carries these habits over when he retires to his bed where his wife sleeps, for he has brought his notes home with him and intends to continue laboring into the night. Kitty wakes up and sings the opera's first aria, a setting of Muriel Rukeyser's "Am I in your light?": "Am I in your light? No, go on reading, / only my fingers in your hair, only my eyes / splitting the skull to tickle your brain with love / . . . Love, am I in your light? / See how love alters the living face / go spin the immortal coin through time / watch the thing flip through space tick, tick."

By way of Rukeyser's elegant, elusive poem, Kitty attempts to distract her husband from his study and to arouse him. She expresses the wish to break through his defenses for greater intimacy and recalls to him the short window between life and its termination. (Note, too, the images of "splitting" and "tick, tick," both of which resonate powerfully with the opera's themes of atomic fusion and the impending countdown.) As Kitty sings, she caresses him, timidly at first, then with greater insistence. In Sellars's production, she drapes herself over the bedstead, allowing us to see both her desire and his reactions: annoyance at first, as if resisting a pesky mosquito, then gradually increasing passion.

The woman here takes the initiative, and through her agency, Oppenheimer leaves his notes and turns his attention solely to her. Most operatic romances involve the male character wooing a passive lady; when the roles are reversed (in *Carmen*, for instance), it is to paint her as temptress. By having Kitty make the overtures, Sellars offers what seems to me a genuinely adult love scene, with a long-married couple who can still manage—even in this time of tremendous stress—to engage in sexual behaviors. Moreover, they act (in bed, at least) as equal partners, once Kitty draws him into intimacy. They no longer present the excitement of seduction, which had occurred years before, but rather the warmth and deep affection that can grow with relationships. As I think through marital duets to find a comparison, the first scene between Verdi's Otello and Desdemona comes to mind.

When Oppenheimer turns to address his wife, he does so with Baudelaire's hallucinatory paean to his lover's hair, "Un hémisphère dans une chevelure." In his text, Baudelaire brings his powers of synesthesia to bear on a moment of erotic excess: he smells perfumes and other fragrances, he feels heat, he becomes drunk on the scents, he hears songs, he bites and drinks, he travels to distant lands, he sails. Such symbolist texts influenced the next two generations of French writers; Mallarmé's faun and Wilde's Salome express themselves in similar fashions, and Proust's remembering of the past relies on this quick shifting among sensory experiences. Adams's score follows the poem into a rhapsodic impressionist idiom (he refers to this aria as "the opium bath").[19] As Oppenheimer sings a translation of "Long let me inhale, deeply, the odor of your hair," the two make love, rapturously, as if reliving the delirium of courtship while also attempting to hold at bay the momentous events unfolding around them. Rosenbaum found this interpolation particularly ridiculous. As it turns out, Oppenheimer carried a dog-eared copy of *Les fleurs du mal* around with him in the tension-filled days presented in the opera.

In any case, having Oppenheimer sing Baudelaire's text greatly deepens this character. If we come to this opera already acquainted with the brilliant physicist and director of Los Alamos, we now see a very different facet of his personality. The Baudelaire poem reveals the vulnerability, sensitivity, and sensuality he necessarily conceals from his colleagues but which blossoms here in the arms of his wife. Absent this scene and Oppenheimer's contribution to it, his performance of "Batter my heart" would seem far less credible. Donne's explicitly sexual imagery resonates in *Doctor Atomic* with that of the

Baudelaire, and both present a male subject baring himself in submission to his beloved, whether earthly or divine.

Oppenheimer recovers his equilibrium, and as he dresses for the lab, Kitty returns to Rukeyser's "The motive of it all was loneliness." The delirium of lovemaking gives way to the harsh reality of the moment, with Oppenheimer again in charge, his wife left to watching helplessly from the sidelines. Most poignantly, given the circumstances of the plot, she concludes: "Those who most long for peace now pour their lives on war. Our conflicts carry creation and it guilt, these years' great arms are full of death and flowers. A world is to be fought for, sung and built: Love must imagine the world."

The second scene oriented toward women occurs early in act 2 with Kitty and the Native American nanny, Pasqualita (Ellen Rabiner), in the nursery with the children. Once again Sellars gives Kitty a poem by Rukeyser, "Easter Eve," as she ponders the causes of war. Written in 1945, the year in which the United States dropped atomic bombs on Japan, "Easter Eve" concludes: "Night of the soul, our dreams in the arms of dreams, / dissolving into eyes that look upon us. / Dreams the sources of action, the meeting and the end, / a resting-place among the flight of things."

I want to focus for now, however, on Pasqualita. Sellars's long-standing interest in Latin Americans manifested itself in the video footage in *El Niño*, but we may trace it back to his festivals of world cultures in Los Angeles and forward to his *The Indian Queen*. A resident of Los Angeles, Sellars witnesses on a daily basis the indispensable contributions of minority individuals to providing comforts (food, gardening, housecleaning, childcare) while remaining invisible at best, at worst castigated and defamed. Consequently, he strives to make us aware of indigenous people as human beings whose customs and rituals can enrich us all.

Pasqualita serves as the Oppenheimers' housekeeper. Most obviously, she watches over the children. Her job, however, extends to her taking care of Kitty, whom we see drinking to excess. Kitty's preoccupations with her husband, the war, and the bomb leave her little time to function as a mother. In the time-honored tradition of service workers, Pasqualita quietly assumes these and other duties as the Oppenheimers spiral further and further away from the responsibilities of family and life itself.

Sellars has Pasqualita sing "The Cloud-Flower Lullaby" as she soothes both the children and her unconscious mistress. Based on a Tewa song collected by Herbert Joseph Spinden in 1933, this lullaby serves several functions within the context of the opera besides the immediate one of comforting her charges as they sleep. The lyrics' images—"the cloud flower blossoms, now the lightning flashes, now the thunder clashes, now the rain comes down"—resonate both with the impending storm the scientists are fearing and, of course, with the bomb blast itself. By implication, Pasqualita brings traditional wisdom into a world dominated by the sciences. The US government had already seized the land of the Tewa and now threatened to annihilate it in its entirety.

Although I understand and sympathize with Sellars's strategy, I also want to point out some risks. First, it sets up a binary opposition between Western and non-Western epistemologies that essentializes the Native position. Given the complexity of the situation he and Adams take on in *Doctor Atomic*, this seems a bit too easy. Second, Pasqualita utters nothing besides the nearly identical verses of this lullaby and another strophic song, inserted into the ongoing arguments concerning the bomb. She serves thereby as a kind of oracle, channeling inherited words without her own intervention. Of course, the Oppenheimers also sing found texts. But they do so in order to create complex, multileveled subjectivities, not to serve as passive conduits of folk wisdom. Moreover, Sellars's deep respect for women sometimes runs the risk of equating them with nature, putting them on pedestals at the expense while weakening their positions as agents. Pasqualita finds herself multiply essentialized—as female, as indigenous, as Nature.[20]

The danger of this characterization becomes particularly evident if we compare Sellars's staging with that of Penny Woolcock at the Metropolitan Opera. Sellars's costume designer, Dunya Ramicova, presents Pasqualita and the other indigenous women onstage in the housedresses usually worn by domestic laborers. Their long black braids identify them as Native American, but they are not exoticized visually. By contrast, Woolcock's designer, Catherine Zuber, outfits her Pasqualita (Meredith Arwady) as a squaw right out of old cowboy movies. The set itself sports a row of Indian headdresses, images of indigenous culture far distant from the 1940s of Los Alamos. As someone of Cherokee descent who was sometimes called "squaw" during graduate school, I cannot watch Woolcock's Pasqualita without squirming. Woolcock, an English director, apparently picked up on the opportunity to insert exotic color into her production. Sellars takes greater care, given his much deeper experience with and commitment to Native people in the Americas. Yet his libretto is vulnerable to caricatures of this sort.

Responding to criticisms of this sort, Sellars plans to revamp this segment of *Doctor Atomic* in a 2018 production in Santa Fe. He is working in dialogue with local indigenous people for his new staging; Meredith Arwady, the Native woman who sang the role at the Metropolitan Opera, will sing the role of Pasqualita, though not in squaw drag. He has even revised the way he presents "The Cloud-Flower Lullaby."

By far the most significant literary appropriation in *Doctor Atomic* is, of course, John Donne's holy sonnet, "Batter my heart, three-person'd God." Prior to this scene, Oppenheimer has been arguing with colleagues and military personnel over the bomb. What had existed as formulas in notebooks and blackboards is now on the brink of becoming a terrifying reality. In a moment of soul-searching, he retreats to consider the potential consequences of his actions. As mentioned above, Oppenheimer not only treasured this particular sonnet but actually named his project Trinity as a direct allusion.

> Batter my heart, three-person'd God; for, you
> As yet but knocke, breathe, shine, and seeke to mend,
> That I may rise, and stand, o'erthrow mee,'and bend
> Your force, to breake, blowe, burn and make me new.
> I, like an usurpt towne, to'another due,
> Labour to'admit you, but Oh, to no end,
> Reason your viceroy in mee, mee should defend,
> But is captiv'd, and proves weake or untrue.
> Yet dearely'I love you,'and would be loved faine,
> But am bethroth'd unto your enemie:
> Divorce mee,'untie, or breake that knot again,
> Take mee to you, imprison mee, for I
> Except you'enthrall mee, never shall be free,
> Nor ever chast, except you ravish mee.

Even within Donne's collected works, "Batter my heart" stands out for its outrageous imagery. Prominent among what later scholars call metaphysical poetry, it deploys metaphors of siege warfare and, especially, invited rape to convey the feelings of an individual striving to submit entirely to God. The final lines—"for I Except you'enthrall mee, never shall be free, / Nor ever chast, except, you ravish mee"—surely exceed in violence and abject horror any prayer ever delivered up in the English tongue. In his sestina "La benigna fortuna," Petrarch expresses the inability of poetry to capture the essence of extreme anguish ("my harsh martyrdom vanquishes every style"), and Donne similarly battles with the severe limitations of his inherited conventions. The intense enjambment of lines that overflow their bounds produces a sense of urgency. He may obey the letter of the law concerning sonnets, but he violates it at every turn.

Adams's score vacillates between agitation in the orchestra and somber lament in D Dorian, thereby simulating the factions warring inside Oppenheimer. The modal quality of this aria echoes Donne's contemporary John Dowland; think, for instance, of Dowland's signature tune "Lacrimae" ("Flow My Tears"). Nowhere else in *Doctor Atomic* does Adams venture into such unabashed diatonic writing, which sets this aria off from the frenetic activities of the laboratory. I would venture to say that this swerve into an archaic mode marks "Batter my heart" as tapping into a realm in which the mask of modernity has been dropped, baring a soul that strives to address a deity who exists outside human time.

Adams abandons Donne's tortured sonnet structure (perhaps the root of Rosenbaum's criticism) for the sake of his own rhetorical shape, which resembles that of a da capo aria. Oppenheimer sings those signal words "Batter my heart, three-person'd God" four times, the second time to preface lines 3 and 4 that begin "That I may rise and stand." Then, after a return to the agitated orchestra, he repeats the entire sequence. Like most da capo arias, the opening section repeats the same words many times over for the sake of emphasis. Adams groups lines 5 through 10 together as a kind of B section, then begins his final peroration and return to tonic at "Divorce mee," which binds the last line of the first sextet with the second—transgressing once again Donne's formal plan.

For most of *Doctor Atomic*, Sellars avoids assigning main characters the stylized gestures he uses elsewhere. Scenes in the laboratory show the scientists interacting in a relatively realistic fashion. But he brings on the gestures in force for Oppenheimer's soliloquy, and he does so for two principal reasons. First, Oppenheimer is not interacting here with anyone else except, he hopes, his God. The social conventions that demand a certain kind of decorum do not obtain here. Second, "Batter my heart" gives us insight into Oppenheimer's interiority—the wracked subjectivity that Donne and Petrarch struggled to put onto paper. Sellars's gestures always function to present visual traces of internal feelings, and his staging of this aria could stand as a textbook example of his modus operandi. For those not accustomed to this aspect of Sellars's dramaturgy, Gerald Finley's physical contortions may come as a shock or even an embarrassment (they always leave time for extensive discussion when I screen this scene in classes). But the aria's choreography matters enormously for the viewer's understanding of Oppenheimer.

In her staging of this scene for the Metropolitan Opera production, Penny Woolcock greatly tamps down Sellars's gestures. Some of Finley's moves at the Met recall his earlier performance, but Woolcock wants us to see Oppenheimer, even in extremis, as a realistic character. He may plead or wince in pain or stretch out his hands in supplication, but he never ceases to appear as a speaking subject. Recital renditions more closely resemble Woolcock's than Sellars's, for she abides within customs of good concert behavior. Sellars most emphatically does not.

When Sellars works with the da capo formula, he usually strives to differentiate the reiterations, with each statement bringing out another potential meaning or psychological dimension. In his staging of "Batter my heart," however, he works to underscore the repetitions. His radical gestures and their insistent returns do not allow the viewer to turn away from the nakedness of Oppenheimer's appeal.

During Adams's orchestral introduction, Finley moves as if hypnotized toward the lighted tent that encloses the bomb, which we see looming in silhouette. Sellars coached him to move as if his heart were pulling him forward. He touches the flap of the tent warily and peers inside but hesitates to confront the nightmarish creature of his imagination. Instead, he turns and begins the aria.

Sellars accompanies the word "Batter" each time with the gesture associated with "mea culpa," with the fist striking the chest. He thereby couples the literal meaning of the word with an age-old sign of ritual penitence. Donne's pairs of injunctions—knock/breathe, break/blow—receive collapses and expansions, the whole body simulating a shuddering interiority. On "o'erthrow me and bend your force," Finley's arms suddenly fly back, even causing his signature fedora to fall from his head. As the orchestra repeats its agitated ritornello, he attempts again to enter the tent but is driven back once more by his apprehension. The fact that the light comes from within the tent makes the bomb all the more magnetic. We see Oppenheimer backlit as if up against the feared nuclear explosion.

The second iteration of the cycle based on the first four lines follows the pattern of the first. Both Adams and Sellars stress here the fact of repetition: we are to hear and see Oppenheimer as stuck, presenting the same appeal many times as if infinitely. A few significant details make this second version differ slightly: Finley now holds his hands out in supplication more often, and he makes direct eye contact with the audience during the fourth statement of "Batter."

So great is the weight of this opening that even when subsequent lines go on to explain its conceit we are to hear them as occurring parenthetically while the opening line and its mea culpa continue to resonate. As he sings those lines, Finley looks up, addressing God. At each reference to the Other ("to another due," "your enemy"), he glances nervously over his shoulder at the bomb. "Reason" leads him to grasp his head in disbelief of his intellect's treachery. With the high pleading pitch on "dearly I love you," he falls ab-jectly to his knees, shrinking in unworthiness on "would be lov'd fain."

The orchestra begins to insert another ritornello, and Oppenheimer re-sponds by turning back toward the tent, as if pulled against his will. But this time, he wheels around with a sense of purpose to begin the last section, starting with "Divorce me." He holds his crossed wrists high above his head, then throws them apart as he demands that God untie him from his reliance on reason, the internal viceroy that holds him captive. Finley's face presents the utmost urgency on those always-shocking words "except you ravish me" before he falls in on himself, his prayer completed. But as Adams's ritornello thunders, Finley seizes his hat and walks resolutely back toward the tent. Af-ter a slight pause in which he glances back as if to God or to the choice he is on the brink of eliminating, he walks inside that inner sanctum, his silhou-ette now together with that of the bomb.[21]

The overwhelming fear of the bomb finds expression in another item from Oppenheimer's reading list, the Bhagavad Gita, which this Renaissance man read in Sanskrit. Sellars takes from the Gita a chorus reacting to a grue-some manifestation of Vishnu. As Adams's music pounds, the chorus stag-gers forward under a blood-red light, matching each shocking image in the text with a histrionic gesture. At times they fall, writhing as if from nuclear fallout. Sellars's DVD cuts between the chorus, an apprehensive Pasqualita, a fitfully sleeping Kitty Oppenheimer, and the horrified face of the young sci-entist, Robert Wilson, who had warned of the bomb's catastrophic potential. In the wake of the bomb's devastation in Japan, Oppenheimer himself quoted the Bhagavad Gita: "Now I am become death, the destroyer of worlds." This phrase hovers over the entire opera.

As in *El Niño*, Sellars makes strategic use of video in *Doctor Atomic*. Most striking is the montage of World War II footage projected during the over-ture. With Adams's electronic sounds providing an ominous soundscape, Sellars presents snippets of American GIs, assembly-line workers, the loading of an aircraft with bombs, the smoldering ruins of a destroyed city, corpses lying in the aftermath of the bomb's detonation. Adams himself engages in montage with the insertion of a fragment of a forties pop song, its sound garbled as if by long-range radio relay or by fading memory. He interrupts this brief sample with a brutal attack from the orchestra's percussion, and Sellars edits his video to synchronize with Adams's impulses, matching the violent rhythms with images of machines turning out weapons.

Sellars and Adams decided against simulating the explosion at the test site in order to focus on the people we have followed over the course of the opera. But Adams creates a coup de théâtre at the end through the music he writes for the countdown. As he explains in *Wonders Are Many*, Jon Else's documentary, he set clockworks in the different parts of the orchestra, thereby simulating various mechanisms moving inexorably forward to the blast; Else then films Donald Runnicles conducting this entire sequence, allowing us to hear the intricacy of Adams's score. The clocks accelerate, punctuated by the sounds of screams and air-raid sirens. Suddenly the motion stops, leaving only the sound of chimes. In the documentary, Adams then taunts Sellars asking, "How are you going to deal with that countdown?" How indeed?

During that almost unbearable countdown, the camera moves nervously between the horror-struck faces of Kitty and Robert Oppenheimer. Backlit by a blue light, dancers writhe and reach upward, recalling Picasso's *Guernica*. As the sound dwindles to that ominous chime, the light turns red. The chorus and principals stand or kneel, facing the audience, staring motionless and transfixed toward the mushroom cloud we cannot see. As he has done repeatedly over the course of his career, Sellars here seeks to implicate his viewers in the moral dilemmas of the characters onstage. And we may have in this shattering final sequence another allusion to John Donne. In his sonnet "No man is an island," Donne famously wrote, "seek not to know for whom the bell tolls, it tolls for thee."

• Adams and Sellars continue to produce work along the lines of *El Niño* and *Doctor Atomic*, and audiences eagerly await their latest offerings. Most recently, the San Francisco Opera premiered their *Girls of the Golden West*: an opera that begins with the Gold Rush of 1848 but then focuses on the social and political upheaval that followed the annexation of California to the United States in 1849. During that transition, Native Americans were slaughtered, and the Mexican inhabitants whose area this was just the year before, when it was still Mexico, were driven off their lands. As Sellars puts it, "They didn't cross the border; the border crossed them."[22]

Sellars and Adams assembled the libretto for *Girls of the Golden West* from a great many sources. Central to their concept is a series of letters by a woman (Louise Clappe), a New Englander who called herself Dame Shirley and who reported to her sister on her experiences in California. At first enchanted by the terrain and the ideals of the would-be miners coming from all over the globe, she also traces the rise of racial animosities, mob rule, genocide, and lynching. Her letters allow Sellars and Adams to locate the descriptions of such atrocities in the mouth of an eyewitness.

Sellars and Adams still regard this opera as a work in progress. To my mind, one of its weaknesses involves precisely this decision to rely so heavily on Dame Shirley's letters. Although Julia Bullock always acts and sings brilliantly, she has difficulty cutting through Adams's busy orchestra as she delivers that written prose, and she comes off as far less vivid than the characters who surround her. This reveals some of the risks Sellars and Adams face with their modus operandi of text assemblage. Not all texts—however powerful in their own right—lend themselves to operatic performance.

But the collaborators reach an extraordinary height with the setting of Frederick Douglass's "What to the Slave is the Fourth of July?"—a speech that ought to be as familiar as Reverend King's "I Have a Dream." Sung by Devóne Tines as a former slave who accompanies Dame Shirley, this set piece will no doubt take its place alongside "Batter my heart" as a staple of recitals. The dramatic positioning of this particular borrowed text has a shattering effect, especially when Tines is marched off at gunpoint as he finishes.

The years since that fateful meeting in 1983 when Sellars first approached Adams have seen the development of one of the most fruitful collaborations in the history of music drama. Although not without its frictions and occasional aesthetic differences, this team continues to produce blockbusters. They have cleared the path for a new generation of American composers—Du Yun, Missy Mazzoli, Kate Soper, Ashley Fure—who regard opera as the obvious genre for expression and experimentation. But Sellars has not limited himself to collaboration with Adams. In the next chapter, I examine the ways Sellars engages with the stylistic priorities of a very different composer, Kaija Saariaho.

# 5 • Spectral Sensualities

## Collaborations with Kaija Saariaho

As we have seen, Sellars heard many of the compositional techniques Adams had developed in his instrumental pieces—his driving pulsations, his long-range vectors—as perfect for opera. The long series of collaborations with Adams has revealed Sellars's uncanny instinct for discerning dramatic potential in unlikely sources and then working with composers to bring their music to the stage. A chameleon, Sellars always adapts his skills to the formal and expressive demands of the repertory at hand; whether the da capo format of the eighteenth century or the idiosyncratic language of Messiaen, he listens and then translates what he perceives into visual analogues. I have subtitled this book *Staging the Music* because of his commitment to begin with the score rather than with plot.[1]

Kaija Saariaho's style bears virtually no resemblance to that of Adams. Trained first in her native Finland, then at Pierre Boulez's IRCAM (the heart of darkness of postwar modernism), she absorbed rigorous procedures—serialism, electronic composition, computer generation—that predisposed her against opera. And although she has tilted those complex procedures in ways her predecessors never could have foreseen, she continues to use them as tools. During her first years of professional success, she composed almost exclusively in instrumental genres, thereby developing an extraordinary ability to write for orchestras, chamber ensembles, and soloists.

Saariaho produces many of her effects through her own version of a process known as spectralism. Everyone can distinguish between a pitch played on the flute and the same pitch played on the oboe: they have different "colors." But we did not know until quite recently how to account for distinctive sonorities in scientific terms. By means of computer-based processes developed at IRCAM, researchers learned how to break a sound down into the spectrum generated by its fundamental, its principal overtones, its higher-level frequencies, and the relative strengths of each. In other words, they were able to chart the minute details that produce what we hear as color.

This scientific breakthrough inspired some of the artists at IRCAM to experiment with spectra in designing their compositions. That is, they took the materials made available by researchers and figured out how to deploy them actively in the creation of new music. Starting from the spectrum of frequencies generated by a fundamental, they could home in on and emphasize one partial or another, thereby manipulating sound color itself as a compositional parameter. The sense of pitch center we may perceive in Saariaho's relatively dissonant music derives from her selective use of such collections.

But it is one thing to select a particular spectrum for use and another to make it into viable music. Devoted spectralists such as Gérard Grisey and Tristan Murail work more closely within the systems they create. After having learned these techniques, however, Saariaho moved in a more intuitive direction. Relying on her ear, she distributes the various partials among ensemble members, thereby creating the shimmering, elusive sonorities characteristic of her work.[2]

Sellars had to bend his theatrical habits considerably in order to accommodate this collaboration. By means of her spectral-related techniques, Saariaho has developed an affective palette that differs radically from the expressive vocabulary of Adams and most other contemporary composers. Although she punctuates the complex counterpoint of her scores with violent eruptions, she does not position these as goals toward which the energy inexorably leads; they do not, in other words, serve to advance narrative. And her long stretches of orchestral sonorities have little in common with Adams's temporal experiments produced through minimalist techniques (e.g. the opening chorus of *Nixon*) or to his dramatic use of ellipses (e.g. the end of the countdown in *Doctor Atomic*).

Saariaho presented a challenge, however, not only because of her musical proclivities but also because of her determination to write from her vantage point as a woman. Early on in her career, she resisted the label "woman composer." She wrote later: "I saw the fact of being a woman as an enormous handicap. I wanted people to listen to my music and not a woman's music. I tried to scrub away the feminine aspect: I smoked cigars; I dressed like a man."[3]

But then in 1989, two events occurred. First, she had a child. She later wrote:

As a mother, I have access to many things that men could never experience. Before having children, I really was up in the air most of the time. The earthly aspect became more present with children. Has my music changed with motherhood? Of course. At the same time, I don't like to say that, because I really felt some people's suspicions when I had my first child, suspicions like: this is the end of her serious music, she'll become too sentimental. (22)

The second event, also in 1989, was her encounter with Peter Sellars when she attended his productions of *Don Giovanni*, Stravinsky's *The Rake's Progress*, and, later, his staging of *Saint François d'Assise*, by one of Saariaho's teachers, Olivier Messiaen. Sellars had been drawn to Saariaho because of the sensual and dramatic power he heard in her instrumental music, and he believed she could become a formidable composer of opera. As we have seen, he had already served as the Johnny Appleseed for luring reluctant composers into opera. Suddenly, the prospect of composing operas seemed not so preposterous to her.

Beginning in the 1990s, Saariaho and Sellars discussed and planned various possible projects. Sellars recommended that Amin Maalouf—the award-winning Lebanese-French novelist and historian—join the group as a librettist, though he, like Saariaho, had never envisioned working in the operatic medium. The three set to work on what became *L'amour de loin* (2000); other collaborations followed, including *Adriana Mater* (2006) and *La passion de Simone* (2006).

In all of these, Sellars labored as an integral part of the team: suggesting themes, helping to shape the scenarios, characters, and structures, then putting the finished works onstage. He also brought with him Dawn Upshaw, one of his veteran performers whose voice Saariaho had come to admire when watching Sellars's productions. Thrown into the mix for good measure were his brilliant lighting designer, James Ingalls, and his innovative set designer, George Tsypin. I should also mention Esa-Pekka Salonen (Saariaho's former classmate and conductor for Sellars's *Saint François* at Salzburg), who first introduced her work to many audiences and who often conducts her premieres. Eventually Sellars himself created the libretto and mis-en-scène for Saariaho's *Only the Sound Remains* (premiere, 2016).

Clearly one of the most effective partnerships in the history of music, Saariaho, Maalouf, and Sellars have produced a series of masterpieces. Maalouf contributes his exquisite skill with the French language and concerns over wartime violence; Saariaho her genius for orchestral color, formal coherence, and musical imagery; and Sellars his lifelong obsession with spirituality, his dedication to art as social action, his unusual sensitivity to the details of musical scores in his staging decisions, and his deep knowledge of world literature, which included his familiarity with Maalouf's writing. His dramaturgical preference for tableaux rather than continuous action also marks all these works.

Finally, Saariaho and Sellars both bring with them a deep commitment to the sympathetic representation of women on the operatic stage. In his collaborations with John Adams, Sellars features poetry by women such as Rosario Castellanos and June Jordan, and he often gravitates toward scenes exploring pregnancy, motherhood, and childrearing, even in his stagings of the Bach passions (see chapter 7). Consequently, when Saariaho described her experience of feeling two heartbeats when she was carrying her baby, she found a particularly sympathetic response in Sellars as well as in Maalouf. Together they drew from that image a series of characters, scenes, and dramatic tensions, thereby fashioning what became *Adriana Mater*: an opera in which a woman raped during wartime struggles with whether to terminate her pregnancy, then watches as her adult son seeks revenge on his own father for that long-ago crime. Recall that Saariaho feared that people would assume that after she became a mother her music would turn "sentimental"— scarcely an adjective anyone would apply to *Adriana Mater*![4]

Which brings me to the issue of essentialism. Twenty-five years ago I wrote a book encouraging women to put some of their energies to articulating life experiences from a female point of view in their music.[5] Writers and visual artists had received considerable acclaim at that time for doing just this: Nobel laureate Toni Morrison writes from the viewpoint of an African American woman, and most of us celebrate the paintings of Georgia O'Keeffe and Frida Kahlo, who similarly brought women's issues—even the female anatomy—into their paintings. But many prominent musicians cringed at my suggestion, and very few composers volunteered for the task. After a while, during which I got written off as an "essentialist," I surrendered and turned my own energies to other purposes.

I suspect that one reason essentialism became such a big deal in musicology—far more so than in literary studies—descends from the legacy, once again, of absolute music. So long as we exalt musics that bear no obvious traces of ethnicity or gender or sexuality or, indeed, social meanings of any kind, we will continue to disparage composers who move in those directions. To my mind, such policing of artistic content poses a much greater threat than essentialism.

Yes, Kaija Saariaho has included themes of female ecstasy, pleasure, pregnancy, childbirth, and motherhood in her work. But just as Morrison, O'Keeffe, and Kahlo do far more than toss unmediated sensations onto the page or canvas, so Saariaho articulates experiences through musical devices she inherited from Messiaen and IRCAM, through the complex manipulations related to spectralism, through her finely honed sense of long-term structure and expressive nuance, through her unusual ability to invoke qualities such as heat, fragrance, light, and physical weight through her combinations of sounds: synaesthesia, in other words, or what Sellars refers to as her deep commitment to embodied knowledge. Along with her accomplices, Maalouf and Sellars, Saariaho has given us access to points of view rarely voiced on the operatic stage.

When she was young, Saariaho immersed herself in literature by women. She writes:

> In the beginning of my compositional studies, I tried in vain to find a model in the world of music; female composers were few and far between. No doubt this is why I was interested in the lives of female writers, and took pleasure in reading their diaries, letters, and biographies, in addition to their works. Besides Virginia Woolf, the two figures who meant the most to me were Sylvia Plath and Anaïs Nin [because] of their urge to combine—at least that's what it seemed to me—a "woman's life," meaning their roles as mother, and their artistic careers. . . . I was searching for a way of life, I was reading these diaries as survival manuals.[6]

Saariaho so treasured the writings of Simone Weil that she carried her Finnish translation with her when she moved to France. If the equivalent of Woolf or Plath or Weil did not exist in music then, they do now, thanks in part to her own brave imagination.

I first encountered *L'amour de loin* when one of my female undergraduates foisted it on me in tears, so deeply was she transfixed by this "woman's life" in sound. Like Saariaho clinging to her dog-eared volume of Simone Weil, my student clutched her DVD to her heart as her first encounter with some kind of truth she had not found in other music—as her own survival manual. When I have played parts of Saariaho's *Château de l'âme* at conferences, I have met with similar reactions. Really? You can do this with music? Wow!

For Saariaho simulates an erotic quality quite different from the goal-oriented trajectories common to the standard concert repertory. Through her astonishing orchestration she creates what I have called smoldering intensities: a fabric of low drones, extended trills, and static ostinatos disrupted occasionally by violent eruptions or rushes of passion. She forgoes the simulation of direct action for a quality of suspended animation with searing undercurrents of desire and foreboding.[7]

This is not to say that Saariaho has tapped into some universal well of how all women understand themselves. Of course not. Nor is it to suggest that female composers have some kind of obligation to make gender relevant to their work. Of course not. But the fact that Saariaho *chooses* to do so in some (*not all*) of her work enriches our shared culture. And that she does so with such musical integrity, communicative power, and ravishing beauty sets a very high standard for artistic creation. Along with her collaborators, Kaija Saariaho has accomplished what she once could only dream of: music of the very highest quality that brings experiences of women's lives onto the operatic stage.

## L'amour de loin

Saariaho herself proposed the theme of Jaufré Rudel, a twelfth-century troubadour who wrote many cansos concerning *fin'amor*, or courtly love. She had encountered Rudel first through Jacques Roubaud, a celebrated French poet who alludes to the troubadour in his own work, and she started to work on a potential opera with Roubaud as librettist. In 1996, she composed "Lohn," a setting of the Rudel poem that recurs throughout the opera.[8] When Roubaud withdrew from the opera project, Gerard Mortier (then-director of the Salzburg Festival, where Saariaho had first encountered Sellars's work) recommended Amin Maalouf, whose name Sellars had already mentioned to her. Together, Saariaho, Maalouf, and Sellars plotted out and produced *L'amour de loin*, which premiered under Sellars's direction in Salzburg in 2000.

This chapter will focus on Saariaho and Sellars, but Maalouf qualifies as a major cultural figure in his own right. A Lebanese Christian who has spent most of his career in Paris, Maalouf was elected to the prestigious Académie Française for his exquisite novels set in North Africa and the Middle East. But his works of nonfiction also have received much attention: his extraordinary *The Crusades through Arab Eyes* should be required reading for anyone still wondering about the history of Western relations with the Middle East.[9] This subject matter shows up explicitly in the person of Clémence, the sister of a Provençal crusader who rules conquered Lebanon from his citadel in Tripoli. Sellars related powerfully to the story because of his lifelong interest in manifestations of Divine Union. As to Saariaho:

I realized in the middle of composing the work that it was my story too. I was at once the composer and the lady, the two parts of myself that I try to reconcile in my life. To be a woman composer is almost impossible. To write music, you need concentration, to listen to what is going on inside you. To be a woman, to be a mother, you must always be available and efficient. It's hard to keep your feet on the ground and your head in the clouds at the same time.[10]

Now both Parisian residents, Saariaho and Maalouf also share the experience of geographic displacement from their homelands—a crucial theme in *L'amour de loin.*

The team based the libretto on the *vida* (biographical sketch) of Rudel composed in the thirteenth century:

> Jaufré Rudel de Blaye was a noble man, Prince of Blaye. He fell in love with the Countess of Tripoli, without seeing her, on account of the fine things he heard about her from the pilgrims who came from Antioch, and he composed many *vers* about her with good melodies but poor words. And desiring to see her, he took the cross and set out over the sea. He fell ill in the ship and was taken to Tripoli, to an inn, as though dead. The Countess was informed of this; she came to him, right up to his bed, and took him in her arms. He recognized that it was the Countess and immediately he recovered his hearing and sense of smell; and he praised God who had kept him alive until he saw her. And in this manner he died in her arms. She buried him in the House of the Temple, with great honor, and then that very day, she took vows on account of the sorrow his death brought to her.[11]

The *vida* itself drew on and often circulated along with Rudel's signature canso, "Lanquand li jorn," verses 2, 5, and 7 of which are sung by the Pilgrim and then Clémence in act 2. In the third act, Clémence sings verses 5 and 7 of the canso in the original Occitan:

| | |
|---|---|
| 1. Lanqand li jorn son lonc en mai | When the days are long in May |
| m'es bels douz chans d'auzels de loing | the sweet song of birds from afar seems lovely to me |
| e qand me sui partitz de lai | and when I have left from there |
| remembra-m d'un'amor de loing | I remember a distant love |
| vauc de talan enbroncs e clis | I walk bent and bowed with desire |
| si que chans ni flors d'albespis | such that neither song nor hawthorn |

no-m platz plus que l'inverns gelatz.
2. Je mais d'amor no-m gauzirai
si no-m gau d'est'amor de loing
que gensor ni meillor non sai
vas nuilla part ni pres ni loing
tant es sos pretz verais e fis
que lai el ranc dels sarrazis

fos eu per lieis chaitius clamatz.
3. Irarz e gauzens m'en partrai
qan veirai cest'amor de loing
mas non sai coras la-m veirai
car trop son nostras terras loing
assatz i a portz e camis
e per aisso non sui devis
mas tot sia cum a Dieu platz.
4. Be-m parra jois qan li qerrai
per amor Dieu l'amor de loing
e s'a lieis plai albergarai
pres de lieis si be-m sui de loing
adonc parra-l parlamens fis
qand drutz loindas er tant vezis

c'ab bels digz jauzirai solatz.

5. Ben tenc lo signor per verai
per q'ieu verai l'amor de loing

mas per un ben que m'en eschai
n'ai dos mals car tant m'es de loing
ai car me fos lai perleris
si que mos fustz e mos tapis
fos pelz sieus bels huoills remiratz.
6. Dieus qe fetz tot quant ve ni vai
e fermet cest'amor de loing
me don poder qe-l cor eu n'ai
q'en breu veia l'amor de loing
veraiamen en locs aizis
si qe la cambra e-l jardis

please me more than the icy winter.
Never in love shall I rejoice
unless I enjoy this love from afar,
for nobler or better one I do not know
anywhere, neither near nor far,
so high is its true, real price
That there in the kingdom of the
    Saracens
I wish to be proclaimed her captive.
Sad and joyous, I will separate from her
when I see that distant love
but I know not when I will see her
for our lands are too far apart
there are so many passages and paths
and in this I am no seer
but may all follow God's will.
I will feel joy when I ask her
for the love of God the distant love
and if it pleases her I will live
near her even if I am from far away
then will come our faithful meeting
when I, the faraway lover, will be so
    close
That I console myself with her lovely
    words.
I trust well in the Lord
through whom I will see the distant
    love
but for something that fails me I have
two sorrows for she is so far away.
Ah, if only I were a pilgrim there
so that my stick and bundle
Could be seen by her lovely eyes.
God who made all that comes and goes
and formed this distant love
grant me the power of my heart
soon to see the distant love
truly in a propitious place
and in that room and garden

| | |
|---|---|
| mi resembles totz temps palatz. | Always appear as palaces to me. |
| 7. Ver ditz qui m'apella lechai | He speaks the truth who calls me greedy |
| ni desiran d'amor de loing | And longing for the distant love |
| car nuills autre joist ant no-m plai | For no other joy pleases me as much |
| cum jauzimens d'amor de loing | As enjoyment of love from afar; |
| mas so q'eu vuoill m'es tant ahis | But what I want is forbidden to me, |
| q'enaissi-m fadet mos pairis | For thus did my godfather decree my fate, |
| q'ieu ames e non fos amatz. | That I should love and not be loved. |

Note that Jaufré himself never sings his celebrated canso in the opera. We hear him trying to compose at the beginning of the opera, expressing frustration over his failure to get his words right. He does, however, present one set of lines that sets the plot in motion:

Belle sans l'arrogance de la beauté,
Noble sans l'arrogance de la noblesse,
Pieuse sans l'arrogance de la piété.

[Beautiful without the arrogance of beauty, noble without the arrogance of nobility, pious without the arrogance of piety.]

In keeping with the aesthetic principles of *fin'amor*, Jaufré describes the idolized lady in the abstract. But the Pilgrim claims that this woman exists and that he has seen her. Later the Pilgrim conveys Jaufré's description to Clémence. Without the Pilgrim's intervention that locates Jaufré's ineffable desire in an actual person, he would never have set out to sea, and Clémence's life too would have remained unchanged. But although flattered by this description, the Countess realizes that she cannot measure up to those ideals, and she castigates herself for her vanity in precisely the areas Jaufré seeks perfection. She understands all too well the difference between reality and dreams. The opera will trace her journey from protected child to sacrificing adult.

Saariaho alludes to Rudel's medieval idiom throughout the opera with open fifths and harp arpeggios, recalling the sound of a lute being tuned and played. But she goes further as she models Rudel's formal songs on the melodic shapes of troubadour cansos, never quite quoting but always evoking the modal melodic shapes of that repertory. She immerses all these archaic references into her signature wash of smoldering sonorities, as if we hear these twelfth-century musical figures from the temporal distance of nearly a millennium: from afar, in other words.

The collaborators decided to focus their drama on the three characters mentioned in the *vida*: Rudel (Gerald Finley), the Countess in Tripoli (Dawn Upshaw), and the Pilgrim (Monica Groop). Rudel and Clémence each has a chorus of companions with whom they converse. In his production, Sellars chose to show only the three principals, and the chorus sounded from off-stage. One of the benefits of Sellars's solution (suggested explicitly in the score as an option) is that these voices may represent either the citizens of Jaufré's Blaye and Clémence's Tripoli or the debates located deep within the characters themselves. In any case, his staging trusts Saariaho's music to carry the show.[12]

Saariaho structures her opera through rigorous symmetries between Rudel and Clémence: each receives a full act, and they split act 3 as they become closer in spirit, echoing their sentiments back and forth. The palindrome shatters, however, when Rudel attempts the sea voyage, abandoning his tower to embark with the Pilgrim on his own pilgrimage; only when the Pilgrim delivers the dying troubadour does Clémence leave her refuge. Neither can return to his or her previous condition, for their protective shells have been destroyed, and what should have been a triumphant union of the lovers in the final act becomes instead a deathbed farewell.

Sellars and his set designer, George Tsypin, scrupulously follow this plan in their production. Rudel inhabits a spiral staircase—a kind of helix—on the left side of the stage, Clémence an identical one on the right. Lighting designer James Ingalls deploys blues and greens on Rudel's side, oranges and yellows on Clémence's, thereby contrasting the lushness of southern France with the desert climate of the Middle East. Sequestered from the world and encased within their own isolated subjectivities, neither can move beyond the narrow confines of those stairwells. Water surrounds them on the stage, and although both occasionally dip a hand into the sea, neither ventures forth until Rudel's ill-fated journey. Only the Pilgrim has free range of motion and access to both parties by way of his boat.

The utter simplicity and elegance of Sellars's concept—two helixes and a water-covered stage—invite the viewer to attend to the resonances of Saariaho's score and Maalouf's libretto without distraction. For the most part, only the music and the corresponding lighting convey the lovers' mercurial shifts between extremes of longing and fear. Until the last two acts, Sellars limits the stage action of the principals to their racing up and down their respective staircases, thereby underscoring their isolation and repressed energies. The effect resembles that of the medieval iconography Sellars studied in preparation for his production of *Saint François*, with individuals peering out from castle towers.

The Pilgrim in *L'amour de loin* serves as a necessary conduit between the troubadour and his lady. He fans the flames of Rudel's imagination by attaching the poet's lofty ideals to a living woman, then spreads the contagion through Rudel's poetry to Clémence. In turn, Clémence succumbs to Rudel's fantasy, igniting a folie à deux that can only end in tragedy when the Pilgrim attempts to literalize their union. Jaufré's fervor cannot withstand its redirection to an actual woman; he expires from his exposure to reality.

Clémence, however, survives. In the final scene, she performs an extended baptismal rite on herself, transforming her earthly love into longing for the always-unknowable Divine.[13] Like Wagner's Isolde, Clémence remains alone to absorb the weight of the failed consummation. Both women redirect their earthly ardor upward: a blaze of ecstatic glory in Isolde's *Liebestod*, a transformation of longing for a troubadour into Clémence's appeal in her finale to God, the ultimate distant beloved. This blurring between the carnal and the sacred had already informed Rudel himself. The culture of *fin'amor* drew on the imagery inherited from the verse of Muslim Spain, which descended in turn from Sufi texts and finally from the Hebrew Song of Songs.[14] As Lacan told us long after all these ancient poets had already established such tropes, the human condition rests upon desire for a never-to-be-attained object, what he labeled as the *objet petit a*.

We might hear the presence of the Mediterranean in Saariaho's music with its oceanic qualities. In fact, Robert Lepage foregrounded the sea in his staging for this reason.[15] But although Sellars acknowledges the sea in his water-covered stage, he also leaves open the possibility of hearing that orchestral wash as psychological obsession and the reverberating sound waves of poetic recitation that bridge the distance between the lovers. Indeed, his staging of "Mer Indigo" (the orchestral opening to act 4 labeled explicitly as pertaining to the sea) focuses exclusively on the Pilgrim, whose face vacillates between hope and angst at this moment of no return. The crashing breakers in the orchestra—a kind of spectralism at its most spectacular (and easiest to hear)—play out against the utter stillness of the go-between.[16]

Throughout the voyage, Jaufré huddles abjectly in the glass boat awaiting what he calls a second birth, and the Pilgrim addresses him as if speaking to a fetus in the womb. The sea here becomes the amniotic fluid that surrounds an unborn child, producing those swooshing sounds that remain with us throughout our lives as the memory of plenitude, of oneness with the mother. But it also represents a violent, indomitable force of nature, as the male chorus relates iconic fragments from legends of warriors lost at sea.

Saariaho's tumultuous music corresponds not only to the storm-swept sea but also to Jaufré's terror at his foolhardy undertaking. Gerald Finley's hysterical face and gestures suffice to project the drama of this scene. Awaking from a fitful sleep, he tells the Pilgrim that he has dreamed of Clémence. As he recounts his vision, Clémence appears beside the boat, singing one of his chansons: "Your love fills my mind, waking and dreaming. But it is dreaming that I prefer because in dreams you are mine." Yet this moment of plenitude occurs only in his fevered imagination, and he sings of his fear and loss of faith in counterpoint to her lyrics. As they approach Tripoli, Jaufré is dying; the Pilgrim has served unwittingly as Charon, ferrying him from the land of the living across the River Styx and into the spirit world.

The story conveyed in the medieval *vida* focuses exclusively on Jaufré, the troubadour. *L'amour de loin*, however, follows Clémence's journey from self-centered noblewoman, smug at her ability to inspire the poet's adoration, to self-sacrificing devotee. Even as Jaufré lands in Tripoli, she continues to rehearse her charms, still oblivious to the mortal danger to which he has subjected himself. Only when her lover arrives moribund at her doorstep does Clémence venture from her helix to descend into the water. A countess, she has never sullied herself with the outside world. Now the sea laps at her dress, and the spreading stain marks her commitment to leave the comforts and luxury of her former life behind. When she curses God after Jaufré's death, she splashes around gracelessly before lying down in the water for her final peroration. Soaked in this baptismal font, she prays for purity and holy union.

The remainder of the opera will involve her process of transforming of that human love into adoration of God. But first she must pass through blasphemy and bargaining. At last she surrenders. Lying in the water over a prolonged drone in the orchestra, Clémence makes her appeals: "If you are called love/goodness/pardon/passion, I love only you." With each of these elements, Sellars has Upshaw reach upward from her mouth, now the only source of poetry, toward heaven. Over and over, her melodic line strains toward fulfillment, only to fall short on what sounds like a leading tone prepared for resolution. Both lights and orchestra fade in a kind of ellipsis. Her redirected desire will remain unrequited for life. And long after the sound has disappeared, many listeners find themselves still suspended in the harmonic field Saariaho first began to unfurl at the very beginning of the opera.

## La passion de Simone

Like Saariaho, Sellars had long admired the mystic works of Simone Weil, a French Jewish woman who converted and drove herself mercilessly to follow the model of Christ. Weil starved herself to death in 1943 to express solidarity with French children who were succumbing to malnutrition and the other horrors of wartime. When Saariaho first left her native Finland in 1981 to study in Germany, she brought her treasured copy of Weil with her. Later, as she and Sellars compared their respective inspirations, they embarked on the project that became *La passion de Simone: Chemin musical en quinze stations*.

As we have seen, Sellars has increasingly returned to the Bach passions for his dramaturgy, and this semistaged monodrama brings that commitment to the fore. He might have assembled a libretto himself, as he did for *El Niño* and *Doctor Atomic*, for Weil's writings abound with concise, powerful statements conducive to musical setting. But the collaborators rejected that solution, in part because doing so could have resulted in a straightforward hagiography. And for all that Sellars and Saariaho loved those writings, they did not want to present a worshipful portrait in the fashion of Messiaen's *Saint François*; Weil elicits far more complicated reactions than does the beatific Francis, removed from us by nearly a millennium of mythology.[17]

Consequently, they turned once again to Maalouf for their texts. As Saariaho has described the creative process:

> The combination of Weil's severe asceticism and her passionate quest for truth has appealed to me ever since I first read her thoughts. *La Passion de Simone* was specifically the result of collaboration with Amin Maalouf and Peter Sellars; together we chose the different parts of Weil's work and life for the libretto before I began composing. Whereas I have always been fascinated by Simone's striving for abstract (mathematical) and spiritual-intellectual goals, Peter is interested in her social awareness and political activities. Amin brought out the gaping discrepancy between her philosophy and her life, showing the fate of the frail human being amongst great ideas. In addition to Simone Weil's life and ideas, many general questions of human existence are presented in Amin's texts.[18]

Weil's own words appear over the course of the piece, but they are spoken rather than sung. The featured soprano soloist represents not Weil herself but rather a somewhat ambivalent devotee: a reader deeply drawn to Weil's ideas who also struggles with the contradictions and sometimes nearly inhumane positions those texts often annunciate. The dialogue between short excerpts from the printed volume and the reader's responses—written by Maalouf—comprises the libretto of *La passion de Simone*. Although he did not write the libretto, Sellars left his fingerprints all over this piece in its structure and its dual commitment to social justice and radical spirituality.

As the subtitle *Chemin musical en quinze stations* indicates, the piece takes its formal structure from the Stations of the Cross ritual of Holy Week. But in place of Christ's path of martyrdom, we follow our reader as she traces the steps of Weil's life. Several of the stations in *La passion* correspond to those in the Catholic rite: in both, station 2 involves the voluntary taking up of the cross, station 4 engages with the martyr's relationship to parents, station 6 relates to facial images, station 13 narrates the deaths, and station 15 looks forward to resurrection. This is not an easy piece to embrace; indeed, the journey proves quite harrowing as the viewer or listener experiences the wild affective swings along with the singer. Rarely has Saariaho deployed her extremes in register in so compact a manner, with quiet, intimate passages juxtaposed with violent eruptions.

Saariaho has not entirely avoided the pitfalls of choosing to simulate the experiences of women such as Weil in her music. One review of her opera *Émilie* describes her main character—a prominent eighteenth-century intellectual who died in childbirth just as she was completing what still stands as the standard French translation of Newton's *Principia*—as a "hormonally ravaged hysteric."[19] *La passion de Simone* could easily provoke similar responses, as we witness the singer writhing on the stage or pacing with rage. Male composers, of course, have always had access to the full range of emotions as they write, and no one ever thinks to suggest that they thereby reveal what all men are really like; they are simply exercising their craft. But critics expect female artists to express some feminine essence, and they receive blame whether they adhere to standards of ladylike behavior or if they violate those codes. This is why so many women simply avoid engaging with gender at all in their work.

Yet Saariaho not only chooses to represent women's experiences but she often risks homing in on profoundly uncomfortable zones: the fiercely protective mother in "Pour repousser l'esprit" (from *Château de l'âme*), the woman in *Adriana Mater* expecting a child engendered by a rapist, the widowed Clémence, or the conflicted reader of Simone Weil in *La passion*. These characters stand far outside the accepted cultural stereotypes of lullaby-singing nurses or sexy singers of torch songs or malicious femmes fatales. Keep in mind that Saariaho produces her sonorities through the techniques of electronic manipulation and spectral-related devices: the raw quality we may perceive results from many layers of extremely complex mediation. Yet this supremely reserved Nordic woman serves up searing imagery on a regular basis. In her own way, she can rival the savagery of Diamanda Galás in her music.[20]

The premiere of *La passion de Simone* took place in 2006 with Pi Freund as the soloist and Susanna Mälkki conducting; subsequent performances featured Dawn Upshaw, who also performed the role on the audio recording with Esa Pekka-Salonen conduction.[21] Although Sellars staged the original production with dancing by Michael Schumacher (the angel in *El Niño*), it never appeared in video format. Fortunately, he staged it again at the Ojai Festival in June 2016, with Julia Bullock singing and Joana Carneiro conducting members of the International Contemporary Ensemble and Roomful of Teeth, and this performance appears on YouTube.[22] My discussion deals exclusively with Sellars's staging at Ojai.

The stage itself is bare save for Ben Zamora's light panel standing like a full-length mirror behind the singer. Over the course of the piece, the panel will glow with a variety of lights signaling visually the singer's changing affective states. It first features a soft violet color, but when Bullock turns to accuse Weil, the panel suddenly goes stark white. The terms of address have changed, from quiet contemplation to confrontation, and the shift in lights underscores that alteration, as do Bullock's gestures and vocal timbre. Except when it turns white, the panel usually has a contrasting vertical stripe down the center—a mystic aperture, perhaps. The striking arrangements of colors may also recall the paintings of Mark Rothko, especially the ways as he contemplated death he began to make the higher part of his canvases dark: as if the horizon and future portended nothing but despair. Other than the panel and a copy of Weil's book, we see no props or scenery. Bullock performs barefoot in a casual tracksuit, and a chorus of four singers stands to the side, their scores resting on the stage.

Station 1 begins with a particularly troubled backdrop in the orchestra. In place of the slow, calm unfolding of the harmonic field at the opening of *L'amour de loin*, Saariaho here presents dissonant sounds in the upper partials. The harp in particular sounds anxious. Over this sonority Bullock addresses Weil both as big sister (as an older role model) and as little sister (as a deeply flawed woman who refused to mature and who died young). The book she carries features on its cover the famous picture of Weil taken for purposes of identification at her factory job, and Bullock raises the book as if elevating the host in Mass as she pledges to follow Weil's path. But as she flashes forward to anticipate Weil's chosen journey to sacrifice, she turns abruptly as if already giving up. Compelled, however, by Weil's ideals, she tries again. Maalouf's libretto offers a concise account of the reader's mixed feelings: "I admire you for making of your life a shining crossing, But I resent that you preferred death." Recall the way Bach starts the *St. John Passion* with a chorus in which congregants pray they might share in the pain of Christ's suffering; here a single voice does much the same. As the sonority fades, Bulloch reads the first of the direct quotations from Weil: "Nothing that exists is absolutely worthy of love, so we must love what does not exist." (We may hear resonances here of Jaufré Rudel's *fin'amor* and Lacan.)

At the conclusion of this first station, Bullock begins to wander off, biting worriedly at a thumbnail. But the entrance of the chorus announcing station 2 causes her to wheel around to face more directly the challenges Weil faced: a woman, a Jew, an individual wracked with chronic illnesses. She crumples to one knee in sympathetic pain. As the chorus warns against seeking consolation, Bullock seems to take on Weil's identity: no longer Self and Other but one entity experiencing Weil's suffering. It is because of this strong tendency toward the reader's assimilation that the moments of separation and castigation become so savage.

A shattering blast and fatalistic drumbeats introduce station 3, sometimes driving the singer to the ground. Such blasts alternate with sonorities of the greatest delicacy as the singer contemplates Weil's desire to disappear into silence against all odds. During station 4, the singer reflects upon Weil's rejection of her own family, and she hurls the book to the floor, picks it up, then hurls it down again several times. As she attempts to justify Weil's behavior (her family would have impeded her path to sacrifice), she approaches the panel and kneels.

In these opening sections, the collaborators emphasize the reader's mixed feelings, rather the way the early parts of the gospel narrations focus on Judas's betrayal and Peter's denial: the reactions of vulnerable human beings to the magnitude of the events in which they find themselves swept up. As we shall see in the final chapter, Sellars's stagings of Bach's passions draw our attention especially to the agony of those who want to follow but lack the courage or strength to do so. The narrator in *La passion de Simone* will similarly pass through a sequence of difficult trials in her attempt at coming to terms with Weil's martyrdom.

Beginning in station 5, the reader imagines herself as Weil in her real life, first as a factory worker. Here Bullock's body mimics the motions of repetitious manual labor as Saariaho's score becomes far more percussive. But the singer also expresses defiance over the enslavement of the masses by industrial forces, and her gestures often take on qualities of martial arts. The reader's singing voice fails altogether in station 6 as the chorus recites the serial number stamped on Weil's ID card: A9660-Weil. Bullock stands as if before a firing squad as the numbers rain down like bullets or needles imprinting the skin with a tattoo—an image explicitly invoked in Maalouf's text.

The reader pulls back into her ambivalent stance in station 7 as she weighs the stakes in Weil's march toward self-destruction. Weil's words, "Two powers hold sway over the universe: light and gravity," occur four times over the course of this section, with light corresponding to purifying flames, freedom, and enlightenment, gravity to greed and servitude. As she recites the two terms, light and gravity, Bullock stands posed on one foot, one arm raised and the other curved inward for balance. But between iterations of these terms, she marches aggressively or sobs silently as a solo oboe plays a lament reminiscent of the sorrowful English horn in the last act of Wagner's *Tristan*. To advance or retreat? To act or mourn? How best to respond to events beyond human control?

Station 8 stands as the still center of the composition. Weil's words appear alone, without commentary: "God withdraws so as not to be loved as a treasure loved by a miser." During the orchestral interlude, the reader picks up Weil's book again, then performs a silent ritual in the front of the stage. She has made peace with Weil's decisions.

By the time we reach station 12, the reader has become Weil, accepting death as the rightful conclusion of her journey. Only the chorus sings over Bullock's still body, as the orchestra plays an elegy simulating suspended animation. Station 13 has the singer comparing Weil's act to those of Alexander the Great and, of course, Christ, both of whom sacrificed themselves for their people at the same age as Weil. And here we hear one of the most chilling of Weil's statements:

> For the privilege of discovering myself before death in a state exactly similar to that of Christ when, on the cross, he said: "My God, why has thou forsaken me?"—for this privilege I willingly would renounce everything that is called Paradise.

She prays, in other words, not for certainty or eternal life but rather to hover forever in that exquisite moment between doubt and determination, to embrace death even without knowing its consequences.

In station 14, Bullock returns to her role as reader. She sings of the world's loss of Weil to the book cover, then holds the book with its picture of Weil next to her own face, cementing their union even if now separate beings. The final station gestures toward the triumph of resurrection, and the light panel changes from its solid colors to a pattern in which a path seems to lead upward toward a lighter horizon, then turns blood red. Maalouf's text resonates with those that appear in Bach's passions: compare "Your passion defeated oblivion, your grace was liberated from the gravity of the world" with Bach's "Durch dein Gefängnis Gottes Sohn ist mir der Freiheit kommen" (Through your imprisonment, Son of God, freedom has come to me, *St. John Passion*). Maalouf then circles back to the quotation that appeared at the beginning: "Nothing that exists is absolutely worthy of love, so we must love that which does not exist."

Yet the collaborators chose not to leave their audiences with a mystical conclusion that would betray Weil's dedication to activism. Maalouf's last words, delivered by the reader, are, "But the earth where you abandoned us still is the kingdom of deceit where innocents tremble." *La passion de Simone* has shown us courage, but Weil's struggle does not suffice. They admonish us to take up her cause, if not her cross, and to continue the fight against injustice.

## Only the Sound Remains

In their most recent collaboration, *Only the Sound Remains*, Saariaho and Sellars worked directly with one another to produce a libretto based on two Japanese Noh plays translated by Ernest Fenollosa and Ezra Pound. Both collaborators had long manifested a keen interest in this terrain: Saariaho had set part of Pound's *Cantos* in a chamber work for baritone, *Sombre*, in 2012, and Sellars staged *Tsunemasa* (the first of the plays set in *Only the Sound Remains*) in 1986. *Tsunemasa* and *Hagoromo* deal with encounters between humans and spirits who have not managed to complete their crossings. In the first, a priest conjures the ghost of a courtier who died in battle; in the second, a fisherman discovers a feathered cloak without which an angel cannot return to heaven.

Anyone who has tracked only Sellars's more activist trajectory might be puzzled by this esoteric turn. Yet as we have seen in these two collaborations with Saariaho, Sellars often concerns himself with the process through which a living being approaches death and attempts to move beyond it.[23] Saariaho's music palette proves especially compatible with this agenda given its ephemeral quality, with its many sound layers fading in and out. Recall that her technique is derived in part from spectralism, and she increasingly uses those sonorities in the service of representing specters. She seems to bring us to that glass through which Saint Paul could see only darkly, right to the instant when we can see face to face.

Noh challenges Western spectators in several ways, making this an especially risky project. First, its ancient texts allude to a wide network of poetic and theological traditions, all of them entirely alien to North American audiences. Second, they often relate stories in which the dead return—not a terrain guaranteed to attract attention of contemporaries unless the revenants happen to be vampires or zombies. Third, they feature actors in conventionalized masks that prevent facial expression. But most important, they unfold at a glacial rate: a single gesture might take a full minute to complete, up against an austere soundscape of slow vocal moans and flute glissandi punctuated with whacks on a dry-sounding drum.

Critics have sometimes complained that nothing happens in *Tristan und Isolde*, but Wagner's opera moves like an action film next to Noh. Of course, Sellars and Bill Viola brought something of a Noh aesthetic to the video footage in their *Tristan Project*, and Robert Wilson similarly adopts this kind of temporality in many of his productions. But taking on Pound's adaptations for operatic staging required a stubborn commitment on the part of Sellars and Saariaho. A friend of mine, also a director of abstract opera productions, complained to me after the Amsterdam premiere of *Only the Sound Remains* that nothing at all happens in it. If he even had difficulty with it, how could less adventurous viewers begin to make sense of this work?[24]

*Only the Sound Remains* has only two soloists: American baritone Devóne Tines, who plays the parts of the mortals in both halves, and French countertenor Philippe Jaroussky, whose high, crystalline voice provides the uncanny sound of the two spirits. Jaroussky needs no introduction, but Tines appeared to many of us to emerge out of nowhere when he sang Caroline Shaw's *By and By* with the Calder Quartet at the Ojai Festival in 2016.[25] Nora Koito Kimball-Mentzos, whom Sellars used to such extraordinary effect in *El Niño*, represents the visual dimension of the angel pressured to dance for the fisherman in exchange for the feathered cloak he has found and wishes to keep.

For his production, Sellars dispenses with the masks central to Noh—not surprising given his signature tight focus on the faces of his performers. In doing so, he violates a crucial tenet of this ancient Japanese genre, for we see modern realistic expressive gestures along with the oblique words they sing. But this decision fits with his career-long commitment to translating foreign texts—whether Mozart operas or Asian theater—into the emotional terms of his present day, Western audiences. In *Only the Sound Remains*, the strain of sustaining this double commitment—static texts versus mobile faces—challenges Tines and Jaroussky, who must present visual intensity and variety to lines that often have no obvious affective import. Especially in the filmed performances, Sellars strives to suture his viewers into the alien subject positions of priest and ghost.

*Only the Sound Remains* ventures into a new domain for Sellars: physical intimacy between two male characters. We might understand this as a manifestation of the phenomenon of Divine Union, which appears in so many of his works, including *El Niño*, *The Gospel According to the Other Mary*, and *L'amour de loin*. At least as far back as Bernard de Clairvaux, male theologians have wrestled with the homoerotic implications of welcoming penetration from the godhead: recall John Donne's shocking "Batter my heart," which Sellars chose for the climactic emotional center of *Doctor Atomic* (see chapter 4). But we usually try to push those implications to the side as mere metaphors.

In his book *Closet Devotions*, however, Richard Rambuss has insisted that we take at least some of these images at face value, as channeling the power of same-sex love.[26] The intensity of the exchanged gazes, embraces, caresses, and prolonged kisses in *Only the Sound Remains* makes it difficult to hold exclusively to a metaphorical reading of these scenes. If physical affection occurs between women throughout Sellars's oeuvre (recall the Countess and Susanna, Theodora and Irene, Kitty Oppenheimer and Pasqualita, Mary and her companions in *El Niño* and *The Gospel*), male intimacy still remains mostly taboo on the operatic stage—nearly five decades after Stonewall. Note that the Noh plays themselves do not call for any particular action. It is Sellars himself who chooses to render contact with the spirit world in this fashion, and he reports that Saariaho was shocked at and pushed back against his decision.[27]

Saariaho assimilates key elements of Noh into her orchestration, which features Camilla Hoitena on a variety of flutes, Niek KleinJan on percussion, the Dudok String Quartet, and Eija Kankaanranta on kantele—a traditional Finnish instrument that resembles a zither. I would guess that she and Sellars chose this one of these plays, *Tsunemasa*, in part because of its line describing the spirit, "only the thin sound remains," but also because of this extraordinary description by the chorus of the piece played on the lute at the climax of the play:

> A moon hangs clear on the pine-bough. The wind rustles as if flurried with rain. It is an hour of magic. The bass strings are something like rain; the small strings talk like a whisper. The deep string is a wind voice of autumn; the third and the fourth strings are like the crying stork in her cage, when she thinks of her young birds toward nightfall. Let the cocks leave off their crowing. Let no one announce the dawn.

The script itself, in other words, invites the composer to give a starring role to her native kantele, identified closely in this play with the ghost's beloved lute—the medium through which the priest summons him. In his staging, Sellars implies that the lute itself, which the priest cradles in his arms, actually becomes Tsunemasa, whom he later holds in similar fashion.

By means of this ensemble, Saariaho produces some of her most ethereal and eerie sonorities. For instance, she opens the first play, *Tsunemasa* (retitled "Always Strong") with the striking of a tam-tam. But she then picks up and amplifies the tam-tam's lingering overtones with overblown flute, plucked kantele, col legno strings, electronics, and nearly inaudible choral voices; she allows the listener to follow the process through which the gong's resonances seem to morph into a rich, complex soundscape. This pattern repeats several times, creating an ominous, even catastrophic atmosphere. When Tines first appears after about three minutes, he appears apprehensive, as though he too hears what we hear: he clutches his hands over his ears, for instance, in response to the sonic assaults. But those sounds might also represent his own terror at the conjuring he is about to attempt. The vocal quartet chants the name of the eponymous ghost with properly haunting timbres.

Synopses of the Noh drama identify Giokei as a priest ordered by a prince to perform a rite that will allow the departed Tsunemasa to turn to Buddhism. Because Tsunemasa served as a musician in the emperor's court before he died in battle, Giokei chooses to use his lute, Blue Mountain, rather than the more typical libation in his service. The summoned ghost of Tsunemasa arrives, first as a voice ("only the thin sound remains"), then eventually as a visible apparition. Neither spirit nor priest truly knows what is transpiring, but Tsunemasa eventually agrees to play a prayer on his lute. He sings:

A flute's voice has moved the clouds of Shushinrei. And the phoenix came out from the cloud; they descend with their playing. Pitiful, marvelous music! I have come down to the world. I have resumed my old playing. And I was happy here. All that is soon over.

When the Priest claims that he can see the figure, Tsunemasa demands that he extinguish the lights. The chorus reports on the conclusion:

The sorrow of the heart is a spreading around of quick fires. The flames are turned to thick rain. He slew by the sword and was slain. The red wave of blood rose in fire, and now he burns with that flame. He bade us put out the lights; he flew as a summer moth.

His brushing wings were a storm.
His spirit is gone in the darkness.

Sellars had to create a scenario that fleshes out this poetic and oblique script. An account of the play online describes it as having "an airy and light atmosphere" that entices many young actors to perform it.[28] I doubt that Sellars and Saariaho were aiming for "airy and light" in their rendering of Pound's translation. Instead, they focused on the erotic, seductive dimension of the encounter, as well as on the violence entailed in spirit possession—its literal violation of the natural order. We see no trace of anyone else ordering Giokei to undertake the séance; he seems to act on his own accord and yet greatly fears the transgression of summoning the ghost of Tsunemasa. Even in the opening section we see him nearly crippled by the aggressive attacks by the instruments and chorus.

Following the terse hints offered by the Noh play, Sellars produces a kind of plot (only slightly less elusive than the original) that resonates with a number of archetypes. Not content with hearing and even feeling Tsunemasa's presence, Giokei demands to see him, finally forcing a harsh light on him. This event occurs in the play, but Sellars's vivid staging brings to mind Psyche, who insisted on seeing her lover, Cupid, or Orpheus or, of course, Jaufré Rudel. In each of these, the failure of faith—the overwhelming craving for visual evidence—leads to tragedy and irrevocable loss.

The tension between sight and sound underlies not only the plot for this play but also the very center of this collaboration. Saariaho's score for *Tsunemasa*, mysterious yet viscerally powerful, presents Giokei's wracking internal conflicts and Tsunemasa's essence more concretely and in greater detail than can corresponding action on stage. Sellars knows this, and here (as elsewhere) he sets as his highest goal to make us attend to the music itself. He first chose Saariaho as an artistic partner and pushed her into writing opera because he perceived such dramatic intensity in her instrumental compositions. This piece, perhaps more than any others, realizes his dream.

Much of the mis-en-scène in *Only the Sound Remains* depends on the use of scrims and lights alone. As in so many of Sellars's productions, James Ingalls brings a kind of genius to his strategies, making it possible for Tsunemasa to appear behind veils or just as a looming shadow or on stage as if fully human. Moreover, Giokei himself sometimes projects an ominous shadow on the scrim: as he performs his service at the beginning, his own body casts a blood-red image behind him. Neither the priest nor the audience can locate the spirit's position or grasp its materiality, and the exchange of shadows often suggests that the ghost is a psychological projection of the priest's desires and anxieties—or, perhaps, a guilty recollection of events in which his own actions precipitated devastating consequences. Adding to the sense of dislocation in the video production, the camera often sweeps back and forth wildly across the abstract scrim painted by the celebrated Ethiopian American artist Julie Mehretu.

Sellars and Saariaho make Tsunemasa's entrance suitably astonishing. Tines has paced nervously, grasped at the air before him as low flute, then kantele, lead him to hope for success. Suddenly the light beams on an unveiled Tsunemasa. Jaroussky's high, clarion tones allow for the character to sound uncanny, and Saariaho has him perform extended melismas, thereby distorting words in a manner reminiscent of Orfeo's celebrated "Possente spirto"; the character even introduces himself singing "I am Tsunemasa," echoing Monteverdi's "Orfeo son io," in which the syllables dissolve into pure ornamental filigree, attenuating verbal meaning.

Yet both priest and ghost seem to experience excruciating physical anguish at this meeting between the living and dead—Tsunemasa at being called back to reinhabit his body, Giokei at having to accommodate the spirit within himself. For that moment of breakthrough, Saariaho's ensemble crescendos to an almost unbearable level. The merging of identities becomes clear when Jaroussky's giant, looming shade diminishes to the size of Tines's and then becomes one with it, their hands superimposed.

As in the Noh script, Giokei sometimes believes he sees, sometimes that he only hears what Tsunemasa refers to as "the faint sound alone that remains." Like so many other doubting disciples (Saint Thomas, Saint Peter), Giokei longs for certainty. As he asserts that he actually sees the form, Jaroussky's hand comes around behind Tines's head, bringing the sense of feeling to bear in what had previously remained as aural and visual imagery. They now face each other and nearly kiss before Jaroussky vanishes. The chorus sings of Tsunemasa's "unstillness": "His voice was heard there, a voice without form. None might see him, but he looked out from his phantom, a dream that gazed on our world." During this sequence, Jaroussky sings from behind the scrim as Tines bitterly laments this absence and conjectures that it all might have been but a dream.

In her writings, Saint Teresa of Ávila attempts to describe moments in which she experienced physical contact with Christ. These ecstatic spells brought radiant joy but also terrible pain. Teresa explains that not even she can determine when and how Christ will manifest himself to her; she can long for full disclosure and union but only rarely achieves that stage of rapture. So Tsunemasa moves in and out of degrees of revelation. No sooner does he touch Giokei than he evaporates. But hearing and seeing no longer suffice for believing, and the bond between priest and ghost moves beyond mere appearance and into the intensely erotic. Sellars, abetted by Saariaho's deeply sensuous music, makes explicit and elaborate this element perhaps only suggested in the play.

The focus shifts abruptly to Tsunemasa's reminiscence of his luxurious life at court as a lute player. He proposes to lead the priest unseen through his music. An extended passage for virtuoso kantele ensues, as Giokei lies prone, writhing, as though in a trance. Jaroussky comes to him, lies down beside him, and caresses him, perhaps bringing the trembling Giokei to climax. The spirit invites the priest to "look yonder," and Tines gazes in amazement at a revelation we cannot see. As the chorus sings the text quoted above ("A moon hangs . . ."), Jaroussky moves around to face Tines for a mutual kiss, after which they both turn toward the spotlight and audience; they have become equal partners, both deeply moved by this moment of contact. They proceed to make love, Tsunemasa now allowing Giokei to take the lead. Up against Saariaho's exquisite vocal quartet, Sellars here choreographs one of the most moving erotic scenes in his career.

But suddenly, with the references to the cocks crowing and dawn, Tsunemasa vanishes, and Giokei finds himself clutching at thin air, bereft. When Tsunemasa reappears to sing his final speech ("A flute's voice . . ."), Giokei violates their implicit contract by shining a bright spotlight on Tsunemasa's face. The ghost recalls the music he played and admits that he was happy on earth. But Giokei has become an aggressor now, announcing proudly that he can now see this figure, who cringes pitifully under the light. Like so many mythological characters, the priest triumphs in making his beloved visible, only at the expense of losing it all. Tsunemasa must shrink back into the underworld, and Giokei is left to gaze sorrowfully at his empty hands.

As the chorus sings "He slew by the sword and was slain"—a line originally referring only to Tsunemasa, Giokei takes upon himself the responsibility for having destroyed the spell through his lack of faith. He has in effect slain Tsunemasa all over again. Jaroussky hovers in a red light, now out of reach. The lights fade along with the sonorities, which dwindle to frail, thin scraping and patchy overtones. Sight has vanquished sound, and both evaporate.

• The second of the Noh plays in *Only the Sound Remains*, *Hagoromo* (here titled "Feather Mantle"), provides an uplifting counterweight to *Tsunemasa*. Although it also deals with human weaknesses, it rewards generosity. The play's opening chorus (not included in the opera's libretto) presents this following synopsis:

> The priest finds the Hagoromo, the magical feathermantle of a tennin, an aerial spirit or celestial dancer, hanging upon a bough. She de-

mands its return. He argues with her, and finally promises to return it, if she will teach him her dance or part of it. She accepts the offer. The Chorus explains the dance as symbolical of the daily changes of the moon. The words about "three, five, and fifteen" refer to the number of nights in the moon's changes. In the finale, the Tennin is supposed to disappear like a mountain slowly hidden in mist. The play shows the relation of the early Noh to the God-dance.

The original script itself merges the figure of the priest who introduces the action and the fisherman—both identified with the name Hakuryo—who performs the role of the antagonist to the Tennin (a spirit or angel).

The script's synopsis itself points to the greater stakes of this allegory. In exchange for the mantle, Hakuryo does not simply enjoy the aesthetic pleasure of a dance. Rather, the dance itself imparts wisdom and knowledge of the lunar cycles by means of which humans measure the passing of the seasons. Much as Moses climbed Mount Sinai to acquire the Ten Commandments, so this humble fisherman who rows to the isle of Miwo receives transcendent insights concerning cosmology, space, and time. As often occurs with prophets, Moses and Hakuryo (as well as Saint Hildegard von Bingen and Saint Teresa of Ávila, and many others) suffered physical pain when chosen to serve as conduits, and the nature of these holy transactions surpasses language.

If the opera stuck solely with the action described above, it would be over in short order. But although Sellars and Saariaho faithfully render the discovery of the mantle, the tug-of-war over its proper ownership, and the demanded dance, they care far more about the metaphysical dimensions of *Hagoromo*, about giving us some faint glimmer of what it would be like to experience a holy revelation. The play strives to accomplish this greater goal through its extended poetic verses for the chorus.

Sellars, however, has among his resources Saariaho's music, James Ingalls's evocative lighting, Nora Kimball-Metzsos's deeply expressive body, and the incandescent voices of Philippe Jaroussky and Devóne Tines. By means of these resources, he attempts to immerse us in a trance state that eradicates differences between Self and Other, human and divine, time and eternity. To be sure, not everyone responds enthusiastically to this project; one review contained the phrase "almost perversely unengaging" in its title.[29] Of course, Saariaho and Sellars knew this perfectly well in advance, but they undertook the risk nevertheless. Clémence's final surrender to God lasted only about six minutes. *Hagoromo* asks us to hang suspended in that state of suspended animation for almost its entire length.

In keeping with the prevalence of descriptive choruses that appear throughout the play, Saariaho's score for *Hagoromo* contains many lush numbers for her vocal quartet; indeed, she often sets parts of the script designated for characters for the chorus. Her score also features birdsong, a crucial dimension of her sonic aesthetic as well as that of her mentor, Messiaen, who understood birds as emissaries from heaven. If the kantele simulated Tsunemasa's beloved lute, the bird calls in *Hagoromo* refer sonically to the Tennin with whom this mortal interacts.

Sellars chose for his staging to present a double vision of the Tennin. As he did with the angel in his production of *Saint François* and with Mary in *El Niño*, he cast both a dancer and a singer in this role. Hakuyro perceives the uncanny phenomenon through all his senses, eventually even by means of erotic contact. If we count Saariaho's birdsongs, the angel manifests itself synaesthetically as nonverbal sonority as well as through sung lyrics, acting, and movement.

*Hagoromo* opens with Tines immersed in an enchanted landscape, simulated in sound by string instruments playing with increased ponticello and by bell-like tones on kantele and xylophone; he gazes around him with awe, apprehension, and supplication. In contrast with the eerie suspended animation that characterizes the island's mystery, Saariaho often accompanies Hakuryo's lines with rhythmic, agitated figures, in keeping with his worldly orientation.

The script indicates that the fisherman happens upon the feather mantle by chance. But Sellars has dancer Nora Kimball-Metzsos offer the sheer white robe to him, as if he were predestined to undergo this rite of passage. Kimball-Metzsos wears diaphanous, white attire; with her exquisite fluid motions—especially her hands—she resembles a creature attempting to take flight but condemned to earth's gravity without her mantle. We first glimpse Jaroussky when he sings "Pitiful, there is no flying without the cloak of feathers, no return through the ether." As the Tennin sings about helplessness without the robe, we see Kimball-Metzsos again, now fluttering and limping in despair. Hakuryo will eventually bargain to return the mantle in exchange for the Tennin's dance.

Up until now, Kimball-Metzsos and Jaroussky have become visible in alternation, with either sight or sound coming exclusively to the fore. With the negotiation, however, all three principals appear on stage, and Saariaho's score turns to delicate dance rhythms. And here Sellars ventures into the tactile, erotic dimension of the encounter. The dance, the induced trance, and the physical union between Tennin and human transmit to Hakuryo the secrets of the moon's seasons. The fisherman has received far more than he had bargained for, and Jaroussky kisses Tines at "I also am heaven-born."

The most extraordinary moment occurs when the Tennin sings "This is the dividing of my body." For the first time, Kimball-Metzsos and Jaroussky line up, their figures now resembling a multiarmed deity, as Tines kneels in reverence. Ingalls bathes the scene in golden light. Then, as Kimball-Metzsos continues her dance, Jaroussky and Tines begin to move in synchronized gestures, evidence that Hakuryo has internalized the Tennin's holy knowledge. Tines then bends to the ground, observing the earth with newfound wonder.

As Hakuryo commences his trip home from the enchanted isle, the music reduces to chimes and high, wavering pitches on violin and kantele. "Fuji is gone; the great peak of Fuji is blotted out little by little. It melts into the upper mist. In this way, she is lost to sight." Jaroussky continues to sing wordlessly above this shimmering sonority. And, as the opera's title proclaims, the sound remains, long after the lights dim and the final curtain.

•    *Only the Sound Remains* is the most recent of the compositions discussed in this book. No doubt, Saariaho and Sellars will continue to produce new pieces of music theater in years to come, but someone else will have to write about those. The next two chapters deal with recent productions by Sellars of much earlier works: Purcell's *The Indian Queen* and Bach's passions. Although these scores predate any of those discussed in previous chapters, Sellars's stagings of them could not have preceded his experiences with Mozart, Messiaen, Adams, or Saariaho. If they qualify as early music, they count for him as relatively late works—works that bear traces of a career-long series of advances and experiments.

# 6 • Peter Sellars's Mayan Passion

Always a stickler for fidelity to his texts, Sellars rarely allows cuts. Even when translating Mozart's *Figaro* from eighteenth-century Spain to New York's Trump Tower, he insists that the libretto be presented in the original Italian. Yet his experience with hands-on creation has often encouraged him to impose his own vision on some lesser-known operas from the past. In some cases, he has even inserted additional music into his scores. To be sure, he draws these supplements from the composers' own oeuvres. Nonetheless, he has given himself license to tamper not only with the settings but also with musical content and trajectories.

Sometimes these intrusions are relatively minor. In his 2008 production of Mozart's early Singspiel *Zaide*, for instance, Sellars interpolates entr'actes from the composer's *Thamos, König in Ägypten* to allow room for dramatic action. Given the opera's Middle Eastern setting, he also introduces improvisations on the oud during the opening materials. His Salzburg production of Mozart's *La clemenza di Tito* in 2017 includes sections from the composer's C Minor Mass and *Masonic Funeral Music*. And near the end of his staging of Tchaikovsky's *Iolanta*, he inserts the composer's sublime choral "Cherubs' Hymn," converting this strange, enigmatic fairy-tale into something resembling an oratorio. In all these productions, Sellars expands upon the scores in order to push the operas closer to his own artistic agendas: political tensions on the one hand, spirituality on the other. He treats Mozart and Tchaikovsky as collaborators—akin, perhaps, to Adams or Saariaho—to whom he might suggest alterations for the sake of enhanced flow, aesthetic effect, or contemporary social issues.

None of these precedents, however, could have prepared us for his reconstitution of Henry Purcell's *The Indian Queen* (2015). Purcell composed only one piece, *Dido and Aeneas*, that fits the criterion that an opera must be sung throughout,[1] and music historians have long treasured *Dido* as seventeenth-century England's principal contribution to the genre—even if we believed until very recently that Purcell wrote it for a girls' school.[2] Yet Purcell wrote a considerable amount of dramatic music for what he labeled as "semi-operas." In collaboration with John Dryden, the foremost poet and playwright of this period, he composed what we usually term "incidental music" to go with plays such as *Oedipus, King of Thebes, The Fairy Queen* (a revision of Shakespeare's *Midsummer Night's Dream*), and *The Indian Queen*.[3] Dryden's plays have long since fallen out of favor, removing the dramatic contexts for which Purcell designed these songs. Of course, singers have kept many of these alive: we know "Sweeter than roses" from recitals, not from *Pausanias, the Betrayer of His Country.* "Music for a while" works well outside its placement in *Oedipus, King of Thebes*—or at least it does so until the weird line about dropping snakes embarrassingly appears. And "I attempt from love's sickness" makes perfect sense as a conventional lover's plaint without reference to *The Indian Queen.*

Purcell composed something less than an hour of music for *The Indian Queen*, and his incidental numbers do not trace a compelling narrative trajectory by themselves. Moreover, the account of political machinations between the Incas and Aztecs penned by Dryden along with Richard Howard often stymies even literary historians who specialize in Restoration theater. The Indian queen referred to in the title, Zempoalla, has usurped the Mexican throne, which a young Montezuma wishes to reclaim. It presents, in other words, yet another play concerning rightful succession—a topic much obsessed over in 1660s England—though most of the plot focuses on the rival love interest of Montezuma and Acacis (Zempoalla's son) for the hand of an Incan princess, Orazia. All that gorgeous music with little of apparent interest to hang it on.

Although Sellars labels his new production "Henry Purcell's *The Indian Queen*," it has virtually nothing in common with the play for which the composer wrote his music. To be sure, all the music belongs to Purcell. But Sellars has culled it (with the assistance of Ryan Dudenbostel) from the extended works of Purcell: from other dramatic works, psalm settings, the song collection *Orpheus Britannicus*, and elsewhere, yielding a nearly four-hour orgy of some of the most effective and profound music of the entire seventeenth century.

But there remained the problem of the play itself. Sellars recalled encountering in the 1980s a novel by Nicaraguan writer Rosario Aguilar, and *La niña blanca y los pájaros sin pies* (*The White Girl and the Footless Birds*) suggested an alternative narrative.[4] Aguilar's novel concerns several generations of women during and following the Spanish conquest. One of the principal characters, a Mayan princess named Teculihuatzin, is given as a concubine to a conquistador, Don Pedro de Alvarado. Like Hernán Cortés, Alvarado relishes the exotic sexuality of his mistress but longs for a "proper" European wife.[5] Leonor, the daughter of their union, grows up despising her abject mother and only gradually comes to understand the horrendous circumstances behind her own birth and upbringing. A third woman, Doña Isabel (the Spanish-born wife of another conquistador), serves to bridge the gap between the warring factions, and her own daughter María wrestles with whether Spain or the New World counts as her rightful home.

As his choice of materials for *El niño*, *Doctor Atomic*, *The Gospel According to the Other Mary*, and his other libretti indicates, Sellars is a voracious reader of world literature. More often than not, he foregrounds the words of women such as Claudia Rankin, June Jordan, or Rosario Castellanos in his work, thereby giving voice to female and minority subjectivities. It is no accident that he collaborated with Toni Morrison on her revision of *Othello* from Desdemona's point of view. Not presuming to imagine for himself what it feels like to be a woman or black or Latina or pregnant or Native American, he scours poetry collections little known to most North Americans to articulate these experiences. Aguilar's novel gave him the words he needed to turn Dryden's play into a very different piece.

Several elements in Aguilar's novel appealed to Sellars. First, it concentrates on the stories and experiences of women rather than on the heroic feats of military leaders. Second, it engages critically with the social oppression of Latin Americans still very much with us. The challenge then was to fashion a scenario from *La niña blanca* that would allow for the showcasing of Purcell's music.

"Henry Purcell's *The Indian Queen*" qualifies almost entirely as a Sellars invention. Just as he relies on found materials in his Adams libretti, he weaves this piece from strands taken from Aguilar, whose words appear spoken by a narrator, and from Purcell's collected works. Although he does use all the numbers Purcell designated for *The Indian Queen*, he lifts most of the music for this adaptation from other contexts. Responsible now for both libretto *and* music, he creates a full-length opera that reveals most clearly his own dramaturgical inclinations. It will come as no surprise that his *Indian Queen* resembles a passion.

Sellars's opera plays out against brightly colored, pseudo-Mayan backdrops designed by Chicano artist Gronk (Glugio Nicandro). Although the Native Americans dress in traditional clothing, the conquistadors wear battle fatigues and carry automatic weapons, identifying them as members of a contemporary army sent to subdue and enslave an indigenous population. Here, as in his productions of *Theodora* and *Zaida*, Sellars reminds us that violent oppression scarcely stopped with the Romans and Spanish. The United States still subjects other peoples to our superior military might, and the problem of mixed-race children has left indelible traces of our conquests on the continent and around the globe for centuries.

As he usually does, Sellars has brought together an extraordinary group of singer-actors for this piece. Physically beautiful as well as musically brilliant, members of the troupe led by soprano Julia Bullock deliver a stunning and profoundly moving spectacle. For all that the plot hinges in part on racial conflict, Sellars casts African American, Asian, Latino, and European performers indiscriminately as Spanish or Mayan. His decision to do so shifts the emphasis from racial essence to the abuse of power—a constant in his productions.

When Sellars's *The Indian Queen* premiered, it garnered mixed reviews, many of the negative ones highly reminiscent of those that greeted the Mozart Trilogy. Critics wrote condescendingly of the attempt at connecting with political themes and of the use of the "semaphore" gestures. And almost all of them took issue with the very foundation of this project: the fact that Sellars saw fit to pillage Purcell's oeuvre for his own purposes.[6]

I happen to admire this production for several reasons. As someone who has studied Sellars's career, I see *The Indian Queen* as a crucial new stage in his creative trajectory, even as it resonates with nearly everything he has done up until this point. Moreover, the dazzling array of familiar and unfamiliar pieces by Purcell offered here ought to qualify as an unexpected bonanza; even baroque specialists will find new treasures here, all of them performed exquisitely. Finally, I find the cultural stakes of this staging timely in this period of undisguised racism in the North American political arena. Recall that Sellars compiled this work before we could have imagined that "Build the Wall" would become an election-winning mantra, before the United States started rounding up and deporting wholesale the descendants of the very people depicted by Dryden, Purcell, and Aguilar. In his *Le nozze di Figaro*, Sellars tried to warn us about Trump. *The Indian Queen* may address the abuses of the colonial past, but it means to serve as a wake-up call for citizens of today and tomorrow.

As Dryden and Purcell designed it, *The Indian Queen* resembles many a baroque entertainment in which a play is interrupted by interludes that foreground spectacle, dance, and extravagant music. The action stops altogether for these interludes or divertissements, which tend to operate according to conventional scenarios: pastorals, Hades, seascapes, military exercises, and so on. Each of these had associated instruments, and the same stage sets often reappeared in play after play; set designers were especially proud of their ability to simulate hell with, literally, smoke and mirrors.

Sellars had to figure out how to work within seventeenth-century musical conventions, which differ considerably from those of Handel or Bach. Whereas eighteenth-century composers relied on da capo arias, a structure Sellars had long mastered, their predecessors preferred free-form procedures: monodies that hover between recitative and arioso, strophic ditties, and the ground bass or ostinato—the cognate of "obstinate"—that features an obsessively repeating figure in the continuo. Each of these calls for a different dramatic response, and Sellars strives to match Purcell's musical strategies and their psychological implications in his staging.[7]

Dryden's and Purcell's piece has only five, widely separated musical sequences: the introductory instrumental music and allegorical prologue, a series in act 2 of choruses and solos in praise of the queen, a conjuring ceremony in act 3, a solo aria in act 4, and a sacrificial rite in act 5. None of these has a lot to do with Dryden's story line, and they did not give Sellars as a dramatist much to work with. Although he incorporates all these sequences, he had to figure out how to weave them into a plausible dramatic narrative. Moreover, he set himself the task of fleshing out that rich but relatively meager score with many more numbers in order to create a full-length opera. To that end, he adopted Bach's passion strategy: choruses of communal expression, airs sung by individual characters, and a narrator who provides continuity.

The other works discussed in this book come to us with full scores, and Sellars's contributions register up against those, even when he participates in the assembling of the libretti. But his *Indian Queen* requires me to shift gears, to tease out the logic by which he chooses particular musical numbers for his dramatic purposes. However well we may know the Purcell choruses or airs that appear in *Indian Queen*, they mean something radically different in their new contexts. I want to examine in some detail the ways he weaves together the various strands—Dryden's play, Aguilar's novel, Purcell's scattered music—to produce his own opera.

The original *Indian Queen* opens with a sequence of brief instrumental numbers. Designated in the score as First Music, Second Music, Overture, and Trumpet Tune, this series of dances and fanfares serves to showcase Purcell's musical brilliance before the play itself commences. Sellars uses this music to present what he calls "Five Mayan Creations": a ballet choreographed by Christopher Williams for four dancers who represent elements from the mythology recorded in *Popol Vuh*. Alternating between abstract gesture and steps that respond to Purcell's baroque grooves, they offer an impression of a prehistoric, perhaps even prehuman universe. Before and between the numbers, the sounds of the rain forest and distant drums surround the audience.

You might think of this ballet as Sellars's *La creation du monde* or *Le sacre du printemps*. Simulating the rituals of Others always raises questions of primitivism, and the cultural gulf between music of the baroque court we hear and the pre-Columbian figures we see deliberately shocks. To be sure, Sellars and Williams base many of their images on those of the ancient Mayans. But few viewers will bring familiarity with the *Popol Vuh* and its creation myths with them when watching this, and much of the dance may seem inexplicably opaque and even grotesque.

Halfway through his dance suite, Purcell inserts an overture, which opens with an anguished Adagio before moving on to its conventional Allegro. During the Adagio, Williams has the performers writhing on the floor, pulling their tongues out in a manner reminiscent of some of the violent images in *Popol Vuh*. If the sprightly dances that frame this moment make the Old and New Worlds seem compatible, the choreography for this slow section registers as disturbingly distant. Accustomed as I am to defending Sellars's strategies, I find myself averting my eyes during this section. I might have advised him to rethink his concept.

Dryden put Restoration-era English in Montezuma's mouth, making the chieftain a noble savage, a stand-in for the European aristocracy. But although Sellars strives to maintain the dignity of the Mayans, he also insists on radical difference, and his staging of this divertissement establishes a barrier between stage and audience. The people whose story we will follow do not share the backgrounds and values of most viewers; they remain in an important sense ineluctably alien. Sellars and Williams call upon us to witness their conquest. And with Purcell's Trumpet Tune, camouflage-clad Western soldiers creep warily onto the stage, assault rifles at the ready, accompanied by Gronk's painting of a military tank.

Following the introductory concert, Dryden presents a prologue in which two Natives—identified only as a boy and a girl—express fear that the Edenic world in which they live is threatened by long-prophesied invasions from the outside. Yet (this being a play presented from the viewpoint of an imperialist culture), the couple also longs for the salvation and superior civilization their vanquishers promise to bring:

If this be they, we welcome then our doom!
Their looks are such that mercy flows from thence,
more gentle than our native innocence.
By their protection, let us beg to live;
They came not here to conquer, but forgive.

The presentation in the prologue of a soon-to-be-destroyed paradise makes immediate sense for a Sellars project. Moreover, the abject words concerning the desire for European domination, rather than distracting from the matters at hand, actually seem to connect the Dryden play directly with the plot in Aguilar's novel, in which this Indian queen does indeed fall in love with her conquistador and suffers abominably as a result.

In other words, the tensions present in *La niña blanca* appear as if foretold in Dryden's own introduction. Sellars has his Indian queen and her attendant sing the prologue, thus stitching what had been a vaguely connected allegorical introduction onto the narrative itself. When the lines concerning the enemy's mercy appear, a missionary walks onto the stage. The two Natives subject themselves to him as though children before a paternal figure.

Several of the other sequences from Purcell fit without too much trouble into Sellars's schemata. It is in the context of an exorcism ceremony in act 3, for instance, that the queen sings the most familiar excerpt from *The Indian Queen*:

> I attempt from love's sickness to fly in vain,
> Since I am myself my own fever and pain.
> No more now, fond heart,
> With pride no more swell;
> *I attempt, etc.*
> Thou canst not raise forces enough to rebel.
> For love has more power and less mercy than fate,
> To make us seek ruin and love those that hate.
> *I attempt, etc.*

This air could well have seeded Sellars's entire project, so accurately does it encapsulate Teculihuatzin's predicament. As he stages it, the ministrations of her attendants cannot fix her, and she stands with the posture of a broken doll at the air's finish. During Purcell's "Third act tune," the Mayan gods move around her in a stately dance; she falls to her knees while reaching up to the heavens then collapses. Her mind has snapped, her will to fight extinguished.

Teculihuatzin will return briefly in act 4 to sing an air originally designed for Montezuma's Incan princess, "They tell us that your mighty powers above."

> They tell us that your mighty powers above
> make perfect your joys and your blessings by love.
> Ah! Why do you suffer the blessing that's there

to give a poor lover such sad torments here?
Yet though for my passion such grief I endure,
my love shall like yours still be constant and pure.

To suffer for him gives an ease to my pains;
there's joy in my grief and there's freedom in chains.
If I were divine he could love me no more,
and I in return my adorer adore.
O, let his dear life then, kind gods, be your care,
for I in your blessing have no other share.

Purcell sets this text as an elegant, simple minuet, its two verses separated by a rendition in the orchestra alone. In collaboration with conductor Teodor Currentizis, Sellars extends this scene by having the chorus sing the first verse after the queen has concluded it, then has one of the dancers perform the instrumental version. As Teculihuatzin sings, she loses strength, reclines, and scarcely breathes the final word. She has died. The music Purcell composed for act 5 accompany a ceremony, and Sellars has no difficulty staging that as the queen's funeral rites.

But the musical sequence in act 2 presents thorny primitivist problems. Following the symphony, a series of marches and songs appears—in Dryden to introduce the queen onto the stage for the first time. As a time-out for music and dance, it resembles the divertissements in French court spectacle and hearkens back to earlier English masques. Divertissements frequently exploited the representation of exotic (and safely conquered) people. Indeed, when enthusiasm for the *tragédie en musique* waned after the death of Lully, opera-ballets such as Rameau's *Les Indes galantes* offered just such song-and-dance scenarios, showcasing their versions of one ethnic group after another.

Dryden and Purcell insert a struggle for domination between the allegorical figures of Envy and Fame into the midst of their celebration, and Sellars stages the debate as a collision between the two still-hostile groups, with a tribal shaman singing the music designated for Envy. But alas for today's political sensibilities, Dryden has Envy open with the text: "What flatt'ring noise is this, at which my snakes all hiss?" Such imagery is standard fare for incantation and sorcery scenes, long staples of opera (even Purcell's *Dido*), but it takes on vastly different meanings in the mouth of a Mayan priest. Later, in act 3, Dryden gives full vent to eighteenth-century European fantasies concerning pagan religions, with verbal imagery recalling that of Shakespeare's Weird Sisters in *Macbeth* or of the Sorceress in Purcell's *Dido*, designed to produce a horrified frisson in his London audience:[8]

By the croaking of the toad
in their caves that make abode,
earthy dun that pants for breath
with her swell'd sides full of death,
by the crested adder's pride
that along the cliffs do glide,
by thy visage fierce and black,
by the death's head on thy back,
by the twisted serpents plac'd
for a girdle round thy waist,
by the hearts of gold that deck
thy breast, thy shoulders, and thy neck,
from thy sleeping mansion rise
and open thy unwilling eyes,
while bubbling springs their music keep,
that used to lull thee in thy sleep.

I don't know that anyone could salvage the air "By the croaking of the toad," especially with its hopping figure in the accompaniment. Although Luthando Qave's performance is electrifying, especially his truly scary rendition of the chromatically ascending line on "from thy sleeping mansion rise," the text remains risible. I usually defend Sellars's gestures, but the Mickey Mousing by the queen's attendants has the effect of forcing the listener to hear as literal the creepy-crawlies in Dryden's text. In my view, a more metaphorical reading might have served better the very high stakes of this scene—much higher in Sellars than in Dryden.

Sellars had to tread very carefully in presenting this material anew, given his own ethical investments. Yet true to his principle of sticking faithfully to his sources, he goes ahead and stages Dryden's primitivist fantasy—literally ("by the croaking of the toad") warts and all. Although he tries to maintain our sympathy for the Mayan characters, Sellars does put those toxic words back into their mouths.

He does much better when he can leave Dryden behind and finds his own materials in Purcell's broader oeuvre. His first interpolation occurs at the beginning of Part I: "Oh solitude," an air Purcell set to a text by Katherine Philips, sung by the wife of one of the conquistadors who develops a powerful bond with the Mayans over the course of the opera.[9]

Oh *Solitude*! my sweetest Choice!
Places devoted to the Night,

remote from Tumult, and from Noise,
how ye my Restless Thoughts delight!
Oh Heavens! what Content is mine,
to see those trees, which have appear'd,
from the Nativity of Time;
and, which all Ages have rever'd,
to look today as fresh and green,
as when their beauties first were seen?

O how agreeable a sight
these hanging Mountains do appear,
which th'unhappy would invite,
to finish all their Sorrows here;
when their hard Fate makes them endure,
such Woes, as only Death can cure.

Oh! how I *Solitude* adore,
that Element of noblest Wit,
where I have learn'd *Apollo's* Lore,
without the pains to study it:
For thy sake I in Love am grown,
with what thy fancy does pursue;
but when I think upon my own,
I hate it for that reason too;
because it needs must hinder me
From seeing, and from serving thee.

Many elements in this text fit Doña Isabel's situation and Sellars's plot perfectly: the longing for relief from the situation in which she finds herself, her admiration for the primordial forest, and her sympathy for the persecution of the Native population.

But just as important as the text is the music. Like many of Purcell's most effective tunes, "O solitude" unfolds over a tortured ground bass—an obsessively repeating pattern that cannot find rest. Beginning with an extraordinary leap downward of a seventh followed closely by a drop by a diminished fourth, the melody twists and turns above the bass, but to no avail. We will watch as this character administers to the Native population, attempting to embody that "goodness" for which the prologue's duo had hoped. Yet even though she resides on the side of the powerful Spanish, she lacks the power as a mere spouse to intervene in matters of state.

A second interpolation accompanies the consummation between Teculi-huatzin and Don Alvarado. As the couple first begins to make love, her attendant sings "Sweeter than roses," a song Purcell composed for Richard Norton's play *Pausanias, The Betrayer of His Country* but identified here by the narrator's introduction as a song of the queen's people.

> Sweeter than Roses, or cool Ev'ning Breeze,
> on a warm Flowry shore,
> was the Dear Kiss; first trembling made me freeze;
> then shot like First all o're.
> What Magick has Victorious Love,
> For all I touch or see;
> since that dear Kiss I hourly prove
> all is Love to me.

First shyly, the queen begins to caress her ambivalent spouse. Then, following the script prescribed by Norton's lyrics and Purcell's erotic music, she arouses him to "the Dear Kiss." They reach a simultaneous climax at "what Magick." Sellars required no nudity to execute this erotic sequence; Purcell's music does it all.

Later, the narrator tells of ongoing atrocities on the part of Don Alvarado and his inability to bestow mercy. Consequently, it may come as some surprise when precisely this character takes up the theme of penance in Part II. Up until this point, we have not heard Alvarado sing, and so great is Noah Stewart's physical beauty that one might have assumed he was a model or dancer. But sing he does, presenting one of the great monodies of the seventeenth century, Purcell's setting of George Herbert's devastating "With sick and famish'd eyes."

> With sick and famish'd eyes,
> With doubling knees and weary bones,
> To thee my cries,
> To thee my grones,
> To thee my sighs, my tears, ascend:
> No end?
>
> My throat, my soul, is hoarse;
> My heart is wither'd like a ground
> Which thou dost curse.
> My thoughts turn round,

And make me giddie; Lord, I fall,
Yet call.

Bowels of pitie, heare!
Lord of my soul, love of my minde,
Bow down thine eare!
Let not the winde
Scatter my words, and in the same
Thy name!

Look on my sorrows round,
Mark well my furnace!
O what flames! What heats abound!
What griefs! What shames!
Consider, Lord! Bow thine ear
And hear!

[flamenco interlude added]

Lord Jesu, thou didst bow
Thy dying head upon the tree:
O be not now
More dead to me!
Lord, heare! Shall be that made the eare
Not heare?

Behold, thy dust doth stirre;
It moves, it creeps, it aims at thee:
Wilt thou deferre
To succour me,
Thy pile of dust, wherein each crumme
Sayes, Come?

My love, my sweetnesse, heare!
By these thy feet, at which my heart
Lies all the yeare,
Pluck out thy dart,
And heal my troubled breast, which cryes,
Which dyes.

Continuing with the early seventeenth-century fascination with echoes,[10] Herbert ends each stanza with a truncated line of two syllables that completes the rhyme while twisting the knife of irony. "With weak and famish'd eyes" ranks with John Donne's "Batter my heart" (set in *Doctor Atomic*) among the great mystic poems in the English language. But Sellars did not need to turn to a contemporary composer in order to include this searing text: Purcell had already done it for him.

Sellars choreographs this monody in ways that highlight the chromatic twists and turns of Purcell's extraordinary setting. No gesture, no matter how extreme, takes place without harmonic justification. In singing this, Don Alvarado demonstrates at least a deep level of inner torment if not exactly remorse. Although she tries to assist, his wife watches helplessly as he writhes in the throes of agony, recalling his misdeeds.

One extraordinary rhetorical move occurs just before the verse that begins "Lord Jesus." As Herbert shifts from matters of internal guilt to a vision of Christ on the cross, Purcell moves to a harmony meant to sound like an abrupt change of gears. Instead of having the bass line press on immediately, conductor Teodor Currentzis has the continuo instruments dwell on that chord in suspended animation and asks them to embellish it with flamenco-style figurations. Herbert himself was deeply influenced by Spanish mystics such as Saint John of the Cross, and this moment offers a prolonged dark night of the soul.[11] Though anachronistic, the intrusion of flamenco is not altogether arbitrary, for it recalls Alvarado's now-distant homeland. In performance it seems that Alvarado is paralyzed by that vision—or perhaps by his fervent desire to be granted that vision. The bass begins to move again only on the word "head."

The insertion of this penitential monody allows Sellars to elevate Alvarado from outright villainy. In doing this, he departs from Aguilar and freights in one of his own moral priorities. Recall his emphasis on the moral weaknesses of Count Almaviva or Don Alfonso and the ways he enacts on stage the process of redemption. He does not, in other words, castigate his male characters for the sake of the women he seeks to champion but always insists on their fundamental humanity; if these men are irredeemable monsters, we will not identify with them and will learn nothing.

In keeping with the theme of penitence, Sellars also interpolates passion-like choruses from Purcell's sacred repertory. As in Bach's passions, these choral insertions step aside from the action to comment or to react. Near the beginning of Part I, a makeshift congregation of Natives appears, performing "O sing unto the Lord" (Psalms 104:33–35).

[33] I will sing unto the Lord as long as I live: I will sing praise to my God while I have my being.

[34] My meditation of him shall be sweet: I will be glad in the Lord.

[35] Let the sinners be consumed out of the earth, and let the wicked be no more. Bless thou the Lord, O my soul.

Initially this seems like the prayer of new converts, as aural evidence of the missionaries' success, as well as a manifestation of the framing choruses Sellars has long drawn from Bach's dramaturgy. Yet the choristers raise their voices at gunpoint, recalling the coerced praise chorus in *Boris Godunov*. When the psalm reaches verse 35 concerning sinners, soldiers draw out a few individuals and summarily execute them while the terrified, cowering chorus continues to sing.

If Purcell's music stands as a pinnacle of European civility, the culture that produced it was soaked in blood—including even the imposition of European sacred music. Gary Tomlinson has written about the conquistadors' particular fear of Native music and their attempts to stamp it out at all cost.[12] The acquiescence of the Indians to Christianity and its liturgical practices did not stop the carnage. The genocide of Native peoples and the destruction of their cultures in the Americas has continued unabated, as has the wanton murder of African Americans by government agents. Smartphones have made it possible for us to witness on a numbingly regular basis how the police gun down nonwhite males (some of them, like Tamir Rice in my city of Cleveland, mere children). Most of the critics who mocked Sellars's political thrust in *The Indian Queen* do not live in this environment.

Continuing in oratorical mode, Sellars interpolates another biblical text, thus presenting two choral numbers in a row. In celebration of the marriage, the choir sings "Blow up the trumpet in Sion," Purcell's setting of Joel 2:15–17:

[15] Blow the trumpet in Zion, sanctify a fast, call a solemn assembly:

[16] Gather the people, sanctify the congregation, assemble the elders, gather the children, and those that suck the breasts: let the bridegroom go forth of his chamber, and the bride out of her closet.

[17] Let the priests, the ministers of the Lord, weep between the porch and the altar, and let them say, Spare thy people, O Lord, and give not thine heritage to reproach, that the heathen should rule over them: wherefore should they say among the people, Where is their God?

As with the previous numbers, it seems as if this text had been designed for this situation in *The Indian Queen*. Joel's verse 16 refers directly to a wedding ceremony he enjoins the entire community to attend, and Purcell's incipit passes an exuberant fanfare through the entire chorus. But Joel opens his chapter 2 by defining this trumpet as an alarm announcing a kind of apocalypse; indeed, his entire prophecy describes in graphic detail the day of destruction rained down by the Lord upon an Edenic world for all those who do not call upon his name. In its original scriptural context, the bridegroom and bride register only as elements of a traditional society, tenuously going forward through matrimony, childbearing, and old age even though threatened with annihilation. And verse 17 brings this all home with weeping priests who pray for deliverance from the heathen and even wonder whether God exists.

Sellars's chorus comprises singers dressed in both Native and Spanish attire, for this ceremony represents a political union between the two peoples. But the sentiments of the words resonate more directly with the condition of the Mayans, gathered there with extended families. On "Sanctify the congregation," soldiers once more herd the Natives into a huddle at gun point. Verse 16 ushers in the bridal couple, and both communities appear to join forces at least for the moment. Teculihuatzin (renamed Doña Luisa after her conversion) and Don Alvarado depart for the marriage bed but with expressions of grave concern.

With Joel's verse 17, the staging allows the weeping priests and "the heathen" to refer both to the pagans, again threatened with weapons, and also to the Christians imposing their faith most brutally on the heritage of Others. Rendered ambiguous by Sellars's narrative context, the final line—"Where is their God?"—will reverberate throughout the remainder of the opera. Each time this line repeats, the gap between "where" and the rest of the query grows longer, with existential angst marking the faces on both sides of the aisles.

The production's first half concludes with the chorus lying as if dead on the stage. From that posture they sing—along with a cluster of soldiers and Catholic priests—Purcell's gut-wrenching setting of another apocalyptic text, Psalms 102:1: "Hear my prayer, O Lord, and let my cry come unto thee." When the music stops, Alvarado steps forward to survey his handiwork. then charges offstage. Gradually the soldiers file out, with a sorrowful young priest departing last. The red lights linger for a very long time on the prostrate bodies. Sellars reports that audiences in Madrid were particularly shocked by this sequence. Yet although the events depicted refer to the Spanish slaughter of indigenous people, the camouflage and assault rifles relate to present-day military aggression by the United States. Just as Bach had to set biblical texts that blamed the Jews but always hastened to take responsibility onto himself and his congregants, so Sellars seeks to indict not sixteenth-century conquistadors but rather his fellow citizens.

If the first half of Sellars's opera focused on the first encounters leading up to the conquest, the second deals with the challenges faced by survivors in cobbling together new identities out of the shards of their forever-broken world. They now suffer in the aftermath of cultural genocide: the traumas of split families, prohibited religious traditions, and children of mixed race whose genetic composition bears permanent witness to historical violence.

In fact, Rosario Aguilar frames her novel with the recollections of a con-temporary Nicaraguan woman whose ill-fated affair with a Spaniard leads her to think back through her own ancestry. Doña Leonor, the daughter of the Mayan princess and the conquistador, passes for white—as did my own grandmother, whose name, Bennie Fawcett, appears on the rolls of the Cher-okee Nation but who hid that heritage from her children and grandchildren for our sakes.[13] In repudiating her background, she protected us from the prejudice and even shame we would otherwise have experienced. Millions of us with Indian blood share Aguilar's sense of lost ties and impossible choices made by mothers and daughters navigating hostile social environments.

Although it details the horrors of military conquest, the core of Aguilar's *La niña blanca* lies here with these women and the consequences for them. Sellars departs for quite a while from Dryden's script in order to pursue this theme in his Part II. As it turns out, Purcell's oeuvre offers a rich array of op-portunities for exploring these new directions. Indeed, some of the most re-markable moments in Sellars's *Indian Queen* appear here before he returns to the original playbook for an incantation scene and the final funereal rites that conclude both versions.

Sellars opens Part II with a penitential hymn Purcell set to an unidenti-fied text, "Remember not, Lord, our offences." Dressed now in contempo-rary garb rather than the costumes of Part I, the chorus faces the audience to ask forgiveness for intergenerational guilt.

Remember not, Lord, our offences
nor the offences of our forefathers.
Neither take Thou vengeance of our sins, good Lord,
But spare us, good Lord.
Spare thy people whom thou has redeemed
with thy most precious blood,
and be not angry with us forever.

Purcell's wrenching harmonies hold up in comparison even with the introductory chorus of Bach's *St. John Passion*. As in a Bach passion, the audience is encouraged to understand the events that follow not as a tale from the distant past but as grievances we continue to perpetuate in our own lives.

Sellars has the chorus sings the word "Remember" twice in isolation from the rest of the text before the hymn proceeds on to "Remember not." Huge silences separate the iterations of this word. If the burden of the text begs for the Lord not to recall, Sellars here enjoins his audience not to forget. At one point, the chorus steps decisively forward, bringing the address even closer to the viewers. Sellars also makes extensive use of his gestures of supplication he uses to such effect in *Theodora*, the passions, and elsewhere. The hymn ends almost below the level of audibility and on a chord that registers as inconclusive.

The ensemble appears again as the queen is dying in act 4, her daughter having just spurned her. Here Sellars inserts Purcell's setting of Psalms 6, "O Lord, rebuke me not," for two solo sopranos and chorus. Resonating with Christ's passion, this anthem also invokes age-old customs in which women assume the task of grieving for the community as well as for themselves.

[1] O Lord, rebuke me not in thine anger, neither chasten me in thy hot displeasure.
[2] Have mercy upon me, O Lord; for I am weak: O Lord, heal me; for my bones are vexed.
[3] My soul is also sore troubled: but thou, O Lord, how long?
[4] Turn thee, O Lord, deliver my soul: oh save me for thy mercies' sake.
[5] For in death no man remembreth thee, and who shall give thee thanks in the pit?
[6] I am weary of my groaning; ev'ry night wash I my bed and water my couch with my tears.
[7] My beauty is gone for very trouble and worn away because of all mine enemies.
*Turn thee, O Lord, and deliver my soul: oh save me for thy mercies' sake.*

In ominous red lighting, a procession of the dispossessed slowly files in, bearing placards as if in a protest march. A drone begins low in the bass, over which the continuo instruments weave flamenco-like arabesques. Isabel (the conquistador's wife) begins singing an intonation that sounds like a Middle Eastern lament, with angular augmented seconds and wavering ornaments.

At last, Currentzis allows Purcell's harmonic progression and rhythmic impulses to take hold, and Isabel sings the opening phrase of "Oh Lord, rebuke me not." We might expect that the music's momentum will continue. But the continuo halts again, and now Teculihuatzin improvises over that unmeasured drone. Purcell's excruciating dissonances grind between the two solo voices, especially verse 4, in which Isabel reiterates the pitch on "O" without resolving it. Purcell's chorus enters in support only for that line, "Turn thee, O Lord," after the soloists have completed it, and all forces return to it as a refrain to complete the setting. Surely one of the most searing expressions of penance in the repertory, "O Lord, rebuke me not" ushers in the opera's final sequence.

For one more divertissement remains for Dryden's play: act 5 opens with an Aztec altar prepared for the sacrifice of Montezuma himself. Over the course of the act, the political tides will turn, sparing him but not his adversary. Sellars refashions this rather incongruous sequence into a funereal rite for Teculihuatzin—not an easy transformation to achieve. Still, Purcell did provide ceremonial music, and this fits the new context quite well.

The shaman arrives to lead the ceremony. As he confronts Alvarado as one of those Dryden has labeled in his lyrics as "unhallow'd souls," the chorus circles the body of Teculihuatzin:

All dismal sounds thus on these off'rings wait,
your pow'r shown by their untimely fate;
while by such various fates we learn to know,
there's nothing, no, nothing to be trusted here below.

The camera trains tightly on the distraught shaman's face, then on that of Alvarado, who hovers over his dead wife. As the chorus reaches its nihilistic conclusion, Teculihuatzin rises to her feet, her hands fluttering upward to trace the path her soul is taking.

Sellars took a great many risks when he decided to construct his own version of The Indian Queen. Most of them, I think, paid off: I particularly admire the ways he weaves Purcell's anthems and airs to create this large-scale work, and he inspires extraordinary performances from his cast. But his initial decision to maintain all segments of the Dryden-Purcell collaboration intact brought with it some unfortunate racial issues—something that would not have bothered Purcell's original audience but that would certainly raise the political hackles of my students. There is considerable irony in the fact that a work that intends to help undo the damage visited upon Latin America by the conquistadors happens to drag Dryden's imperialist rhetoric along with it.

Sellars developed his *Indian Queen* at the same time he was staging the Bach passions in Berlin, and the powerful influence of Bach's dramaturgy can be felt throughout his posthumous collaboration with Purcell. But, as we have seen, Bach's passions have hovered over virtually everything Sellars has done. My final chapter turns finally to those performances in Berlin.

# 7 • Back to the Source

## The Bach Passions

The convention of quasi-theatrical performances of those portions of the Gospels relating the betrayal, trial, and crucifixion of Christ dates back to medieval times. During Holy Week services, the clergy would occasionally distribute roles among a few singers, some intoning the narrative portions of the scriptures, others presenting the words ascribed in the gospel texts to Pilate, Peter, Judas, or Christ. During the Renaissance, as polyphonic practices developed, composers sometimes set the text in the contemporaneous fashion of motets, which lessened its dramatic impact considerably. But the seventeenth century saw the rise of the *stile rappresentativo*. First applied to pastoral plays in northern Italian courts, this set of techniques allowed performers to sing a script all the way through. The resulting genres of opera and secular cantata emerged and flourished, initially in Italy, then throughout Europe; the oratorio developed by midcentury as a way of relating Bible stories to devotees by means of the operatic medium.

In 1700, Erdmann Neumeister published *Geistliche Cantaten* (*Spiritual Cantatas*), a collection of libretti designed to merge Lutheran materials (e.g. chorales or quotations from the scriptures) with the recitative/aria pairs then fundamental to operatic dramaturgy. The German cantata quickly became the centerpiece for upscale church services, and composers such as Georg Philipp Telemann and J. S. Bach wrote hundreds of them during the next few decades. Conservative congregations often complained that such works brought the opera house into the sanctuary, but their condemnations did little to stem the tide.

Almost immediately, similar libretti for the passions began to appear, the most famous among them Barthold Brockes's 1712 *Der für die Sünden der Welt gemarterte und sterbende Jesus* (*Jesus, Martyred and Dying for the Sins of the World*). As in the Middle Ages, eighteenth-century German passions pre-

**163**

sented the biblical text itself intact, with one singer—called the Evangelist—assigned to sing the gospel narrative and others to present the roles for which the Bible offers direct speech. Also present, however, were chorales familiar to congregants, as well as operatic recitatives and arias in which individual voices reflected upon and reacted to the recounted events.

Bach's passions flow directly from these traditions. Although he never wrote an opera as such, Bach reportedly loved taking his sons with him to attend the opera house in Dresden. Yet the recent merger of Italian operatic styles with Lutheran church music invited him to exercise his dramatic talents. He composed his *St. John Passion* in 1724, soon after his arrival in Leipzig, and the *St. Matthew* followed three years later in 1727; his settings of Saint Mark and Saint Luke do not survive. As he might have anticipated, some members of his congregation carped about his hauling secular theater into the Holy Week services. In other words, Bach's passions and cantatas, like those of his contemporaries, already violated the boundary between sacred and profane genres. And beginning with Felix Mendelssohn's famous revival of the *St. Matthew* in 1829 (an event that marks the widespread rediscovery of Bach),[1] the passions moved into the concert hall, leaving far behind the church services for which Bach had composed them.

Before examining Sellars's staging decisions, I want to mention some of the ways Bach has already imbued his passions with dramatic flair. Bach is responsible, for instance, for shaping the dialogue that allows each character to come vividly to life with just the right melodic intervals, rhythmic declamation, and chord progressions. No one ever wrote more dynamic recitative than Bach, and one of the joys of watching Sellars's performances is getting to recall how genuinely outrageous Bach could be—something obscured by many traditional performance practices.

Several of the coups de théâtre that may startle viewers of Sellars's productions already exist in the score. The most obvious of these are earthquake scenes, for which Matthew's graphic description of temple curtains ripping, graves opening, and the dead walking bears much of the responsibility. Bach leapt at the chance to experiment with musical imagery of catastrophe, long a staple of operatic spectacle. In fact, so enamored was he of this scene that he cut and pasted this part of Matthew's text into his libretto for the *St. John*, for John had neglected to mention the violence God unleashed when his son died. Bach's sweeping scales in these scenes of divine retribution come straight from French *tragédies lyriques*, the low tremolos from Monteverdi's *stile concitato*, the ominously rising chromatic bass line from all those incantations through which sorceresses in Venetian opera conjure up demons (compare this with the end of *Don Giovanni*), the distraught Evangelist from any number of seventeenth-century mad scenes.

Moreover, Bach controlled the pacing throughout, deciding when to offer affective relief from the unrelenting horror of the passion narrative and when to knock us upside the head. Sellars does everything he can to highlight these dimensions of Bach's score, but he does not invent them. For instance, it is Bach who precedes the earthquake sequence in the *St Matthew* with a somber presentation of the Passion Chorale. He takes us from the most profound moment of contemplation to hellzapoppin' special effects. Throughout the passions, Bach revels in quick affective turnarounds, constantly catching the listener off guard in order to bring home an important rhetorical point. When the apostles at the Last Supper ask, "Lord, is it I?" in response to Christ's prediction that one of them will betray him, the chorus pivots from its spiky "Herr, bin's ich?" to the chorale "Bin ich, ich sollte büssen"—It is I, *I* should atone. Bach does not allow his congregants to feel superior to or distant from the naive disciples but immediately sutures them into those subject positions with one of their own hymns (a contrafactum of Heinrich Isaac's pre-Reformation "Innsbruch, ich muss dich lassen"). He repeats this strategy in Part II, when a jeering chorus asks mockingly, "Who has struck you?" juxtaposed again with "Innsbruch," with new lyrics that deflect the blame from the mob to the congregants. In fact, he had already exploited precisely this connection, complete with the "Who has struck you" contrafactum of "Innsbruch," in Part I of the *St. John*.

As mentioned before, Sellars already aspired to stage Bach's *St. Matthew Passion* when working as a Harvard undergraduate with Craig Smith at Emmanuel Church in Boston. Smith had proven game when Sellars experimented with some of the cantatas, but he drew the line with the *St. Matthew*. Yet, as we have seen, the Bach passions have cast a shadow over nearly all the work Sellars has produced over the course of his career. Those weighty choruses—one by Palestinians, the other by Jewish Israelis—that frame *The Death of Klinghoffer* owe their genesis to "Kommt, ihr Töchter," the choral lamentation that opens *St. Matthew*. Indeed, the drift toward oratorio we have seen in his libretti and in his stagings, perhaps even as early as in his staging of Mozart's finales, can be traced to his lifelong obsession with these overwhelming compositions. Only in 2010 did he collaborate on this monumental task of staging the *St. Matthew* with Sir Simon Rattle and the Berlin Philharmonic; in 2014 they presented their version of the *St. John Passion*.

Sellars's calls his staging of the passions "ritualizations," a term he has used to describe many of his other efforts as well (see chapter 2). In highlighting ritual, he draws attention away from the usual trappings of stage works—costumes, plotlines, scenery (the *St. Matthew* features only a bier; the *St. John* eschews even that prop). Instead Sellars focuses on those elements that a society needs to repeat in order to strengthen its ties to the past and to pass its cultural values on to subsequent generations. Surely the prescribed reading of the four Gospels' accounts of the passion during Holy Week counts among Christendom's highest ceremonies. Over the course of his tenure at Leipzig, Bach performed his settings many times.

The two productions share many theatrical strategies. First, Sellars involves the musicians of the Berlin Philharmonic, along with the handful of period-instruments players brought in to supply obbligato parts for which modern instruments cannot adequately substitute. Not only do the players sit center stage, but the choristers and soloists move around in their midst, making them participants in the unfolding narratives. In rehearsal Sellars had the choristers face the orchestra when they sang, so that the orchestra members would pick up on their expressive nuances. "The chorus gave personal responses, and so the orchestra gave personal responses—not as a corporate member but individual artists."[2] In performances, the chorus entreats them, as it does the assembled audience, to bear witness and to share responsibility for the martyrdom.

Sellars regards Bach as having composed this feature into the double forces required for the *St. Matthew*. In his words, he and choral conductor Simon Halsey envisioned

> this space with two choruses, two orchestras facing each other, where there's no proscenium, where people are performing *into* each other, and what you're getting is a community engaging with itself, and you're watching a community work through the issues together. . . . Bach wrote the music of that kind of mutual engagement and mutual regard, and one of the most moving things is one orchestra has to listen while the other orchestra plays, one chorus has to listen while the other sings. So equal time is spent playing or singing and listening silently, having to be receptive and take something in. As a performer you're usually putting stuff out, and what's so fulfilling about the structure of this piece is you spend half the night having to open yourself to receive, which for an orchestra member or chorus member is extraordinary.[3]

During the arias, Sellars often has the vocalists face and interact with the obbligato instruments that play along with them. He sometimes even requires the instrumental soloists to memorize their parts, dispensing with the mediating presence of the score. In so doing, he insists that all the performers engage bodily and emotionally in this social ritual of penitence; he leaves no room for bystanders.

Moreover, he wants to make the viewer acutely aware how Bach produces his effects, the ways he weaves his lines together in taut, sometimes confrontational counterpoint. This is the same impulse that frequently leads Sellars to include dancers, as, for instance, in the opening tableau of *Doctor Atomic* or the close of *Nixon in China*. As we watch virtuosos execute the fiendishly difficult parts Bach has written for them, we see them struggle kinetically, pushed to the very limits of their technical capacities. If many stage directors strive for verisimilitude, thereby distracting spectators from the means of production, Sellars enjoins us to attend to the music in all its complex detail, which is where he locates affect and the essence of the drama.

Second, both productions feature tenor Mark Padmore as the Evangelist, the designated messenger of bad tidings. The Evangelist knows the horrors and despicable deeds he will have to recount to his flock, and some of Bach's most dissonant and chromatic harmonies occur in his recitatives. As he often does, Sellars trains the camera tightly on Padmore's stricken face so that we see the effects of Bach's anguished changes; his sorrowful face often recalls paintings by El Greco. Yet even while thoroughly embodying those twisted progressions, Padmore seems to address us directly and utterly without artifice.

Sellars not only has Padmore sing the parts designated for the Evangelist, but he also has him engage in the dramatic action, variously assuming the poses of the tortured Christ or performing the deeds ascribed to Jesus in the Gospels. In doing so, he offers himself as an ideal role model. If Bach intended his congregants to experience rather than simply witness, Padmore illustrates with his own body how deeply we should feel the events onstage.

Third, Sellars finds ways of presenting the passion characters in theatrical scenarios. Needless to say, the trial and execution of Christ remain central. But Sellars goes much further, especially in his horrific depiction of torture in the *St. John*. Few basses singing the role of Jesus have had to withstand the physical punishment he metes out on Roderick Williams. The stories concerning Peter's denial, Pilate's interrogation, and Joseph of Arimathea's request to bury the body also receive vivid stagings, with soloists sometimes interacting with those singing the scriptural lines.

The two productions also share tenor soloist Topi Lehtipuu and bass Christian Gerhaher. Anyone inclined to intertextuality will note that Gerhaher sings the role of Jesus in the *St. Matthew*, and he acts the parts of both Peter and Pilate in the *St. John*. The Gospel according to John focuses particularly on the travails of Peter in the first half of his narrative, on those of Pilate in the second half. Drawing on this structure, Sellars shapes the *St. John* around these bass characters, making it nearly as much their passion play as it is Christ's. Gerhaher sings both roles, as well as the bass solos typically performed by a separate vocalist, thereby forging significant connections between Peter and Pilate and the sentiments voiced in the contemplative arias. I will return to the consequences of these strategies below.

But Sellars's most daring moves involve the soprano and alto soloists. In Bach's day, boys or countertenors would have performed the arias designated for these voice types. Sellars not only hired women to sing these parts, but he gives them consistent roles: the soprano as a mother (of Judas Iscariot, of the sons of Zebedee, of Jesus himself) and the alto as Mary Magdalene. In the production of the *St. John*, soprano Camilla Tilling wears blue and alto Magdalena Kožená red, the colors conventionally assigned respectively to the Blessed Virgin and Magdalene in traditional iconography.

As it happens, Camilla Tilling was pregnant during the performance of the *St. Matthew*, Magdalena Kožená during the *St. John*. Sellars not only makes use of the fact that these performers are female but also of their impending motherhood. We already know from many of his other projects (e.g., *El Niño, Adriana Mater*) how deeply the phenomenon of motherhood matters to Sellars. While never deviating from Bach's score, he positions Tilling in the *St. Matthew* as Judas Iscariot's mother.

I want to trace the way Sellars draws upon the work of Bach and Picander (librettist and collaborator for the *St. Matthew*) to weave her into this side narrative. The Evangelist has just turned from his account of the woman who bestowed precious ointments on Christ to introduce Judas and his demand for thirty pieces of silver. At this point, the soprano sings "Blute nur, du liebes Herz" (Bleed only, dear heart), a lament that might come from anyone observing the betrayal. But as Tilling sings the B section of the aria ("Ah, a child that you raised, that suckled at your breast, threatens to murder its guardian, for it has become a serpent"), she holds her pregnant belly, aware of the terrible consequences of bringing this infant into the world.[4] The aria becomes very particularly the expression of a woman who bewails the treachery of her still unborn child in the aria. When she returns to the da capo, the chorister who has voiced Judas's line strides menacingly in front of her and the Evangelist. Whereas she sang this part of the text first while walking onto the stage, the realization of the B section and the vision of her miscreant son force her to the ground; she sings the da capo leaning on the bier singing of her own anguish as well as that of the buried Christ.

The next passage takes us to scene of the Last Supper. As they hold each other's faces, the Evangelist confirms to Judas that he is indeed the betrayer. But when Jesus blesses the bread that is his body, Padmore offers this sacrament to Judas, who will sit and partake of it beside the bier. The wine he presents to Judas's mother, who now realizes that she has paved the road to redemption, and she beams in gratitude at Padmore throughout her next aria, "Ich will dir mein Herze schenken" (I want to give you my heart). As Tilling finishes her joyous aria, her son stands and strides purposefully off to commit his criminal deed. Sellars has taken several successive units of the passion and tailored them to dramatize the trials of a woman who gives birth to a monster—but a monster who proves to be part of God's plan. The Communion ritual here involves only Judas and his mother, which elevates them substantially as characters.

Sellars's strategy for the *St. John* has Kožená impersonate Mary Magdalene as the expectant lover of Christ. I will deal with these sequences below. But suffice it to say for now that Sellars insists here—as always—on the centrality of women and their experiences.

Although they share the same basic modus operandi, Bach's two passions have remarkably different priorities, in part because of the ways Matthew and John wrote their scripts. Matthew's account emphasizes Christ's benevolence in the face of death, and he makes use of relatively few direct quotations. Picander tilted his interpolated arias toward the contemplation of affects such as remorse, guilt, and gratitude.

Saint John's Gospel, on the other hand, aims for immediate dramatic effect, with rapid-fire exchanges between antagonists: Simon Peter versus those who seek to identify him, Pilate versus the crowd, Pilate versus Jesus. Writing much later than Matthew, after it had become clear that most Jews would not convert to Christianity, John presents the Jews in direct quotations as they scream at the Roman governor for Jesus's blood. When Bach duly sets this text, he does so with the precision and rhetorical intensity only he could summon. Over and over again, the Evangelist sings: "Die Juden aber sprach" (but the Jews said), answered by a chorus of rabid avengers. So savage are these sections that many of us feel the need to address the issue of anti-Semitism in classes before having students listen to the piece. Musicologist Michael Marissen has written in depth on this problem, for the *St. John Passion* continues to disturb.[5] Indeed, Bach strove for nothing less.

Sellars had to confront this explosive issue when he decided to stage these works. In an interview concerning the *St. Matthew*, he comments:

> The Jewish choruses—[there is] a very complicated history of those things. We have received a performance tradition of how to perform

the music of the Jews that is, frankly, anti-Semitic, and I don't think Bach's score is anti-Semitic. But the way we have been taught to expect to hear these choruses is. How do we detox that? How can we imagine that these are also human beings, and how do we imagine that Bach wrote music for human beings? Why would he not have written human music for the Jews? . . . We need to rethink it from the ground up, we need to go back to the score, which has no tempo marking and no dynamic marking. Why does it have to be fast and loud and stupid? Why can't it be mysterious and strange and have a whole range of feeling and a whole range of haunted, conflicted hurt, anger, regret, confusion, and deep understanding?

I am not entirely sure Sellars—or anyone else—succeeds in "detoxing" these sections, though the performance of "Sein Blut komme über uns," the chorus in *St. Matthew* in which the crowd accepts that Christ's blood will be on them and their progeny, does exactly what he suggests: the choristers sound and look as if quietly contemplating the magnitude of what they have done. Filled with remorse, they complete the chorus on their knees.

But being faithful to the affective nuances of Bach's music often means presenting a hysterical mob specifically identified as Jews, especially in the *St. John*. To be sure, the same choristers who scream "Kreutzige!" also perform the comforting chorales and interact sympathetically with the soloists. But the words Saint John gave to the Jews and Bach's powerful setting of them overwhelm any attempt at softening. Still, however violent, these voices ring as authentically human—perhaps all too human. We have heard their like at Nuremburg rallies and, more recently, at Donald Trump's rallies at which his followers chanted, "Lock her up!": a slogan uncomfortably close to "Kreutzige!"

The dramatic impulses of the two passions lead Sellars to very different theatrical solutions. Yet he does not willfully impose these choices on the pieces. He derives them rather—as did Bach—from the narrative strategies of the individual apostles themselves.

For his staging of the *St. Matthew*, Sellars presents a tableau in which the characters we observe are watching beside the tomb, recalling past events.[6] He uses a minimal set: an austere bier in the center of the stage in front of the orchestra. Christian Gerhaher, the bass delivering the lines Matthew ascribes to Christ, stands in the balcony. When he sings, a spotlight causes him to emerge from the darkness in a kind of halo, similar to the red print with which many Bibles highlight Christ's words and to the warm string accompaniment in which Bach envelops his statements. Visually the lighting recalls the chiaroscuro effects of, say, Caravaggio. With this arrangement, Sellars underscores the fact that Jesus is already dead when the passion begins. The onstage personae hear his voice only as if in their memories; they do not interact with him or look in his direction. From the very first chorus, they devote their attention to the bier and to each other.

If Christ appears in this production as a recollected voice, his body enters the action by way of Padmore's performance. At times he serves only as the conveyor of Matthew's narrative text, a task that clearly weighs heavily on him. When the lights first come up, he sits in deep meditation, girding himself to undertake the difficult journey that lies ahead of him. Over the course of the performance, he frequently seems to lose heart and has to force himself onward. Although the ritual telling of this story drains him of emotional energy, he still must fulfill his role as the leader of this spiritual community regardless of the personal costs. Sellars and Padmore worked to strip away much of the continuo support conventional for recitation. This minimal accompaniment allows Padmore great rhythmic freedom, especially for the very long silences he often indulges in, and it leaves him sonically isolated.

But Sellars also directs Padmore to identify with Jesus as he narrates, thereby animating the events. In the scene of the betrayal, for instance, Judas approaches the Evangelist and kisses him; the two exchange a long gaze of mutual hurt yet deep understanding concerning their respective destinies. When the tenor sings vividly of Christ's anguish at Gethsemane, Padmore lies down on the stage to pray. So devastated is he by his sleeping disciples that he requires the soothing aria "Gerne will ich mich bequemen," sung touchingly by bass Thomas Quasthoff, who gently embraces the Evangelist and reminds him why we have to go through this wrenching ritual. The gestures of mutual tenderness delivered by the alto as the Magdalene similarly involve Padmore's body. When the Evangelist reports the flogging, he mimes being bound at the stake and convulses as if feeling the whip himself, calling attention to the twisted harmonies Bach gives him by writhing as if in great pain. And as the account of the burial unfolds, he lies stretched out on the bier. The implicit identification of the preacher with the story's protagonist makes Christ's physical agony far more immediate, insisting that viewers too grasp the enormous suffering reported in the scriptures.

John's Gospel, however, focuses much more on the vivid description of ongoing events. For his production of the *St. John*, Sellars switches to action mode. Bass Roderick Williams both sings and acts the part of Jesus, and we see his body subjected to scourging, binding, and torture. When the crowd comes to arrest Christ, one of them—played by the tenor soloist—blindfolds him and pushes him to his knees. Williams spends much of the production's length in that posture under a harsh interrogation lamp. Sellars never loses sight of contemporary social issues, and here, as in *Theodora* and *The Indian Queen*, he draws important parallels to Abu Ghraib, Guantánamo, and other recent human rights abuses perpetrated by the United States. He does not permit the viewer to transcend into abstract contemplation but insists that we acknowledge the experience of torture inflicted upon human flesh, both then and now. He requires us to view Jesus as the political prisoner he actually was.

Both productions foreground the relationship between Jesus and Mary Magdalene, whom the Gospels place at the crucifixion and the tomb; she will be the first to view the risen Christ. In Sellars's productions, the alto soloist manifests an unusual degree of physical intimacy with Christ, whether represented bodily on stage by Padmore or by Williams. But Sellars does not make this up. He draws on a tradition that goes back to the gnostic gospels and even the scriptures in which the apostles express jealousy at the Magdalene's special status.[7]

Long before Dan Brown's *The Da Vinci Code*, artists and writers had considered the bond between Jesus and Mary Magdalene as one of lovers or spouses. Brown argues that Leonardo included her in his painting of the Last Supper, Metaphysical poet Richard Crashaw nearly exhausted the ways she related to her Savior in his "The Weeper," and Girolamo Frescobaldi composed a monody in which Mary achieves Divine Union with Christ at the foot of the cross.[8] Bach's Pietistic background made him particularly susceptible to tropes of erotic bonding with Jesus,[9] and Mary fits well within such scenarios.

This character first enters Sellars's staging of the *St. Matthew* as the Evangelist describes the scene in which a female devotee anoints Jesus's head with an expensive ointment. Matthew does not name her, but John relates much the same story in which Mary, the sister of Lazarus, anoints Christ's feet with costly spikenard and then dries them with her hair (John 12:1–8). In both scriptures, the disciples object vehemently to this squandering of resources, but Christ defends the woman for preparing his body for burial and demands that she be remembered for all time. John Adams and Sellars base much of their *The Gospel of the Other Mary* on this episode (see chapter 4).

Sellars identifies the woman here with Mary Magdalene, another woman Jesus defended against his followers. As Padmore sings "Kommt zu ihm ein' Weib," Magdalena Kožená enters as if summoned. During his recitative and Christ's peroration from the balcony, Kožená and Padmore gaze into each other's eyes and embrace tenderly. The care this woman lavishes on Jesus's living body, her grief that it will soon be taken away from her according to his own prophecy, become palpable. We are used to thinking of this body principally as the locus of torture. To reimagine it as a site of pleasure and eros puts the emphasis on his profoundly human dimension.[10]

Picander's alto recitative and the aria "Buß und Reu" follow, and Sellars's setup now illuminates the corporeal aspects of this pietistic text. Kožená continues her anointing gestures, adding her tears as precious liquids—as does Crashaw's weeper. Bach accompanies this aria with two intertwining flute lines, thereby simulating lovemaking, as he does so often in his duos.[11] Sellars does not have the flutes act anything out, yet he features them visually, making sure the viewer understands their contrapuntal interactions as the mutual affection between the soul and Christ.

| | |
|---|---|
| Buß und Reu | Penance and remorse |
| knirscht das Sündenherz | make the sinful heart break |
|   entzwei; |   in two; |
| daß die Tropfen meiner | so that the drops of my tears |
|   Zähren |   may offer |
| angenehme Specerei | pleasing spices |
| treue Jesu, dir gebähren. | to you, dear Jesus. |

But his staging of the return to the aria's A section brings out a different set of metaphors potentially present in Bach's music: the image of violent sundering.[12] The two flutes start their lines in unison, then diverge, and the text refers to the ways remorse rips the heart in two. Here Kožená places her fists together on Padmore's chest then forces them apart for the "knirscht" as if rending soul from flesh. Sellars comments:

> Bach is more the composer of doubt than of affirmation, the music is at its most intense depicting struggle, depicting the divided mind, being torn apart.... "Knirscht" from "Buss und Reu"—he gets his music language from that *knirscht* of the spirit and the body, the *knirscht* of the person you want to be and the person you are every day instead, the struggle between your multiple selves and your multiple impulses and what you've achieved and what you've totally failed to achieve. And that struggle is at the heart of the composition.

At the end, as Kožená realizes that she will have no further contact with this beloved body, she reluctantly leaves the stage and a visibly heartbroken Padmore behind. It takes him a very long time to compose himself sufficiently to continue his narrative.

Bach opens Part II of the *St. Matthew* with the alto searching for her Jesus, to which the chorus replies: "Where has your friend [Freund] gone, you most beautiful of women?" Allegorical readings might link this woman with the Daughters of Zion summoned in the opening chorus, but Sellars identifies her more specifically as the Magdalene—the individual who will indeed show up at the empty tomb looking for him. As she laments, the female choristers try to calm her, gently caressing her. But she recoils in horror, imagining "her lamb is caught in the claws of a tiger." As she becomes increasingly distraught, Padmore rushes to embrace and comfort her. Bach's aria ends on a half-cadence, however, and Kožená holds his face, aiming the question directly at him: Where has my Jesus gone? After a long pause, Padmore recites to her the next part of his ritualized narrative: Jesus has arrived at the court of the High Priest.

Later, when Matthew's narrative proceeds to the flogging, Kožená races onto the stage, alarmed at the turn of events, while Padmore assumes Christ's position. Bach's orchestra slashes violently as the alto prays for God's intervention, then harangues the torturers—both choral and orchestral—to cease. In her aria "Können Tränen meiner Wangen" (If the tears on my cheeks), she recognizes the impotence of her weeping and offers her heart in exchange. As she sings, her face distorted by rage and horror, Kožená attempts to soothe Padmore's shredded back with her tears and cradles his broken body to her own. Recall that the Magdalene once anointed Christ's feet with her tears and wiped them with her hair.

The image of Christ nailed to the cross might have inspired an expression of deepest agony. During the alto ritornello "Ach Golgotha!," Kožená does indeed contort her body as if hanging on the cross. But in her subsequent aria, "Sehet, Jesus hat die Hand," Bach and Picander choose to read his outstretched hands as reaching out to embrace us, and the aria moves along with a rejoicing dance rhythm. In Sellars's production, Kožená spins slowly in ecstasy, then invites the choristers to join her in Jesus's arms. They reply in puzzled monosyllables as she pulls up one person after another to participate with her; she even gives the concertmaster a peck on the cheek. Now that she has glimpsed the divine plan, she can convert the horror of this scene into a spectacle of triumph.

In his staging of the *St. John*, Sellars raises the stakes even more concerning his linking of the alto with the Magdalene, for Kožená was pregnant when she performed this role in Berlin. She dashes onto the stage just after Jesus has been bound. During her aria "Von den Stricken" (From the bonds), she addresses him but also gestures for assistance from the Evangelist and flails in anger at the prison guard. At the end of the first strain, she kneels and kisses Jesus, who smiles tenderly and embraces her; later he mouths what seem to be words of comfort to her while she sings. When the initial set of words return, she returns to the mode of the penitent Magdalene for whose sins Jesus will sacrifice himself. As he often does, Bach accompanies this aria with two instruments (oboes in this case), the lines of which simulate lovemaking.

Koženás other solo in the *St. John* appears just after Christ has uttered his last words, "Es ist vollbracht," which Bach then expands into an aria. Sellars had positioned Kožená and Tilling as two of the Marys at the foot of the cross, supporting him as he is given vinegar to drink and as the soldiers cast lots for his clothing. As she sings "Es ist vollbracht," Kožená hovers over the dead Jesus, holding his hand. Bach creates searing dissonances between the voice and the accompanying viola da gamba, and the performers hold onto these as if trying to maintain life in this unresponsive body. But Bach also broke convention in this aria by inserting into it a defiant warlike section, "Der Held von Juda siegt mit Macht" (The hero of Judah fights with might), reminding us that this death is only a step forward on the path to victory. Kožená stands to sing this section in defiant triumph. Yet the reality of the death itself impresses itself again as the aria goes back to its initial words. Kožená stops for long pause before conceding to the return, and when she goes back to her former place on stage, Jesus's body is no longer there. She kneels, groping for it, smiles sadly inhaling his scent. She holds her last appoggiatura for a very long time, finally resolving by herself without the attendant instruments.

Sellars's other major interpretive intervention shapes his staging of the *St. John*. The score features only two major speaking characters other than Jesus and the Evangelist: Peter dominates Part I and Pilate Part II. As mentioned above, Sellars has Christian Gerhaher perform both roles, thereby suggesting significant parallels between the two.

No one viewing Gerhaher's distant performance of Christ in the *St. Matthew* could have anticipated the acting acumen he brings to these roles. Whether as Peter or as Pilate, he offers a figure of male authority brought low by cowardice. Each one believes in Jesus yet fails to stand up for what he knows is right. Saint John's Gospel makes both dangle for a very long time in indecision before they cave in to external pressures. In an important sense, they are the principal figures of this morality play, and Sellars's staging invites us to see them as sharing the same basic decency and the same inability to act.[13] Sellars says of the moral struggle in Bach's music:

You take each step with Bach, and Bach takes you and guides you though the next steps of your life, through turning things around toward recovery. . . . The reason there's so many notes is because the path is steep toward changing your own life. And the reason Bach is making the most extreme demands of the instrumentalists and the vocalists is because changing your life is really hard, it involves thinking you can go forward and you go back, you're making progress but then you lose the way, so it keeps repeating, but not quite, the actual struggle in the phrases; and of course these amazing moments of harmonic convergence where even when you stumble actually the harmony tells you you're coming home. And this incredible way in which Bach puts hope even in the most tortured path is through these incredible moments of harmonic enlightenment where you sense even at the crisis point that you're coming closer to your real self and that you shouldn't give up, you should keep going, and Bach uses the harmonies to keep drawing you on.[14]

Gerhaher's haunted face and abject posture tell us everything we need to know about these men. When Gerhaher then moves from portraying scriptural figures to singing an aria, "Eilt!" (Hurry!), in which he urges the racing choristers to rush to Golgotha, he does so not as the standard bass soloist but as an extension of the dramatic figures he has been playing.

The very short Part I of the *St. John* contains only three arias, the first of which, "Von den Stricken," I discussed above. The other two respond explicitly to the Evangelist's references to Peter: the first a neutral mention, the other after the denial. But even before Peter enters into the gospel text, Sellars highlights his role as antagonist in this first half of the narrative. When the chorus has concluded its gloomy introduction (see below), the Evangelist enters accompanied by Jesus and Peter. As he describes the arrival of the disciples at the garden, Peter and Jesus silently embrace, their bond still firm; a few minutes later, Jesus will show deep affection while admonishing Peter for having used his sword. Even during the marital interpolation between Jesus and the Magdalene, Gerhaher sits dejected at the lip of the stage. The Evangelist goads him to turn around to face what both know will prove an excruciating trial.

An innocuous line—"But Simon Peter followed after him"—leads into the soprano aria, "Ich folge dir gleichfalls" (I follow you likewise). This perky, childlike number may be read as ironic, given the circumstances, or perhaps as a reminder (especially when sung by an innocent boy soprano) that we all intend to follow Jesus, however we much may fall short. Although Camilla

Tilling performs the music Bach wrote, Sellars keeps our attention focused on Peter.

As she begins, Tilling follows behind Jesus, shadowing his welcoming motions. Then she and the Evangelist try to encourage Peter, who stands diffidently across from Jesus. As Jesus walks toward him, holding out his arms, Peter stumbles forward a bit before recoiling in fear. Again they all try to strengthen his resolve, and with baby steps he falls into Jesus's arms. During the da capo, Williams mimes washing Peter's feet and giving him the first communion.

Many moments from the story of Peter come to mind here: his reckless attempt at walking on water, from which Jesus must rescue him, and his presence at the Passover seder at which the foot-washing and communion ceremonies take place. None of these appear in the libretto. But with Tilling as a gentle mother, Jesus as loving father, the Evangelist as an avuncular figure, Sellars stages a moving family drama in which a toddler learns to walk. Peter qualifies as an exemplary failure in most of the stories involving him, yet Christ chose him to lead the Church, and Sellars invites us to see him as beloved despite his flaws, as an infant in the faith who will eventually (but not yet) grow to fill the role for which Christ ordains him. The choreography of "Ich folge dir gleichfalls" allows us in the subsequent scene to watch Peter's attack with his sword and his fearful denials as evidence of human weakness, heartbreaking yet all too familiar. Jesus has forgiven sins even this horrendous in advance.

The narration focuses next on Jesus's arrest and the beginning of the physical abuse meted out on him. Sellars shows him blindfolded (incidentally, by Topi Lehtipuu, the tenor who will sing the next aria), thrust under a harsh interrogation lamp, and struck in the face. Throughout these events, Gerhaher looks on passively. The spotlight then turns to him as various individuals identify him as a disciple, which he vehemently denies. When the cock crows after his third refusal, the Evangelist reminds him of Jesus's prediction. He crumples to the floor in deep shame; the Evangelist kneels beside him to describe his bitter weeping, then lies down beside him, implicitly making his own human shortcomings parallel to those of Peter.

Although Gerhaher remains lying on the floor, it is the tenor aria "Ach, mein Sinn" (Ah, my troubled mind) that gives voice to his intense blend of remorse, denial, and hopes of self-annihilation. Lehtipuu races onto the stage, stares at the writhing Gerhaher, flees up the stairs, then returns to embrace Jesus. Bach gives this aria no da capo: it leaps in anguish from emotion to emotion, none of which serves as a solution to Peter's guilty conscience. Indeed, the composer offers no real respite at all but instead ends Part I with a moralizing chorale about Peter, drawing a stern connection between his hubris and our own.

Part II opens with a stern chorale that leads into the action of the trial. Or perhaps it is not a trial. Sellars explains:

> In the Book of John, there's no formal trial. You get what we would now call extraordinary rendition or extrajudicial execution. Jesus is kidnapped at night and moved from one basement to another, where random people interrogate him unofficially. And then he's brought to the Roman court but kept in the basement. There's no record of the trial. And Pilate is furtive, going to him in his interrogation cell and then coming out and talking to people in the lobby. At no point are we in a formal courtroom or formal trial. So you get this scabrous, disgusting perversion of justice which is someone deciding—this guy has to go. And then what the deals that have to be made, who pressures whom, who says "OK, I'm looking the other way." So the piece has this weird, furtive side and at the same time this in-your-face level of violence. Whereas the time we're living in, where in my country the crowd votes for violence, the crowd votes for maximum violence, and you're getting the angry, violent temper of our societies, where people are really voting for something aggressive and out of control level of response. So those images of people who are being rendered in some Black Site. What we forget is the fact the world will hear their truth, that truth will come out of that basement cell and echo up around the planet.[15]

Now representing Pilate, Gerhaher sits with his back to the chorus; Lehtipuu, who reassumes his duties as guard, prods the blindfolded and bound Williams back onto the stage and under the interrogation lamp. The Evangelist enters and kneels beside Jesus.

Sellars has the choristers end their chorale with their backs turned. But when Pilate requests that they tell him the charges they bring against Jesus, they spin around angrily to sing their denouncements: "If this man were not a malefactor, we would not have delivered him up to you!" As mentioned above, Sellars worked to "detoxify" the choruses sung by the Jews. But not much can be done to counter the viciousness of Bach's writing here, with its rising hysteria and repeated "nicht, nicht, nicht, nicht!" And so the staging follows the music: the choristers point accusingly at Pilate, their faces distorted in fury. Padmore looks on in shock, Gerhaher in bewilderment.

In an interview, Sellars addresses Bach's dramaturgical strategy for these choruses:

The Book of John is deeply anti-Semitic, and it attacks Jews every time it has a chance the whole length of that book. So what Bach does is every time there's a painfully anti-Semitic comment in John's gospel, Bach interrupts the narrative and says, "I'm sorry—we can't accept this, and we will answer this with a chorale that I'm now inserting here." And that chorale says, All of us just killed Jesus again this morning. This is not about the Jews—it's about us.

To be sure, Bach does dot this horrific scene with chorales, though we sometimes have to wait uncomfortably for them to show up. After "Wäre dieser nicht ein Übelthäter" we also get "Wir dürfen niemand tödten" before the chorus repents with "Ach, grosser König." Yet the transformation of those vicious faces into attitudes of supplication does offer some solace. As Sellars points out, Bach does his best to edit John's text, and Sellars tries to convey Bach's interpretation. If the ceremony requires the ritual repetition of John's words, these interpolations can push them in a different, more humane direction.

When the action resumes, Pilate interrogates Jesus, who answers stoically. Twice Gerhaher inflects his words with facial expression: once when he spits out indignantly, "Am I then a Jew?" and second when he asks, "What is truth?" With the latter, his voice trails off and he gazes at the floor, his own metaphysical angst surfacing. The chorus continues to alternate between its murderous taunts and loving chorales: at one moment they scream for blood, at the next they express their adoration, creating a whiplash effect.

The Evangelist has principally stuck to the business of narrating. But he loses control entirely when the mob begs for Barabbas: he shrieks. "But Barabbas was a murderer!" then melts down in a grotesque melisma meant to simulate flogging. In other words, Bach has him step out of the neutral zone and move toward stirring up violent indignation in his listeners; he participates in the anti-Jewish foment usually identified with the chorus. When the preacher himself explodes, how are his parishioners to remain objective? This is Bach at his most dramatic—and also most problematic, and Sellars does not try to diminish the effect.

Bach pulls away from this nuclear moment to invite his congregants to contemplate the long-term purpose of Christ's torture. In his staging of the *St. Matthew*, Sellars keeps the vocalists who perform arias separate from those who sing passages from the scriptures. But at this point in the *St. John*, he has Gerhaher depart briefly from his role as Pilate to sing the arioso "Betrachte, meine Seel'" (Consider, my soul). He does not do this for want of additional vocalists, which traditionally just get culled from the chorus, but rather to link the activities of this particular character with the lyrics of the arioso. In breaking the realistic representation we have been watching, Sellars also reminds us of its artifice much as Brecht did.

In the contemplative arioso, accompanied so gorgeously by two violas d'amore and lute, the bass reflects on how the agonies we witness can convert into sources of bliss for the believer. Gerhaher interrupts Pilate's interrogation here to amplify the ambivalence he has already displayed but also to call to mind the spiritual benefits of these deeds. Up against the very gentle throbbing of the instruments, he sits singing while the Evangelist attempts to soothe the wounds. Only at the end does Gerhaher look up as if searching for hope.

| | |
|---|---|
| Betrachte, meine Seel' mit änstlichem Vergnügen mit bittrer Lust und halb beklemmtem Herzen | Consider, my soul, in anxious pleasure, in bitter joy, with a heart torn between grief and consolation, |
| Dein höchstes Gut in Jesu Schmerzen, wie dir aus Dornen, so ihn stechen, die Himmelsschlüsel- blumen blühen; Du kannst viel süsse Frucht von seiner Wermut brechen, drum sieh ohn' Unterlaß auf ihn. | how Jesus's suffering is your highest good. Think how from the thorns that pierce him the primroses spring; You can derive sweetest fruit from his wormwood, so fix your gaze on him. |

If images such as wormwood in the bass's arioso seem far-fetched to us, the tenor aria goes much further in the direction of pietist excess. The poet invites us to compare the lashes on Christ's back with the sign God gave Noah as a promise not again to destroy the earth by way of flooding. Bach took this metaphor very literally in his setting, in which the two violas d'amore and the bass line continually trace out arch shapes; he festoons his score with big and little rainbows.

| | |
|---|---|
| Erwäge, wie sein | Consider how his back, |
| blutgefärbter Rücken | stained with blood, |
| in allen Stücken dem | is just like the sky. |
| Himmel gleiche geht. | |
| Daran, nachdem die | After the floodwaters of our |
| Wasserwogen | sins |
| von unsrer Sündflut sich | have passed by, |
| verzogen, | |
| der allerschönste | the most beautiful rainbow |
| Regenbogen | appears |
| als Gottes Gnadenzeichen | as a sign of God's grace. |
| steht! | |

During both arioso and aria, the spotlight remains focused on Jesus's prone body. Gerhaher and Lehtipuu sing in semidarkness, lit with by a dark blue light. If Gerhaher remains absorbed in guilt, Lehtipuu goes through a kind of conversion process over the course of "Erwäge." He moves from his position as flogger and stands looking at the body, as if viewing his own deeds. The middle section, however, takes him up to stand with the chorus, and the lengthy melisma on "Regen-BOG-en" seems to take him into another realm. By the time he reaches the da capo, he has redirected his words to address individual choristers, pointing to Christ as he explains the mystery. He ends kneeling over the body and attempting to soothe the injuries. The torturer's conversion may recall the way Sellars presented the Roman soldiers in *Theodora* abandoning their master to sing a hymn glorifying the Christian God. Even the most bestial of sinners may find redemption.

But the beautiful parenthesis allowed by these two numbers has to end. The Evangelist brings us back, as he must, to the scripture with its accounts of the crown of thorns, the sneering taunts of the mob, and their demand for crucifixion. Pilate cringes in impotence and shame, then even lies on the floor with Jesus, who can scarcely eke out his lines concerning responsibility. Watch Gerhaher pick nervously at his fingernails and try desperately to avert his eyes while the chorus threatens his job, "Lässet du diesen los, so bist du des Kaisers Freund" (If you let him loose, you're no longer Caesar's friend). After he has capitulated, however, he rises and sings the aria "Eilt, ihr angefocht'nen Seelen" (Hurry, you troubled souls), in which the soloist urges the chorus to flee to Golgotha. In fact, as soon as the Evangelist mentions Golgotha, the choristers have scampered away, and we hear only faint echoes from them. Gerhaher delivers this not as a Christian beseeching others but as

Pilate's rage aria spilling over from his disgust with the crowd he has had to confront. Only at a moment when he mentions the cross as the site of spiritual welfare does he lift his eyes in supplication.

Bach offers one last aria for the bass, "Mein theuer Heiland" (My dear savior), after Jesus has died. Gerhaher poses his burning questions—Am I free from sin? Am I free from death?—hovering over the spot where Jesus had lain under the interrogation lamp. At the very end, as his text reports the dying Christ's head nodding "ja," a light finally shines on his face, wordlessly granting him salvation. In this beautiful conclusion, Gerhaher seems to represent simultaneously Peter and Pilate, both penitents pleading for forgiveness, both finally redeemed.

Throughout this book, I have drawn attention to the influence of Bach's framing choruses on Sellars's libretti. He has long opened his own libretti with choruses that similarly engage the audience, and his editing of these prologues for DVD trains in obsessively on specific faces, breaking the social unit down into its individual constituents. Whether the Chinese singing Maoist slogans while awaiting Nixon's arrival or Mayan peasants offering psalms (see chapter 6), his choral groups always feature *this* woman and *this* man. I claimed in chapter 3 that *The Death of Klinghoffer* would have fared better if he had released a DVD with close-up shots of lamenting Israelis and Palestinians. With his staging of the *St. Matthew*, he returns to his original source.

Bach opens his setting of Matthew's account with perhaps the most stunning of all chorale preludes: a double chorus calling for the Daughters of Zion to join a ceremony of mourning and penance, a double orchestra playing a dirgelike gigue, presided over by a cantus firmus, "O Lamm Gottes, unschuldig," trumpeted by high boys' voices (words highlighted in bold below). Although the cantus firmus first appears nearly two and a half minutes into the movement, it actually controls Bach's whole structure, producing a modified repetition of the first section, a modulating middle part, and a resolving conclusion. I might also note that the key of the chorale, G major, stands in affective contradistinction to the E minor of the chorus and orchestra. The boys chorus continually holds out hope to a world so benighted that it seems not to notice.

| Kommt, ihr Töchter, helft mir klagen, | Come, you daughters, help me grieve! |
| Sehet, *wen?* Den Bräutigam, | Behold! *Whom?* The bridegroom! |

Seht ihn, *wie?* als wie ein
  Lamm.
**O Lamm Gottes,
unschuldig,
Am Stamm des Kreuzes
  geschlachtet.**
Sehet, *was?* Seht die
Geduld,
**Allzeit funden geduldig,
wiewohl du warest
  verachtet;**
Seht, *wohin?* Auf unsre
Schuld,
**all Sünd hast du getragen,
sonst müßten wir
  verzagen.**
Sehet ihn aus Lieb und
Huld
Holz zum Kreuze selber
  tragen.
**Erbarm dich unser, o Jesu.**

Kommt, ihr Töchter, helft
mir klagen,
Sehet, *wen?* Den Bräutigam,

Seht ihn, *wie?* als wie ein
  Lamm.

Behold him! *How?* Just like
  a lamb.
**O Lamb of God,
innocently slaughtered
on the stem of the cross.**

Behold! What? Behold his
forbearance!
**Always found forbearing,
however much you were
  despised;**
Look! *Where?* Upon our
guilt!
**You bore all sin;
otherwise we would have
  despaired.**
Behold him, out of love and
grace,
Bear the wood that forms
  his cross.
**Have mercy on us, O
  Jesus.**
Come, you daughters, help
me grieve!
Behold! *Whom?* The
  bridegroom!
Behold him! *How?* Just like
  a lamb.

Universally regarded as one of the most powerful movements in the entire repertory, "Kommt, ihr Töchter" commands listeners' attention and prepares them to enter into Matthew's painful narrative. Bach would have expected his congregants to hear themselves hailed with phrases such as "Look! *What?* At our guilt." He thereby insists on the responsibility of contemporary Christians, along with that of the Romans and Jewish prosecutors, for Christ's suffering. The other interpolations in the libretto—chorales, arias, recitatives—similarly serve to address those who attend as complicit and in need of clemency. When Bach dresses those sentiments in the musical garb of the eighteenth-century Dresden opera house, he produces an updating not unlike those Sellars brings to the Mozart Trilogy, and he does so for precisely the same reasons: to translate traditional cultural texts into terms that speak to contemporary audiences and the moral dilemmas they face on a daily basis.

In his staging of "Kommt, ihr Töchter," the choruses file onto the stage in silence to stand vigil around the bier. When the orchestra begins its throbbing pulse, they move slowly through the orchestra to arrive at their appointed places on two platforms, one in back, the other at the side of the stage. The camera zooms in on their haunted, searching expressions, on their slumped and stumbling bodies. A choir of boys in the balcony hovers above the action, overseeing it like angels, as Mark Padmore, the Evangelist, sits motionless and deep in thought beside the bier.

In accordance with Bach's score, one chorus initially remains uninvolved as the other pleads for help. Only when the direct questioning commences do the choirs interact, and we see the formerly silent group pulled into action. This, of course, is Bach's theatrical concept, and it already strongly suggests the staging Sellars brings to it. As always, Sellars concerns himself with the music's structure—not for the sake of analysis but because he believes that much of the emotional weight of music resides in this aspect of it. To mark the formal start of the second section, Sellars has the singers sit as if overcome with grief. Suddenly, with the move to "Sieht! *Wohin?* auf unsre Schuld" (the start of the chorale's restless middle section), choristers rush down from both sides to intermingle. The conversation, usually presented antiphonally from opposite ends of the stage, now features pairs of singers, one from each chorus. They face one another, urgently soliciting replies, always answered by the acknowledgment of mutual shame. When the Q & A ceases, the choruses join together to sing the concluding lines and the return of "Kommt, ihr Töchter"; though some of the choristers retreat to their separate platforms, others cluster again around the bier, their momentary solidarity apparently shattered.

Bach concludes Part I as he opened it with an elaborate chorale prelude, this time on "O Mensch, bewein dein Sünde groß" (O man, bewail your grievous sin). But he has led into this extended number with a dramatic explosion: the soprano and alto soloists sorrowfully lament the fact that Jesus has been arrested, as the chorus throws in indignant, percussive demands that he be unbound. Sellars has withheld gesturing for the most part up until now, but here the two soloists together signal the heavens on "Mond und Licht ist vor Schmerzen untergangen" (from pain the moon and light have disappeared). Suddenly the chorus erupts with a furious fugue calling down the wrath of God with "Sind Blitzen, sind Donner in Wolken verschwunden" (Have lightning, has thunder disappeared into the clouds). With each new fugal entrance, a group of choristers rise, creating a visual analogue to Bach's tempestuous plea.

After a brief recitative in which Jesus chastises his follower for cutting off the ear of one of his adversaries, the final chorus, "O Mensche bewein," begins. Once again, the boys choir delivers the chorale in its clarion tones, while the adult voices elaborate. As the orchestra presents an agitated accompaniment, Sellars has the choristers race wildly through the concert hall (fleeing as had the disciples), to take up positions throughout the hall, where they sing from the midst of the audience. If in the opening chorus, the members of the two choral groups come together to admonish each other, now the viewers find themselves incorporated into the body of mourners who have to accept responsibility—like Bach's original congregation—for the events unfolding onstage. In contrast to the relative stillness of the staging up until this point, the action explodes here, spilling over past the performance boundaries and engulfing everyone. When the last bars have sounded, the orchestra too abandons the stage, leaving only Padmore lying crumpled on the bier.

The *St. Matthew* ends with a funereal tableau. In preparation, Thomas Quasthoff, representing Joseph of Arimathea, claims the remains in order to place them in his own tomb. He sings lovingly that his heart should purify itself so that Jesus can be buried in it, and at his conclusion, he bends down and kisses the bier.[16] While he sings, the two Marys identified by Matthew as having followed the body to the sepulcher stand embracing Padmore. Next, the four soloists—seated around the bier on which Padmore lies stretched out in state—say their farewells one by one.

Only the final lament, "Wir setzen uns mit Tränen nieder" (We sit with tears streaming down) remains. Bach shapes this chorus as a rondeau, with the principal refrain coming back several times to signal infinite, unending mourning. As they sing, the choristers located on the side of the stage file past the bier, then sit in watch. For the last iteration of the lament, the choristers who had stood behind the orchestra also process down until all have clustered around the bier. If at the opening the chorus urged that we attend to the passion narrative, at the end they mount their vigil over the tomb. They have assumed again the positions they held at the very beginning of the entire performance, bringing it full circle.

As we have seen, the *St. John Passion* presents quite different challenges throughout, and Sellars's strategies for this staging differ markedly from those he brought to the *St. Matthew*. If Bach chose to open the *St. Matthew* with a stately dance, he composed one of his most dire, guilt-ridden movements for *St. John*, in keeping with the focus on Peter's and Pilate's abjection.

The opening movement lasts for more than nine minutes—about a quarter the length of Part I in its entirety.

Bach creates his most brilliant effects in this chorus through the ways he makes us perceive time. In the orchestral ritornello, the bass instruments present nothing but repeated eighth notes on a low G for the first nine measures. Not only do they refuse to budge from that pitch, but their constant eighth notes have the effect of marking beats, making those bars seem interminable. Over this pedal the strings play groups of sixteenth notes, very low in their ranges to produce a muddy quality. Moreover, they just rotate around a single pitch, as if simply spinning their wheels. Although the strings eventually rise in pitch, prodding the bass note to change, they too contribute to producing this very low level of rhythmic activity. Bach's music usually moves at the level of the half note, but his score here seems stuck in mire: exactly the image he seems to have sought.

Over this accompaniment, the flute and oboe present melodic lines that strongly resemble those of Corelli's trio sonatas. These lines do try to move at the half-note level, their dissonances all the more aching because of the grinding pattern and incessant pulsations underneath them. They seem to hang there in agony as if suspended on the cross. When the bass line finally does change in m. 10, it goes into free fall, mechanically dialing down by fifth until latching back to a cadential arrival in m. 19, where the choristers enter crying out, "Herr" (Lord!). But soon after they deliver that word, they too assume the low, groveling pattern already introduced by the strings.

In anybody else's score, this would count as extremely bad writing. Bach, however, designs this texture to sound like souls condemned to the lowest rungs of hell. They call out for help in vain from never-ceasing torment. Occasionally they try to establish a higher level of rhythmic activity, as, for instance, in the imitative section on the words "Herr, unser Herrscher" (Lord, our ruler) or in the B section on "Zeig uns durch deine Passion" (Show us through your Passion). But each time they get dragged back into that grinding pattern. Although Bach experiments with many different formal arrangements in the *St. John*, he gives us no such relief in this opening movement but rather demands a full-blown da capo. Just when we might hope to hear the end of this tortured material, it starts up all over again, as if in an endless loop. I might add that for all its concern with praise, the text itself is also stuck, with its multiple ways of twisting the word "Herr," which may well have inspired Bach's bizarre approach: "**Herr**, unser **Herr**scher dessen Ruhm in allen Landen **herr**lich ist! Zeig uns durch deine Passion daß du, der wahre Gottessohn, zu alle Zeit, auch in der größten Neidrigkeit, ver**herr**licht worden bist" (Lord, our ruler, whose name is glorified in every land. Show us through your Passion that you, the true Son of God, at all times, even in the deepest humiliation, have been glorified).

Sellars responds to this music by having the choristers lying on the floor, writhing in time with the omnipresent pulses that will not release them. On "Herr!" they stretch their hands out in appeal, on the second presentation of "Herr," they rise to a sitting position. Eventually they will stand, yet continue to fall back again, just as Bach's score has the voices reaching out, then sinking back into the morass. As he often does, Sellars marks imitative subjects by having the various parts of the choir rise or gesticulate as they enter, especially on the words "Ruhm" and "Zeig," thereby highlighting Bach's jagged entrances and desperate appeals for rescue. At the word "Niederichkeit" (humiliation), they kneel in abjection.

Sellars usually aims to show psychological growth in his stagings of da capo forms, and he constantly seeks ways of making us hear the return of the A section as different. That is not, however, his vision of this opening chorus. He has the choristers perform the da capo just as they did its first iteration, underscoring the futility of their journey. Redemption might come eventually, but not here at the beginning. As we have seen, Sellars makes minimal use of his gestural vocabulary in his *St. Matthew*. But *St. John* requires a very different set of affects, and the kinetic violence that will characterize this entire production already appears here at the outset. Notice also the way the choristers later move their hands as if flicking off something extremely disgusting for "Weg, weg" (Away, away with him!) or their shaking a rolling of the dice when casting lots for Jesus's garments.

Bach does not articulate the end of Part I or the beginning of Part II of the *St. John* with anything more than a chorale. Those framing movements that help to anchor the *St. Matthew* formally fail to materialize here, thus allowing for greater continuity and dramatic momentum. Only at the end does the chorus offer an extended presentation when they sing "Ruht wohl" (Rest well) at the tomb. Bach shapes this lullaby as a rondeau, with a refrain and a series of episodes. Sellars marks each of these moments with a variety of gestures: kneeling, the crossing of hands over hearts standing, and finally gazing away as if numb from the center where Jesus had lain. During the last ritornello, the Evangelist comes forward into the light that had previously designated the site of Christ's body and kneels, his task now completed, while the chorus sings their final chorale. The light holds steady for a very long time before it gradually fades. Sellars explains his understanding of Bach's strategy here:

And then this beautiful thing of "Ruht wohl," the last long chorus, of "rest now and let us rest and bring me peace," because now I know I don't need to cry for you anymore. Which is really different from the *Matthew Passion*, where everyone sits down and cries and cries and cries. And Bach says, No, actually we don't need to weep anymore. It's not gonna help you, and it's not helping us. We need to actively search for peace and go forward as best we can. So this music, just when you wanted to sit and have a big sad moment, doesn't. It opens and moves forward and says: "Your grave opened the gates of heaven and shut the gates of hell. So the gates of heaven are open. Let's go." To end a piece that has this much violence and this much self-hatred and this much "How weak are you, and why don't you have the courage to say what you really believe in and what you really care about"—to end with this tender, generous "Go ahead, it's open, it's open. Step into it. Jesus's death is not the end, it's the beginning; Jesus's death is not the closure, it's the opening. Death itself is not the end, it's the beginning." For all of this to be stated musically in this long sweep of arias that take you through the stages of grieving and then out to the other side to this other kind of freedom. Delicate freedom. Tender freedom. Freedom that's so new that you can't breathe on it. You just taste it. Which is where the piece ends.

As he does in Saariaho's *Passion de Simone* and *Only the Sound Remains*, Sellars addresses not only social action but also the moment of death for the individual and for the community. He says concerning the *St. John*: "And then the last third of the piece is this deeply quiet meditation of, what is a good death? What it means to die well, with integrity, with kindness, taking care of the people around you, and having them take care of you." Bach ends in a place of profound spirituality and yet a place that ought to provoke change. Sellars learned well from his study of these scores at Emmanual.

In most performances of the passions, the instrumentalists merely accompany. Sellars, however, brings them into the drama, most remarkably in arias in which he has the singer and the player of the obbligato instrument interact with one other as they perform. Doing so requires that he find ways of interpreting the players' gestures so as to illuminate the texts with which Bach associates them.

In the scene in the *St. Matthew* describing the flogging of Jesus, for instance, Bach offers an extraordinary accompanied recitative and aria concerning forbearance for tenor soloist and viola da gamba, played here to extraordinary effect by Hille Perfl. Mimicking the sound of whiplashes, Bach has the viol slash across its strings in multiple stops to produce dry, isolated chords while two oboes add even greater impact through sharply tongued, staccato pitches. Up against this unrelenting attack, the tenor sings of Jesus's response and how the Christian should attempt to emulate his behavior.

Sellars then has the tenor, Topi Lehtipuu, kneel before the viol player as he sings the following aria, "Geduld!" (Patience) in response to the lies of false tongues. Bach's melody alternates between a short sighing motiv and passages of brutally dotted patterns. By putting the two performers face to face, Sellars insists that we witness the extreme physical exertion required of the viol player and demands that we try to make sense of the dialectic between them. Sphinx-like in her refusal to acknowledge the singer, she may be seen either as a torturer impervious to the singer's plight, or herself stoic, despite her own misery. Another aria shaped unconventionally, "Geduld!" (Patience!) does allow the tenor to return to his initial words, though he enters "impatiently" in the middle of the viol's phrase and concludes quickly, leaving the viol to reiterate its enigmatic ritornello.[17]

A different tension occurs in "Gebt mir meinen Jesum wieder" (Give my Jesus back to me) in Part II of the *St. Matthew*. We last saw Judas near the beginning of Part I when he made his bargain. Judas returns in Part II when he attempts to return the bounty he had received, then hangs himself. Bach might have reacted to this event by mourning it, but he anticipated that his audience would need an emotional break from the ongoing expressions of guilt and agony. Consequently, he and Picander insert a bass aria that single-mindedly pursues a heroic affect, with extravagant embellishments in the solo violin. One could envision this virtuosity as an extension of the heroic character who demands an exchange. But Sellars has violinist Daishin Kashimoto fling those runs and swirls as contempt in the singer's face. Bass Thomas Quasthoff glares defiantly at the violinist, never conceding an inch. Even while the text acknowledges him as a prodigal son, he insists that he now stands by Jesus—surely the lesson Bach's congregants were to draw from the aria.

Bach gives voice to Peter's great shame with the aria "Erbarme dich, mein Gott" (Have mercy on me), with solo violin. A pizzicato cello simulates both heartbeats and the teardrops to which Picander's lyrics refer. It begins as if to present the emblematic tetrachord descent that had stood for lament for at least a hundred years. But just as the tetrachord would seem to have reached its resting point, Bach has the harmonies open up so that the lament continues far past its usual goal. This, the music suggests, is mourning that surpasses immeasurably its conventional expression. The violin shares the vocalist's starting melodic gesture, with its beseeching upward leap that redoubles its efforts when the bass line opens out. But then the violin line dissolves into extravagant ornamentation that traces the flood of tears and maps the inner anguish Peter now experiences. Once more Bach eschews the da capo form that lends a kind of certainty to most arias. The A section ends not on the tonic, which would ground the lament formally, but rather in a key that demands an ongoing search for tonal resolution. When the two soloists return to the initial words, they still must forge their path back to the original key. Structural repetition has no place in this emotional journey.

Although "Erbarme dich" occurs in response to Peter's betrayal, Bach writes it for the alto voice. In order to attach the aria to Peter, Sellars has the bass who performed his lines in the recitative collapse on the bier, as Padmore gazes in sorrow at him. But it is Kožená who sings the aria. Has she ceased to be the Magdalene? Perhaps, but recall that Mary stood as an emblem of penitence, and the lyrics of the aria refers over and over to tears—also identified strongly with her (recall Crashaw's "The Weeper"). In other words, we can read Sellars's staging as offering a double image of boundless remorse from two of the individuals closest to Christ. For the duration of this number, Kožená kneels as if begging forgiveness at the feet of violinist Daniel Stabrawa. She addresses him in the aria's middle section, "Schaue hier" (Look at me here), then shrinks back into her personal grief. At the close, the violin wordlessly echoes back the tearful lamentation, not yet answered.

Although every number in both of these productions warrants commentary, I will limit myself to these. Sellars had waited his whole career to realize the Bach passions on the stage. In the meantime, he honed his skills, thinking through potential interpretations, bringing dramaturgical elements from these two works to virtually everything else he did. When he finally had the opportunity in Berlin to bring together a world-class group of performers, he met the challenges with what I can only regard as genius.

• Peter Sellars shows no signs of slowing down: within the last four years he has premiered Saariaho's *Only the Sound Remains*, Adams's *Girls of the Golden West*, and Purcell's *The Indian Queen*, for all of which he composed the libretti. Meanwhile he has also mounted new high-profile productions of Ligeti's *Le grand macabre* and Mozart's *La clemenza di Tito*, as well as Orlando di Lasso's *Lagrime di San Pietro*. As I complete this volume, he is busy designing an interpretation of Robert Schumann's *Das Paradies und die Peri*.

I would love to keep going with this project, but I have to draw the line somewhere. Like others around the globe, I will try to keep track of Sellars's inventions, now including not only staging and libretti but also full-scale assemblages for which he selects the music as well. He will continue to challenge, annoy, and enchant those who attend to his audacious work. No doubt, many more studies of Sellars will follow in the wake of this one. I hope, however, to have shed light on some of his achievements—particularly on the processes by means of which he stages the music, on the ways he has made his passions the shared passions of anyone who cares about contemporary music theater.

# Notes

## Introduction

1. Anthony Tommasini, "Trump Has Changed a Night at the Opera, Too," *New York Times* (May 26, 2017). Tommasini mentions productions of Rossini's *Barber of Seville*, Strauss's *Der Rosenkavalier*, and an updated *Nozze di Figaro*, *¡Figaro!*, but not Sellars. See, however, Michael Cooper, "Remember When 'Figaro' Was Set in the Trump Tower?," *New York Times* (November 25, 2016), which includes a brief interview with Sellars. I discuss his *Le nozze di Figaro* at length in chapter 1. See also the discussion of Sellars's *Theodora* in chapter 2 for another possible Trump reference.

Not surprisingly, updated performances featuring Trump-like characters have received some pushback since the election. Delta Air Lines and Bank of America withdrew financial backing from New York Public Theater's production of Shakespeare's *Julius Caesar* in which the ill-fated emperor looked and acted like the current president. "Delta Air Lines and Bank of American Won't Back Trump-Like 'Julius Caesar,'" *New York Times* (June 11, 2017).

2. For more on Sellars's early career, see Don Shewey, "Not Either/Or but And: Fragmentation and Consolidation in the Post-modern Theatre of Peter Sellars," in *Contemporary American Theatre*, ed. Bruce King (New York: Palgrave Macmillan, 1991), 263–82. See also the entry on Sellars by Maria Shevtsova in *Fifty Key Theatre Directors* (Routledge Key Guides), ed. Shomit Mitter and Maria Shevtsova (New York: Routledge, 2005).

3. "Sellars: Laughing All the Way to a National Theater," *Los Angeles Times* (February 24, 1985).

4. I allude here to Robert Lepage's production of Wagner's *Die Walküre* (Metropolitan Opera, 2011), Michael Mayer's of Verdi's *Rigoletto* (Metropolitan Opera, 2013), and La Fura del Baus's of György Ligeti's *Le Grand Macabre* (Gran Teatre de Liceu, Barcelona, 2011).

5. For a slightly earlier culprit, we might point to Patrice Chéreau's production of Wagner's *Ring* at Bayreuth in 1976, which situated the epic in nineteenth-century Germany.

6. In fact, my project was conceived the evening following the *Tristan Project* performance when Victoria Cooper—then music acquisitions editor at Cambridge University Press—encouraged me to consider a Sellars book. Although the venture with Cambridge

did not work out, I want to thank Vicki for instigating the process that migrated first to University of California Press and then, along with my longtime editor, Mary Francis, to University of Michigan Press.

7. Sellars uses a similar image to describe his enterprise. In his account of his initial suggestion to John Adams in 1983, he says: "I think he believed I was not serious. About a year later he called back to see if I was still interested. You never know when the right moment is, but we're always planting seeds." Interview with Thomas May, "Creating Contexts: Peter Sellars on Working with Adams," in *The John Adams Reader: Essential Writings on an American Composer*, ed. Thomas May (New York: Amadeus Press, 2006), 240.

8. John Adams, *Hallelujah Junction: Composing an American Life* (New York: Picador, 2008), 126–27.

9. In *Lettera a Peter: Saint François a Salisburgo*, a film for television by Jean-Luc Godard associate Jean-Pierre Gorin (1992), available for viewing at www.youtube.com/watch?v=J4iOdeesrTs

10. It also helps explain why he rarely receives requests from the Metropolitan Opera, which depends on a less rehearsal-intensive process. See chapters 3–5 for a comparison between his versions of operas for which he staged the premieres and those for which the Met engaged other directors.

11. Zachary Woolfe, "Can Opera Become an Agent of Change?," *New York Times* (July 15, 2016).

12. Christopher Small, *Musicking* (Middletown, CT: Wesleyan University Press, 1998).

13. Small, "Pelicans," in *The Christopher Small Reader*, ed. Robert Walser (Middletown, CT: Wesleyan University Press, 2016), 229.

## Chapter 1: American Mozart

1. Sellars's production of *Le nozze di Figaro* had its premiere at the PepsiCo Summerfare in Purchase, NY, in 1988. His *Così fan tutte* had appeared at PepsiCo in 1986, followed by *Don Giovanni* in 1987. PepsiCo presented all three operas in subsequent seasons, allowing the interpretations to settle before filming. In 1990, performances in Vienna of all three, featuring the Wiener Symphoniker, appeared on DVD (Decca Records and Polygram Video), and this chapter focuses on these. A version of *Don Giovanni*, starring James Maddalena, appeared at the Monadnock Music Festival in 1980, but no footage exists from that production.

2. See the review by Donal Henahan, *New York Times* (August 3, 1984). If you Google "Donal Henahan, Peter Sellars," you will find a long stream of attacks, not only on the Mozart Trilogy but also on *Nixon in China* and other productions. See also Richard Trousdell, "Peter Sellars Rehearses *Figaro*," *TDR* 35, no. 1 (Spring 1991), for critical responses.

3. Karrie Jacobs, "Peter Sellars Digs Up 'The Cabinet,'" *New York Times* (February 17, 1991).

4. *Destination Mozart: A Night at the Opera with Peter Sellars* (Kultur, 1990).

5. David J. Levin has written persuasively about Sellars's overriding concern with cultural translation in this production. See his *Unsettling Opera: Staging Mozart, Verdi,*

*Wagner, and Zemlinsky* (Chicago: University of Chicago Press, 2007), chapter 3. See also Marcia J. Citron, "A Matter of Time and Place: Peter Sellars and Media Culture," in her *Opera on Screen* (New Haven: Yale University Press, 2000), 195–226.

6. See Horner's brief description of his process in the *New York Times* obituary (June 23, 2015): "If the music is too emphatic and emotional, it might drown the comedy. But if the music is toned down too much, the scene might not give the audience the emotional catharsis it wants from the climax. It's like being a tightrope walker with one foot in the air at all times. When it makes me cry, then I know I've nailed it. I can't do any better."

7. Wye Jamison Allanbrook, *The Secular Commedia: Comic Mimesis in Late Eighteenth-Century Music*, ed. Mary Ann Smart and Richard Taruskin (Berkeley: University of California Press, 2014).

8. For a sensitive examination of both the Mozart mystique and also the technical ways in which Mozart achieves what many hear as unearthly perfection, see Scott Burnham, *Mozart's Grace* (Princeton: Princeton University Press, 2013).

9. Bach also identifies brass and timpani with royalty, especially with the divine nobility of the godhead, which is why he chose the key of B minor for his mass. This key shares its signature with D major, thus allowing the composer to pivot from the despair of the Kyrie into the triumph of the Gloria and Resurrection.

Mozart relies on the same set of associations but often positions signs of royalty critically. The Prague Symphony, for instance, also presents a highly topical argument by way of scoring. See my "Narratives of Bourgeois Subjectivity in Mozart's 'Prague' Symphony," in *Understanding Narrative*, ed. Peter Rabinowitz and James Phelan (Columbus: Ohio State University Press, 1994), 65–98.

10. See also, however, David J. Levin's extended queer reading of Larson's performance here and the ways it destabilizes the economy of desire in the opera. Levin, *Unsettling Opera*, chapter 3. As the essays in *En Travesti* argue, pants roles have long afforded women in audiences with the spectacle of same-sex encounters, if they choose to ignore the convention. *En Travesti: Women, Gender Subversion, Opera*, ed. Corinne Blackmer and Patricia Juliana Smith (New York: Columbia University Press, 1995).

11. John Corigliano's opera *The Ghosts of Versailles* relies in part on *La mère coupable*. Only Massenet has composed an opera based entirely on this third of Beaumarchais's Figaro plays.

12. Concerning the cleaning up of this aspect of Beaumarchais, see Daniel Heartz, *Mozart's Operas* (Berkeley: University of California Press, 1990), 109–10.

13. For a brilliant discussion of the functions of dance types in Mozart, see Wye Jamison Allanbrook, *Rhythmic Gesture in Mozart: "Le nozze di Figaro" and "Don Giovanni"* (Chicago: University of Chicago Press, 1983).

14. The very long da capo arias of Handel and Bach will demand much more invention when Sellars stages them, and he often speaks to audiences before performances about the psychological rationale behind this apparently hoary convention. See chapters 2 and 7.

15. The music director at Emmanuel Church in Boston, Smith had encouraged the young Sellars in his dramatizations of Bach cantatas, and his influence can be discerned throughout Sellars's career. Smith started out serving as rehearsal accompanist for the Mozart productions and then moved into the position of conductor. As a core part of the team and longtime collaborator at Emmanuel, he gave Sellars license to experiment with translating Mozart's musical phrases, gestures, structures, timing, and affect onto the

stage. Smith's decisions, and those of continuo player Suzanne Cleavendon, might be read in these performances as extensions of Sellars's *Gesamtkunstwerk*, but they brought their own considerable musical expertise to the collaborations.

16. Allanbrook, *Rhythmic Gesture in Mozart*, 119–36. Sellars reports that he made extensive use of Allanbrook's book as he planned his Mozart productions.

17. Film scholars often use the term "Mickey Mousing" to describe a kind of slavish mimicry between image and sound; it alludes to Walt Disney's earliest animations, featuring Mickey, which served as models for many subsequent cartoons and films. See Daniel Goldmark, *Tunes for 'Toons* (Berkeley: University of California Press, 2007), and Daniel Batchelder, "Mickey Mousing, Performance, and Dramatic Integration in Disney's Early Animation," in his "American Magic: Song, Animation, and Drama in Disney's Golden Era Animated Musicals" (PhD dissertation, Case Western Reserve University, 2018).

18. Allanbrook, *Rhythmic Gesture in Mozart*, 197.

19. The #MeToo movement, which arose in late 2017, involved women who dared to come forward to testify publicly to such abuses. Nearly every awards ceremony in 2018 has featured a carefully coordinated protest by female stars who stand together in solidarity against sexual exploitation.

20. Musicologist Tim Carter presents a similar argument concerning this scene in his Cambridge Opera Handbooks companion to *Le nozze di Figaro* (Cambridge: Cambridge University Press, 1987), 113–15; he also presents an astute comparison between the Count's and Bartolo's rage arias, the latter of which resides comfortably within the conventions of opera buffa. In "La vendetta," Bartolo even spills over into patter declamation. Mozart and Sellars both highlight the Count's apparently genuine anguish.

21. See David Levin's comments concerning this moment: "The Sellars production arguably offers a dramatization of the dramatic *irresolution*, of the jarring and unprepared nature of the resolution of *Figaro*" (*Unsettling Opera*, 88). I am reading the scene in terms that help to set up many of Sellars's later projects, many of which emphasize including the audience in communal union.

22. Concerning the feminist dimension of Figaro, see Heartz, *Mozart's Operas*, 112. See also Kristi Brown Montesano, *Understanding the Women of Mozart's Operas* (Berkeley: University of California Press, 2007).

23. For more on these operas, see Nicholas Stevens, "Lulu's Daughters: Portraying the Anti-heroine in Contemporary Opera, 1993–2013" (PhD dissertation, Case Western Reserve University, 2017).

24. Edward Said reads these performances as misogynist because of the punishments inflicted on the female characters. Edward W. Said, "Peter Sellars's Mozart," in his *Music at the Limits* (New York: Columbia University Press, 2008), 89. I see these same moments as demanding that we attend to the antiwoman sentiments that appear as a matter of course in these classic operas. But the differences between my understanding and Said's may also have to do with the ways Sellars foregrounds women's issues in his subsequent work.

25. Richard Dellamora, "Mozart and the Politics of Intimacy: The Marriage of Figaro in Toronto, Paris, and New York," in *The Work of Opera: Genre, Nationhood, and Sexual Difference*, ed. Richard Dellamora and Daniel Fischlin (New York: Columbia University Press, 1997), chapter 11.

26. On the history of this term, see Heartz, *Mozart's Operas*, 196.

27. Compare Sellars's footage with Queen Latifah's video of "Ladies First" (1989). See also the still-powerful essay by Marshall Berman, "Roots, Ruins, Renewals: City Life after Urbicide," *Village Voice* (September 4, 1984).

28. In this multiracial cast, Zerlina is Asian and Masetto black, while the "noble" characters are all white. As we shall see, Sellars often strives for mixed-race casting, and he makes use of Eric Owens, Willard White, Julia Bullock, and Devóne Tines in ways that do not emphasize race—or, better, that challenge assumptions about race.

29. Technically speaking, the Commendatore challenges Don Giovanni to a duel to save his daughter and her honor. But the disparity between the elder statesman and the young thug scarcely make this a fair fight, and the burden of this crime weighs on the entire opera, finally demanding retribution from on high.

30. See Burnham, *Mozart's Grace*. See also my "A Musical Dialectic from the Enlightenment: Mozart's Piano Concerto in G Major, K. 453, Movement II," *Cultural Critique* 4 (Fall 1986): 129–69.

31. A French production in 1834 transposed Giovanni's part into the tenor range, because the French found the low voice of this protagonist so distasteful. See Mary Hunter, *Mozart's Operas: A Companion* (New Haven: Yale University Press, 2008), 150.

32. Søren Kierkegaard, *Either/Or* (1843). In his story "Don Juan" (1831), E. T. A. Hoffmann similarly made Giovanni into a Romantic hero, as have a great many male critics over the years. For more on this reception, see Hunter, *Mozart's Operas*.

33. See, for instance, the 2000 Metropolitan Opera production starring Bryn Terfel.

34. The silencing of women has become an important theme in the wake of Donald Trump's election. Colleagues have shut down outraged senators such as Kamala Harris during formal hearings, triggering an outpouring of shared experiences by women similarly admonished to keep quiet. See "The Universal Phenomenon of Men Interrupting Women," *New York Times* (June 16, 2017).

35. Mozart famously pulls a similar stunt in the coda to the last movement of his Jupiter Symphony, in which he juggles five tunes until the attentive listener nearly implodes. But as with the ballroom scene, one can simply float along on the smoothly flowing surface without noticing.

36. This identification also foreshadows Sellars's career-long concern for returning soldiers and the effects of post-traumatic stress. His interpretation of Handel's *Hercules* dealt most pointedly with this issue. For each production, he invited war veterans to attend the performance and then participate in a panel concerning post-traumatic stress and its effects on families. Some of these panels may be viewed online.

37. See also Burnham, *Mozart's Grace*: "This crystallization of the relation between beauty and the loss of innocence, lingering in the aura of so much of Mozart's later instrumental music, becomes explicit in *Così fan tutte*. There the main characters are disabused of their idealized view of love and fidelity to the accompaniment of astonishingly beautiful music; and the audience witnessing the ignoble deceit practiced upon the women by their male lovers also observes the demise of the cherished equation of truth and beauty" (52–53).

38. For a thoughtful account that compares this staging with more a conventional one at Glyndebourne, see Mary Hunter, "Window to the Work, or Mirror of Our Preconceptions? Peter Sellars's Production of *Così fan tutte*," *Repercussions* (Fall 1995): 42–58. Hunter admits that she dislikes Sellars's ending. Yet "in refusing the gestures that make the Glyndebourne production seem smug . . . Sellars's angst-ridden, atomized ending

forces us to think about what the end of this most unsettling off comedies is 'really' about" (45). Later she states: "I would suggest that one of the most precious gifts that Peter Sellars gives his audiences is a chance to be jolted into facing... what we have done to Mozart" (50).

39. David Cairns, *Mozart and His Operas* (Berkeley: University of California Press, 2006), 185.

40. Hunter, "Window to the Work," 56.

## Chapter 2: Ritualizing

1. Peter Sellars, interview with Simon Halsey, included in the Berlin Philharmonic DVD of the *St. Matthew Passion*. President Trump plans to round up those same Salvadorans and send them back to the death squads and extreme poverty.

2. Sellars compiled performances from the 1990 Los Angeles Festival, available on DVD.

3. The Vienna Festival compiled a lavish book documenting Sellars's New Crowned Hope Festival (Vienna: Verlag Wien-Bozen, 1996). At this month-long event, Sellars also presented his collaborations with John Adams (*A Flowering Tree*) and Kaija Saariaho (*La passion de Simone*).

4. Musicologist Anthony W. Sheppard has charged Sellars with orientalism because of his penchant for drawing on non-Western sources for much of his work. See "The Persistence of Orientalism in the Postmodern Operas of Adams and Sellars," in *Representation in Western Music*, ed. Joshua S. Walden (Cambridge: Cambridge University Press, 2013). See also, however, Kenan Malik, "In Defense of Cultural Appropriation," *New York Times* (June 14, 2017); Malik writes: "The accusation of cultural appropriation is a secular version of the charge of blasphemy." I will discuss this potential problem in Sellars's oeuvre when I deal with some of these productions and libretti over the course of this book, especially *Doctor Atomic* and *The Indian Queen*. For now, I will simply emphasize that Sellars's interest in non-Western cultures emerges from his deep commitment to presenting Asian musicians and dancers performing their own music.

5. Gorin, *Lettera a Peter*.

6. He was even nervous about using period costumes in this production. In *Lettera a Peter*, Sellars expresses how he faced the arrival of costumes with great trepidation, for he feared that the singer-actors whose moves he had choreographed so carefully would revert in their monks' habits to traditional operatic behavior, with all its standard gestures.

7. Sellars had initially wanted a multistory Sony Jumbotron (then a state-of-the-art technology), but even Salzburg balked at this expense. See Sander van Maas, "Dorsal Monuments: Messiaen, Sellars, and Saint Francis," *Opera Quarterly* 27, no. 4 (Autumn 2011): 420–42.

8. *Lettera a Peter*. Critics have sometimes suggested that Sellars does not qualify as a musician because he does not perform. But one has only to watch him working from Messiaen's extremely complicated score to recognize his expertise. Even my advanced graduate students blanch at tackling this opera in its original format.

9. *Lettera a Peter*.

10. Sellars will continue to deploy this strategy of double casting of a singer and dancer for a single role in, for instance, *El Niño* with Adams and *Only the Sound Remains*

with Saariaho. Both these works also present complex emotional vacillations in angels.

11. *Destination Mozart* also includes footage of Sellars coaching, especially a scene between Giovanni and Zerlina. But the gestures he asks for in *Don Giovanni* proceed from the rhetoric of the score; they have little to do with the codified kinetic moves he develops for *Saint François* and continues to utilize.

12. All the footage of Upshaw—particularly the clip tracing her entrance down a long ramp (7:19)—glows with childlike wonder and benevolence. Sellars worked to keep her as a regular, featuring her also in his *Theodora*, *El Niño*, and *L'amour de loin*. The possibility of using Upshaw for her works also helped to lure Saariaho into vocal and theatrical music.

13. Sellars has Don Alfonso adopt this prayerful gesture in his staging of "Soave sia il vento" in *Così fan tutte*, thereby offering a radical rereading of this character. See the discussion in the previous chapter.

14. Walz shot this photo at a rehearsal of Saariaho's *La passion de Simone*, but it might have come from any number of productions.

15. Said, "Peter Sellars's Mozart," 87–90.

16. For more on the long-standing ideologies that discourage or prohibit kinetic engagement in musicians, see my "The Bodies of Angels," in *Desvelando el cuerpo: Perspectivas desde las ciencias sociales y humanas*, ed. Josep Martí et al. (Barcelona: CSIC, 2010), 137–44.

17. Edward Seckerson, "Classical Theodora Glyndebourne," *Independent* (May 19, 1996).

18. Alan A. Stone, "Report and Recommendation: Concerning the Handling of Incidents Such as the Branch Davidian Standoff in Waco Texas," November 10, 1993. Stone (Touroff-Glueck Professor of Psychiatry and Law at Harvard) headed a panel appointed by the US Justice and Treasury Departments, reporting to Deputy General Philip Heymann.

19. He will use similar images of American military aggression in his productions of *The Indian Queen* and Bach's *St. John Passion*. See chapters 6 and 7.

20. Imogen Tilden, "How We Made: Peter Sellars and William Christie on *Theodora*," interview by Imogen Tilden, *Guardian* (August 27, 2012).

21. Tilden, "How We Made."

22. Although the characters in this scene briefly simulate rape, everyone remains fully clothed. Neither here nor elsewhere in his work does Sellars present nudity or sexual violence for purposes of titillating the audience. Never shying away from an opera's implications of assault, he carefully avoids prurience. If he often attempts to shock his viewers, his reasons—as in *Theodora*—remain political. For a recent critique of gratuitous rape scenes in opera productions, see Micaela Baranello, "When Cries of Rape Are Heard in Opera Halls," *New York Times* (July 19, 2015).

23. Robert Freeman, *Opera without Drama* (Ann Arbor: UMI, 1981). Freeman's title alludes, of course, to Richard Wagner's famous tract, *Opera and Drama*.

24. See especially Martha Feldman, *Opera and Sovereignty: Transforming Myths in Eighteenth-Century Italy* (Chicago: University of Chicago Press, 2007). See also my "What Was Tonality?," in *Conventional Wisdom: The Content of Musical Form* (Berkeley: University of California Press, 2000), chapter 3.

25. For anyone who cares, the aria starts in E♭ major (I), with an initial modulation to B♭ major (V). Handel then goes to G minor (iii) for an internal cadence. When the text

begins again, it is in F minor (ii), before the aria works its way back to E♭. The B section remains in C minor (vi) throughout. Neither iii nor ii appears frequently as a secondary key in eighteenth-century music, especially during an A section.

26. Sellars often uses this gesture himself in interviews when expressing astonishment or referring to the mind. See, for instance, his responses to Simon Halsey's first comments in the DVD bonus track for the *St. Matthew Passion*.

27. This is why the lyrics given above have the designation "Dal segno" (from the sign) instead of "Da capo," which would take us back to "the top."

28. The Largo establishes G minor as its tonic, but Theodora begin her recitative in G major. Handel then moves quickly through A to B minor. Her aria is in F♯ minor.

29. The aria was in F♯ minor; the new iteration of the Largo takes place not in its original G minor but in E minor—a key extremely remote from either G minor or F♯ minor. The rest of the scena, including the aria "Oh if I had wings," remains in E minor.

30. See Gary C. Thomas, "Was George Frideric Handel Gay?," in *Queering the Pitch: The New Gay and Lesbian Musicology*, ed. Philip Brett, Elizabeth Wood, and Gary C. Thomas (London: Routledge, 1994); Ellen T. Harris, *Handel as Orpheus* (Cambridge, MA: Harvard University Press, 2004).

31. Mozart and Da Ponte often share this predisposition. See again chapter 1.

32. Anthony Tommasini recently cited this 1996 performance as one of his favorites. See "A Beatific Gesture: This Week's 8 Best Classical Music Moments on YouTube," *New York Times* (July 14, 2017).

## Chapter 3: Inventing New Operas

1. See Adams, *Hallelujah Junction*, for Adams's account of their first meetings.

2. Adams, *Hallelujah Junction*, 144. A few modernists, such as John Cage and Luciano Berio, did produce some works they labeled as operas, though these scarcely occupied the center of their oeuvres.

But some of the most exciting composers in opera today work to weave together elements from high modernism within a much more eclectic palate: George Benjamin, Thomas Adès, Salvatore Sciarrino, Unsuk Chin, Du Yun, and Kaija Saariaho come to mind. John Adams too makes full use of electronic and highly dissonant idioms when they suit his needs. Concerning this postmodernist rapprochement with modernism, see my "The Lure of the Sublime: Revisiting Postwar Modernism," in *Transformations of Musical Modernism*, ed. Erling Guldbrandsen and Julian Johnson (Cambridge: Cambridge University Press, 2015), 21–35.

3. I criticized Adams in a (mercifully still-unpublished) paper, "The Gentrification of Postmodernism," at the New Music American Festival, Philadelphia, in October 1987. For more on goal-oriented versus minimalist teleologies in music, see my "Getting Down Off the Beanstalk," in *Feminine Endings: Music, Gender, and Sexuality* (Minneapolis: University of Minnesota Press, 1991), chapter 5. Both these essays took shape under the editorial guidance of Greg Sandow, then the advocate for Downtown music in the *Village Voice*.

4. For my infamous attack on academic modernism, see "Terminal Prestige: The Case of Avant-Garde Music Composition," *Cultural Critique* 12 (Spring 1989): 57–81. But see also my "The Lure of the Sublime."

5. Glass's influence on film music is particularly apparent, not only because of his own much-admired scores for *Koyannisquatsi*, *The Thin Blue Line*, *The Last Emperor*, *The Hours*, and many others, but also because so many other composers shamelessly copy him. See my "Minima Romantica," in *Beyond the Soundtrack: Representing Music in Cinema*, ed. Richard Leppert, Lawrence Kramer, and Daniel Goldmark (Berkeley: University of California Press, 2007), 48–67.

6. Interview with Thomas May in *John Adams Reader*, 244.

7. Interview with Thomas Hampson, Metropolitan Opera HD transmission of *Nixon in China*, 2011, available on Nonesuch DVD.

8. As quoted in Richard Scheinin, "John Adams on His First—and Perhaps Favorite—Opera, 'Nixon in China,'" *Mercury News* (June 7, 2012). I shouldn't have to add that Verdi and Puccini scarcely wrote "dozens of operas before they got it right." Adams and Sellars succumb to hyperbole as much as I do.

9. See my "Music and Culture in the Wake of *Einstein*," foreword to *Einstein on the Bach: Opera Beyond Drama*, ed. Jelena Novak and John Richardson (Abingdon-on-Thames: Routledge, forthcoming). I teach a graduate seminar every two years titled "Opera after *Einstein*," and I owe many of the insights in this book to the students in that seminar and our stimulating discussions.

10. Quoted in interview with Elena Park, in liner notes to DVD of the Metropolitan Opera production.

11. May, *John Adams Reader*, 241.

12. Thomas May, in the introduction to *John Adams Reader*, xvi. Alex Ross claims that "*Nixon in China* helped set off a fad for operas with contemporary subjects: Charles Manson, Marilyn Monroe, Harvey Milk, and Rudolph Valentino, among others, have been set to music. The genre has been given such condescending labels as 'CNN opera' and 'docu-opera,' but Adams bristles at the idea that *Nixon* was some sort of trendy exercise. 'Anyone who uses these terms,' he said, 'just doesn't begin to understand what opera is about, potentially or historically.'" Alex Ross, "The Harmonist," *New Yorker* (January 8, 2001), reprinted in *John Adams Reader*, 38. See also Yayoi Uno Everett, *Reconfiguring Myth and Narrative in Contemporary Opera* (Bloomington: Indiana University Press, 2015), especially chapter 4.

13. Adams, *Hallelujah Junction*, 135.

14. *Nixon in China*, Metropolitan Opera, DVD. The first production with the Houston Opera in 1987 was broadcast on PBS and may be viewed in full on YouTube: https://www.youtube.com/watch?v=DXXmjR0aCug

15. Alice Goodman, program note, 1987, included as the introduction to the piano-vocal score to *Nixon in China* (New York: Boosey and Hawkes, n.d.).

16. See Rupert Christiansen, "Breaking Taboos (Portrait of Alice Goodman)," *Opera* (May 2003), reprinted in May, *John Adams Reader*, 249–57.

17. Interview in 2005 with Thomas May, *John Adams Reader*, 220. In his liner notes to the original sound recording of 1988, Michael Steinberg writes; "Goodman's *Nixon in China* is a wonder of human perception, generosity, wit, and poetic resource. . . . But an opera is, in the end, the composer's. It stands or falls by its music. We can read a few opera librettos with pleasure away from their music, and *Nixon in China* is one of them, but when we hear an opera . . . what we encounter and respond to is not the text itself, but the text as the composer read it and wanted us to hear it. It is the music that delivers the words."

18. See Scheinin, "John Adams on His First." Goodman's libretti, plus her translation of *The Magic Flute*, are now collected in a book, *History Is Our Mother: "Nixon in China", "The Death of Klinghoffer", "The Magic Flute"* (New York: New York Review Books, 2017).

19. Adams, *Hallelujah Junction*, 139. Mark Morris already knew these socialist-realist ballets before Sellars approached him, and he joined the project with great enthusiasm in part because of this element.

20. Cecilia Zung, *Secrets of the Chinese Drama: A Guide to Its Theatre Techniques* (New York: Benjamin Blom, 1964).

21. Michael Steinberg, "*The Death of Klinghoffer*," in May, *John Adams Reader*, 129.

22. Maddalena also sang the part of the Captain for the premiere of *Klinghoffer*, but he appears neither in the audio CD conducted by Kent Nagano nor in the version filmed by Penny Woolcock.

23. Tim Page, review of *Nixon in China* in *Newsweek* (March 28, 1988), reprinted in May, *John Adams Reader*, 295.

24. Sellars says of Maddalena's performance: "He inhabits the character of Nixon with astonishing depth and insight—the neuroses, the strange humor, and Nixon's own sense of grandeur, self-importance, and ruthlessness, but also, together with Janis Kelly's fierce, tender, and heartbreaking Pat, he gives you the remorse, the doubt, the better angel, and the private sense of failure that could never appear in public." Liner notes to the DVD of the Metropolitan Opera production.

25. Sellars singles out Zung's *Secrets of the Chinese Drama* as his principal source for dramaturgy in *Nixon*. The film of Chiang Ch'ing's ballet, which inspired this project, exhibits gestures are similar to those Sellars uses here and elsewhere. See https://www.youtube.com/watch?v=ZHTPcs3lQPU. Tom Sutcliffe associates these gestures (which he calls—courtesy of Johnny Otis—"hand-jive") with Indonesian and South Asian performance practices, both of which Sellars knows; see the chapter on Sellars, "Americanizing Everything," in his *Believing in Opera* (Princeton: Princeton University Press, 1996). Michael Steinberg also cites multiple Asian traditions in Sellars's work ("*The Death of Klinghoffer*," 129). See also the interview with Sellars in Matthew Daines, "Telling the Truth about *Nixon*: Parody, Cultural Representation, and Gender Politics in John Adams's Opera *Nixon in China*" (PhD dissertation, University of California–Davis, 1995), 82.

26. May, *John Adams Reader*, 244–45.

27. For more on this problem, see Sheppard, "Persistence of Orientalism." But see also Malik, "In Defense of Cultural Appropriation"; Malik writes: "The accusation of cultural appropriation is a secular version of the charge of blasphemy." I will have more trouble with aspects of *Doctor Atomic* and *The Indian Queen* (see chapters 4 and 7).

28. Edward Said, *Orientalism* (New York: Pantheon, 1978).

29. See my *Georges Bizet: "Carmen"* (Cambridge: Cambridge University Press, 1992). I spend about a month every year in the area around Barcelona, and I find that many of my American colleagues assume that Catalonia is the same as Bizet's Andalusia.

30. In contrast to the Houston version, the Metropolitan production features a multiracial ensemble, enhancing the sense of individuality and helping to break the possible implication of yellowface in having Caucasians playing Chinese people. The latter production also goes lighter on the eye makeup.

31. Adams mentions the influence of *Satyagraha* in particular. See the Scheinin interview, "John Adams on His First."

32. See again n. 3.

33. Interview with Hampson, Metropolitan Opera DVD.

34. Sellars has reported that he meant Nixon's "Fathers and sons" speech to sound "highly ironic and suspect." Matthew Daines and Peter Sellars, "'Nixon in China': An Interview with Peter Sellars," *Tempo*, new series, no. 197 (July 1996), 19. Once again, Maddalena may have presented a more sympathetic figure than the collaborators had intended.

35. Interview with Hampson, Metropolitan HD transmission.

36. Interview with Adams, part 8 of PBS broadcast of *Nixon*: https://www.youtube.com/watch?v=hDoHLafyPU

37. See https://www.youtube.com/watch?v=ZHTPcs3lQPU

38. For a harrowing account of the impact of Chiang Ch'ing's Cultural Revolution on musicians in the Shanghai Conservatory, see Madeleine Thien, *Do Not Say We Have Nothing* (New York: Norton, 2016).

39. Quoted in Daines, "Telling the Truth," 94. Daines also includes an interview with Adams in which the composer voices his and Goodman's misgivings; see Daines, 111.

40. Richard Taruskin, "Music's Dangers and the Case for Control," *New York Times* (December 9, 2001), reprinted in May, *John Adams Reader*, 331–39, and also in Taruskin, *The Danger of Music: And Other Anti-utopian Essays* (Berkeley: University of California Press, 2009). But see also the rejoinder by Robert Fink, "*Klinghoffer* in Brooklyn Heights," *Cambridge Opera Journal* 17, no. 2 (July 2005): 173–213.

41. This controversy continues to flair, especially with Donald Trump's preemptory naming of Jerusalem as Israel's capital. For two recent articles articulating the Palestinian position, see Raja Shehadah, "This Land Is Our Land," and Sarah Helm, "Homeless in Gaza," both in the *New York Review of Books* (January 18, 2018).

42. Interview with Elena Park for *Web* magazine, quoted in Bernd Feuchtner's excellent account of the controversy provoked by this opera, "The *Klinghoffer* Debate," *Opernwelt Jahrbuch* (2004), trans. Thomas May and reprinted in May, *John Adams Reader*, 305.

Critic Alan Rich argued that Goodman, "A 'nice Jewish girl' from Chicago in 1991, has assumed the brunt of the reproach leveled at *Klinghoffer*'s controversial message and stands by her words. Whether because or despite, she has in that time abandoned Judaism and now preaches at an Anglican church in London, to a largely Palestinian congregation." *LA Weekly* (November 20, 2003), reprinted in May, *John Adams Reader*, 342.

43. Mark Swed, "Seeking Answers in an Opera," *Los Angeles Times* (October 7, 2001), reprinted in May, *John Adams Reader*, 321–22.

44. Personal correspondence (June 24, 2017).

45. See, however, John Rockwell's review of the Sellars production, *New York Times* (March 21, 1991), reprinted in May, *John Adams Reader*, 313–20. See also the account in Sutcliffe, *Believing in Opera*. The best way to experience something like the original is through the CD conducted by Kent Nagano, though one has to imagine the mis-en-scène for oneself.

46. According to Adams, Woolcock had particular difficulty dealing with the opening choruses when she made her realist film of *Klinghoffer*. Her solution—to mount footage

of both the Holocaust and displacements of Palestinians during the singing of those choruses—contributed to the controversy.

47. Mark Swed describes Sellars's staging of Klinghoffer's death as "a dance between Klinghoffer and his body: a dancer slowly drags the singer across stage on a flowing white shroud." Swed, "Seeking Answers," 325.

48. Adams, *Hallelujah Junction*, 166–67. For a comparison between the staged production and the film, in addition to the film's reception, see Feuchtner, "The *Klinghoffer* Debate."

49. See especially Alex Ross, "Long Wake: 'The Death of Klinghoffer,' at the Met," *New Yorker* (November 3, 2014); Anthony Tommasini, "Distress at Sea, and Offstage: *The Death of Klinghoffer* at the Metropolitan Opera," *New York Times* (October 21, 2014); and Mark Swed, "Met Opera's *The Death of Klinghoffer* Is a Compassionate Feat," *Los Angeles Times* (October 21, 2014).


## Chapter 4: A Libretto of One's Own

1. We can observe him in the act of assembling on Jon Else's documentary *Wonders Are Many: The Making of "Doctor Atomic"* (Docurama Films, 2007). Else films Sellars in his studio as he cuts paragraphs from photocopied materials and tapes them onto a sheet that becomes part of his libretto.

2. Adams, *Hallelujah Junction*, 130.

3. Adams, *Hallelujah Junction*, 239.

4. I suspect that the collaborators' negative portrayal of Henry Kissinger in *Nixon in China* reflects our generation's deep suspicion of his shadowy activities in the White House during those turbulent times.

5. For more on this phenomenon, see my *Desire and Pleasure in Seventeenth-Century Music* (Berkeley: University of California Press, 2012), chapter 5.

6. Although I admire these experiments and will write positively about the ways in which they function, I should mention that Adams at one time expressed misgivings concerning the presence of video in both the *Tristan Project* and *El Niño*, believing that they detracted from the music and onstage performers. Adams, *Hallelujah Junction*, 249. He has changed his mind, however, and now endorses the use of the video in performances of *El Niño*.

7. Adams, *Hallelujah Junction*, 244.

8 Sellars uses the translations in *The Selected Poems of Rosario Castellanos*, trans. Magda Bogin, ed. Cecilia Vicuña and Magda Bogin (Saint Paul, MN: Graywolf Press, 1988). "La anunciación" appears on facing Spanish and English pages, 61–66.

9. See Ann W. Astell, *The Song of Songs in the Middle Ages* (Ithaca: Cornell University Press, 1990), 15–16.

10. Adams credits Sellars for transforming Hunt Lieberson from a violist who performed in some of Adams's instrumental premieres to the celebrated singer-actor she became. *Hallelujah Junction*, 247.

11. Castellanos, *The Selected Poems*, 78–79.

12. Adams, *Hallelujah Junction*, 251.

13. See *Wonders Are Many*. Adams displays a military book from the 1940s concerning nuclear weapons and shows the lines that appear in the opening chorus, "The end of

June 1945 finds us expecting from day to day to hear of the explosion of the first atomic bomb."

14. Interview in *Wonders Are Many.*

15. In an interview concerning the 2018 production of *Doctor Atomic* in Santa Fe. https://www.youtube.com/watch?v=ByXZlGO6agA

16. Adams recalls, "The atomic bomb was the ultimate archetype, the ultimate looming presence. And I do remember, as a kid—I don't know how old I was, maybe seven or eight years old—living in the most secure, Steven Spielbergesque, idyllic village in New Hampshire ... getting into bed one night, and my mother gave me a kiss and turned out the light. I heard a jet plane way, way high up in the sky, and I went into a panic, because I wondered if that was the Russians coming to bomb us." Quoted in Alex Ross, "Countdown: John Adams and Peter Sellars Create an Atomic Opera," *New Yorker* (October 3, 2005).

I grew up in southern Illinois, and I experienced precisely the same terror. Even though the United States had carried out the only deployment of nuclear weapons in wartime, we were taught to project that threat exclusively onto that potential aggressor, the Soviet Union; my high school friends and I fully expected to die during the Cuban Missile Crisis in 1962. When I teach *Doctor Atomic*, I have to make sure my undergraduates realize that we were the ones who bombed Japan.

17. Ron Rosenbaum, "The Opera's New Clothes: Why I Walked Out of *Doctor Atomic*," *Spectator* (October 24, 2009).

18. Adams and Sellars wrote this role for Lorraine Hunt Lieberson, who died before she could sing it.

19. Quoted in Ross, "Countdown."

20. I owe some of these insights to my student Taylor McClaskie, who has written persuasively on the hazards of ecofeminism.

21. Several times in *Wonders Are Many*, Jon Else superimposes footage of nuclear explosions over the ritornello of "Batter my heart," thereby linking Adams's agitated music with the consequences: the bombing of Nagasaki and Hiroshima.

22. See the online panel discussion on YouTube: https://www.youtube.com/watch?v=cFygj4EyVTs. Among Sellars's and Adams's source materials for *Girls of the Golden West* was Benjamin Madley, *An American Genocide: The United States and the California Indian Catastrophe, 1846–73* (Berkeley: University of California Press, 2016).

## Chapter 5: Spectral Sensualities

1. See the quotation in the introduction.

2. For a technical account of Saariaho's musical language, see Spencer Lambright, "*L'amour de loin* and the Vocal Works of Kaija Saariaho" (PhD dissertation, Cornell University, 2008). Lambright describes Saariaho's distribution of sonorities through this work as a harmonic field.

3. Kaija Saariaho, "Earth and Air" (2005, Strasbourg Conservatory), trans. Jeffrey Zuckerman, *Music and Literature* 5 (2014): 20–21.

4. Because only fragments of Sellar's staging of *Adriana Mater* are available, I will not focus on it in this chapter. Yayoi Uno Everett, however, has published an excellent account of that opera. See her *Reconfiguring Myth and Narrative*, chapter 3.

Although I have written on it elsewhere, I also will not deal with Saariaho and Maalouf's opera *Émilie* (2008) because Sellars was not involved in this work. This monodrama focuses on the last hours of Émilie le Tonnelier de Breuil, Marquise du Châtelet—the translator of the standard French version of Isaac Newton's *Principia*, philosopher, pioneering game theorist, astronomer, harpsichordist, and close companion to Voltaire. Over the course of the piece, Émilie reflects on her intellectual achievements, her personal affairs, and her premonition that she will soon perish in childbirth. Saariaho invited me to write the program notes for the North American premiere of *Émilie*, and I also spoke about it in "Da Capo: Women Representing Women," American Musicological Society Committee on Women and Gender Lecture Series, November 2017.

5. See my *Feminine Endings*.

6. Saariaho, "My Library, from Words to Music" (1987), trans. Jeffrey Zuckerman, *Music and Literature* 5 (2014): 13–14.

7. See my "Lure of the Sublime." See also Yayoi Uno Everett, "Trope of Desire and Jouissance in Kaija Saariaho's *L'amour de loin*," in *Music and Narrative since 1900*, ed. Michael Klein and Nicholas Reyland (Bloomington: Indiana University Press, 2012), 329–45.

8. Saariaho, "Lohn, for Soprano and Electronics" (Dawn Upshaw, soprano), on the album *Private Gardens* (Ondine, 1997).

9. Amin Maalouf, *The Crusades through Arab Eyes*, trans. Jon Rothschild (New York: Schocken Books, 1984). See also his book concerning the dangers of identity politics, *In the Name of Identity: Violence and the Need to Belong* (1998), trans. Barbara Bray (New York: Arcade Publishing, 2012). Maalouf's novels include *Léon l'Africain* (1986), *Samarcande* (1988), *Les jardins de lumière* (1991), *Le premier siècle après Béatrice* (1992), and *Le rocher de Tanios* (1993).

In a panel discussion with Saariaho at the American Musicological Society in 2015, Anthony Sheppard labeled *L'amour de loin* as Orientalist. I have already discussed how he brings this critique to the work of Sellars and Adams (see chapter 3). In the case of *L'amour de loin*, however, Saariaho had a Lebanese librettist and collaborator who writes professionally about such issues.

10. As quoted in the liner notes for the CD of *L'amour de loin* conducted by Kent Nagano (Harmonia Mundi, 2009), 17.

11. Translation from *Songs of the Troubadours and Trouvères: An Anthology of Poems and Melodies*, ed. Samuel N. Rosenberg, Margaret Switten and Gérard le Vot (New York: Garland, 1998), 54.

12. By contrast, Robert Lepage, in his Metropolitan Opera production in 2016, made the choristers visible, having them poke their heads up between the rows of LED lights representing the Mediterranean. The Cirque du Soleil–inspired production shared between London and Toronto filled the stage constantly with choristers, dancers, streaming banners, and acrobats. Both these productions seemed to me to assume a very short attention span in their audiences, and the music became an elegant soundtrack to the visual spectacles.

13. Anyone who has seen *The Tristan Project* may recall here the elaborate ablutions Sellars and Bill Viola presented in video footage during the opera's opening act. The production of *L'amour de loin* by Daniele Finzi Pasca in Toronto dangled an effigy of the dead Rudel over Clémence during this sequence, thereby collapsing the double meaning. When Saariaho objected, Pasca explained that he had recently suffered the death of a

close relative and that maintaining this image of life after death helped him. Saariaho reported this exchange in a panel discussion at the American Musicological Society Meeting in 2015.

14. For more on the history of such imagery, see María Rosa Menocal, *The Shards of Love: Exile and the Origins of the Lyric* (Durham: Duke University Press, 1993). As we have seen, Sellars draws on the poetry of divine union in his libretti for Adams, and his stagings of the Bach passions dwell on the ambiguities between carnal and Divine Love (see chapter 7). I will deal later in this chapter with *Only the Sound Remains*, which focuses intensely on this theme.

15. Robert Lepage, interview with Michael Cooper, "With 28,000 LEDs, It's Lights! Lights! Lights! Action!," *New York Times* (November 30, 2016).

16. Lepage's rendering of the Mediterranean with LED lights does succeed in tracking Saariaho's rhythmic sequences, and it encourages us to notice the chorus that contributes a human, if ominous, tone to the orchestration. But surely my entourage wasn't alone in giggling when a puppet representing Clémence swooped around within the waves.

17. Sellars discussed this matter in a pre-performance discussion at the Ojai Festival, 2016.

18. Quoted in liner notes to the recordings featuring Dawn Upshaw (soprano), conducted by Esa-Pekka (Ondine, 2013).

19. See Igor Torony-Lalic, "Kaija Saariaho's *Émilie*: A New Compositional Turn from the Finn Undermined by Misogynistic Madness," *Arts Desk* (March 9, 2010).

20. See the discussion of Galás in my "Madwomen," *Feminine Endings*, chapter 4. My husband, Robert Walser, once had the task of taking Galás to lunch when she visited Dartmouth College, where he was teaching. After reading about her, he panicked. I assured him, however, that she was just a small academic woman. In fact, she showed up in standard academic gear: jeans and a tweet jacket. When Rob mentioned that he was married to me, she replied: "Oh, people think she's so scary. But she's really just a small academic woman." She was responding to the perception—common at that time—that my writing seethed with rage.

21. The sound recording appears on YouTube, https://www.youtube.com/watch?v=gsdTvcFhNOw

22. *La passion de Simone,* dir. Peter Sellars, Julia Bullock, soprano. https://www.youtube.com/watch?v=1auH7AtE7Fg

23. Sellars's staging of Claude Vivier's *Kopernikus* at the Ojai Festival interpreted the entire opera as an Indonesian-inspired ritual by means of which an individual moves through this liminal stage from life into death. Performance accessible at https://www.youtube.com/watch?v=mhugEOl2vug

24. The Dutch National Opera production of *Only the Sounds Remains* is now available on DVD (Warner Classics, 2017).

25. Tines starred in the December performance of *El Niño* in Los Angeles and in the premiere of Adams and Sellars's *Girls of the Golden West* in San Francisco, November 2017. See Christopher Smith, "At 29, this *El Niño* Singer Is the Buzz of California's Opera World," *Los Angeles Times* (December 8, 2016).

26. Richard Rambuss, *Closet Devotions* (Durham: Duke University Press, 1998).

27. Private conversation with Sellars, December 2017.

28. Noh Plays DataBase, Tsunemasa: Synopsis and Highlights, http://www.the-noh.com/en/plays/data/program_042.html

29. Andrew Clements, "Only the Sound Remains Review—Almost Perversely Unengaging," *Guardian* (March 23, 2016).

## Chapter 6: Peter Sellars's Mayan Passion

1. Somehow, we put this criterion to the side when it comes to Bizet's *Carmen*, originally performed with spoken dialogue with sung recitative composed by someone else only after his death. Many recent productions of *Carmen* have returned to the original performance practice.

2. See, however, Ellen T. Harris, "The More We Learn about *Dido and Aeneas*, the Less We Know," *New York Times* (December 17, 2017). Long an international authority on Purcell, Harris reviews the received wisdom concerning *Dido* and also recent findings that have called the date and circumstances of the opera's genesis into question.

3. Recall that Shakespeare's plays also had numerous musical interpolations. Ross Duffin has published extensively on this music, much of which he has recovered. See his *Shakespeare's Songbook* (New York: Norton, 2004), and *Some Other Note: The Lost Songs of English Renaissance Comedy* (New York: Oxford University Press, 2018).

4. Rosario Aguilar, *La niña blanca y los pájaros sin pie*, translated as *The Lost Chronicles of Terra Firma* by Edward Walters Hood (Fredonia, NY: White Pine Press, 1997).

5. In fact, Dryden produced a sequel to *The Indian Queen*, *The Indian Emperor*, which deals specifically with the conquest and even Cortés's relationship with Montezuma's daughter. Purcell did not contribute to this second play, however.

6. See, for example, Fiona Maddocks, *Guardian* (March 1, 2015); Rupert Christiansen, *Telegraph* (February 27, 2015); Alexandra Coghlan, *Spectator* (February 2, 2016); Miranda Jackson, *Opera Britannia* (February 26, 2015). The slightly later production in Madrid received far more positive reviews, perhaps because the Spanish are not so invested in Purcell. A review in *La Pais* called it "one of the best theatrical operas in recent years" (quoted in www.larkreviews.co.uk, posting of February 16, 2015).

7. Many prominent productions of seventeenth-century opera go in the other direction and pair the music with deliberately incongruous gestures. See, for instance, the performance of Monteverdi's *Orfeo* staged by Trisha Brown.

8. For more on the obsession with Native religions in early modern Europe, see Olivia Bloechl, *Native American Song at the Frontiers of Early Modern Music* (Cambridge: Cambridge University Press, 2008). Bloechl demonstrates how Quakers and other sects borrowed some of their practices (e.g. "quaking") from what they thought they knew about Native customs.

9. Katherine Philips, "O Solitude" (her translation of "La solitude" by Marc-Antoine Girard de Saint-Amant). Purcell sets verse 1, half of verse 3, and all of verse 20, the poem's concluding stanza. The song appears in Purcell's *Orpheus Britannicus*.

10. For a discussion of the ideological uses of echoes in the seventeenth century, see Ljubica Ilic, *Music and the Modern Condition* (New York: Routledge, 2010).

11. See my *Desire and Pleasure*, chapter 5.

12. Gary Tomlinson, *The Singing of the New World: Indigenous Voice in the Era of European Contact* (Cambridge: Cambridge University Press, 2009).

13. I have not managed to trace the lineage of my grandfather, who may have adopted "McClary" as a surname for similar reasons. Nevertheless, my father, Dan McClary,

served during World War II in an all-Indian regiment—a regiment charged with attracting the attention of the German soldiers so that "real" Americans could shoot them. Recipient of a Purple Heart, he was the only survivor of his regiment.

## Chapter 7: Back to the Source

1. For more on this historic performance and its consequences, see Celia Applegate, *Bach in Berlin: Nation and Culture in Mendelssohn's Revival of the "St. Matthew Passion"* (Ithaca: Cornell University Press, 2005). For a thorough tracing of Bach's original sources to their acquisition by collectors in Berlin to the making of modern editions, see Daniel Boomhower, "The Manuscript Transmission of J. S. Bach's Mass in B Minor and the Development of the Concept of Textual Authority, 1750–1850" (PhD dissertation, Case Western Reserve University, 2017).

2. Sellars, interview included in Berlin Philharmonic DVD of the *St. Matthew Passion*. The conductor of the chorus, Simon Halsey, mentions that Sellars spent eight days rehearsing with the choristers after they had learned their parts.

3. Sellars, interview, DVD of *St. Matthew Passion*.

4. Note the parallel between this scenario and that of Saariaho's *Adriana Mater*, in which a rape victim struggles with the possibility that her child will inherit his father's brutality. Recall also Lorraine Hunt's transformation of Sesto in Sellars's *Giulio Cesare* from devoted son to terrorist. Sesto and Pompey's wife, Cornelia, become the center of this 1990 production.

5. Michael Marissen, *Lutheranism, Anti-Judaism, and Bach's "St. John Passion"* (New York: Oxford University Press, 1998), and *Bach and God* (New York: Oxford University Press, 2016).

6. Sellars used a similar concept with his 2016 Ojai Festival production of Vivier's *Kopernikus*.

7. See the discussions of the tropes of Divine Love in *El niño* (chapter 4) and *L'amour de loin* (chapter 5).

8. For more on the Frescobaldi and the theology of Divine Love, see my *Desire and Pleasure*. For more on Crashaw's "The Weeper," see Richard Rambuss, "Crashaw and the Metaphysical Shudder; Or, How to Do Things with Tears," in *Structures of Feeling in Seventeenth-Century Cultural Expression*, ed. Susan McClary (Toronto: University of Toronto Press, 2013); see also his *Closet Devotions* (Durham, NC: Duke University Press, 1998).

9. See, for instance, the bride-and-groom interactions in his Cantata 140, *Wachet auf*. I discuss this cantata in my "The Blasphemy of Talking Politics during Bach Year," in *Music and Society: The Politics of Composition, Performance and Reception*, ed. Richard Leppert and Susan McClary (Cambridge: Cambridge University Press, 1987).

10. Art historian Leo Steinberg has traced the prevalence of this theme in earlier periods and the ways we now attempt to deny this aspect of Jesus's life. See his *The Sexuality of Christ in Renaissance Art and in Modern Oblivion* (Chicago: University of Chicago Press, 1983).

11. See again n. 8. So pervasive was the association of Jesus with the longed-for bridegroom that several of the duets in the B Minor Mass simulate lovemaking between the soul and Christ.

12. See again chapter 2 for a discussion of Sellars's understanding of da capo arias.

13. Simon Peter's ambivalences and anguish have clearly mattered enormously to Sellars throughout his career: recall his staging of Orlando di Lasso's *Lagrime di San Pietro* but also his unusual emphasis on flawed, penitent men beginning with Count Almaviva in *Figaro* and Don Alfonso in *Così fan tutte*, as well as Nixon, Chou, and Oppenheimer.

14. Interview, DVD of *St. Matthew Passion.*

15. Interview included in the Berlin Philharmonic DVD of the *St. John Passion.* Recall that this interview took place in 2014, before Donald Trump won the presidential election in 2016.

16. Quasthoff was on the brink of retirement and his brother was dying when he agreed to perform with some reluctance to sing this role. Sellars encouraged him to dedicate this aria, "Mache dich, mein Herze, rein," to his brother. I find this perhaps the most moving moment in this remarkable production.

17. The viol player returns for the sequence in which the bass offers to carry the cross. Note in particular the accompanied recitative for which the viol plays arpeggios, bowing across all the strings. As she did in "Geduld," she presents an extraordinary counterpart to the voice in the aria, "Komm, süsses Kreuz" (Come, sweet cross). Padmore lies facedown, his arms outstretched, for the duration of the sequence.

# Index

**211**